# Continuity and Change in France

# Continuity and Change in France

*Edited by*

VINCENT WRIGHT

London
GEORGE ALLEN & UNWIN
Boston             Sydney

**George Allen & Unwin (Publishers) Ltd,**
**40 Museum Street, London WC1A 1LU, UK**

George Allen & Unwin (Publishers) Ltd,
Park Lane, Hemel Hempstead, Herts HP2 4TE, UK

Allen & Unwin, Inc.,
9 Winchester Terrace, Winchester, Mass. 01890, USA

George Allen & Unwin Australia Pty Ltd,
8 Napier Street, North Sydney, NSW 2060, Australia


First published in 1984

**British Library Cataloguing in Publication Data**

Continuity and change in France.
1. France - History - 1958-
I. Wright, Vincent
944.083'7      DC412
ISBN 0-04-354028-7


**Library of Congress Cataloging in Publication Data**

Main entry under title:
Continuity and change in France.
Includes index.
1. France - Politics and government - 1969-
- Addresses, essays, lectures. 2. France - Economic
policy - 20th century - Addresses, essays, lectures.
3. France - Social policy - Addresses, essays, lectures.
4. Giscard d'Estaing, Valéry, 1926-    - Addresses,
essays, lectures. I. Wright, Vincent.
DC422.C663  1983      320.944      83-11739
ISBN 0-04-354028-7

Set in 10 on 11 point Plantin by Graphicraft Typesetters Limited
and printed in Great Britain by Billings & Sons Limited, Guildford, London and Worcester

# Contents

# Preface

This book started life as a collection of essays on President Giscard d'Estaing, his personality and politics. It was intended to be a contribution to understanding the man who was elected President of the French Republic in May 1974 and whose re-election in May 1981 seemed assured. Most of the book was completed before the May 1981 presidential election, only the finishing touches were required. However, the French electors were to change their President, and more irritatingly, dictate a change in the nature of the book: for the first time, the editor of the book fully appreciated the Brechtian character's advocacy of the need, on occasion, not to elect a new government but a new people.

Yet, on reflection, it was clear that a great deal of the book needed no change. First, a record of the Giscard d'Estaing presidency was useful in itself. Secondly, it became increasingly apparent that in many areas, in spite of the rhetoric of the new Socialist administration and the fears of its opponents, Mitterrand would be continuing many of the policies and practices of his predecessor – often with the aid of the same or similar personnel. The book comprises, therefore, a series of essays which are concerned largely with the balance-sheet of the last presidency, but which also pinpoint some of the changes of direction dictated by the new President as well as outlining the areas of continuity.

V. Wright
*Florence*

# List of Contributors

| | |
|---|---|
| Pierre Birnbaum | *University of Paris I* |
| Roger Formesyn | *Ealing Polytechnic* |
| Xavier Gardette | *Portsmouth Polytechnic* |
| Diana Green | *City of London Polytechnic* |
| Jack Hayward | *University of Hull* |
| Raymond Kuhn | *Queen Mary College, London* |
| Howard Machin | *London School of Economics* |
| Yves Mény | *University of Rennes and European University Institute* |
| Ella Searls | *University of Newcastle* |
| Vincent Wright | *Nuffield College, Oxford, and European University Institute* |

# Introduction: The Change in France

*V. WRIGHT*

At exactly 8 p.m. – the time of the closing of the polling-booths in Paris – on 10 May 1981 the computers of two television channels confidently predicted the victory of François Mitterrand in the election to the presidency of the French Republic. The prediction was quickly to be confirmed, and before midnight the incumbent President, Valéry Giscard d'Estaing, had conceded defeat, and the new President, François Mitterrand, had made his victory speech. In all the major towns of France there were spontaneous outbreaks of noisy joy. In Paris a vast crowd gathered in 'the Republican heart' of the town – the Bastille and the Place de la République – to celebrate, in festival mood, the victory of Mitterrand and, often more pointedly, the defeat of Giscard d'Estaing. Cries of *on* [not Mitterrand] *a gagné* were frequently drowned by *Giscard au chômage*. It was a sad end to a presidency which had commenced seven years previously in an atmosphere of breezy good humour and optimism.

Many reasons have been advanced to explain the result of the May 1981 presidential elections. Some observers see in the results the consequence of the vast socio-economic changes that were taking place in France: the country was becoming 'sociologically left-wing', as the result of urbanisation, industrialisation and secularisation. It was argued that what had been surprising was that the Right had managed to stave off defeat for so long: *France de gauche, vote à droite* was the revealing title of a book which attempted to explain why an intrinsically left-wing country – in socio-economic terms – had given its votes to the Right in the 1978 election.[1] Other observers explained the result in terms of the defection of the floating Centre voters to the Mitterrand camp, whilst others presented the results in economic terms. Giscard d'Estaing was presented as the victim of *la crise*, the deepening depression which had afflicted the world economy since the first energy crisis of 1973–4. Or his defeat was attributed to the immediate *conjoncture*, since in 1980–1 almost all the electorally sensitive economic indices (particularly on employment) were poor. Another set of explanations for the result related to sectoral discontent: specific groups such as the Jews, the farmers, the managers and the environmentalists expressed their discontent with the incumbent President for the policies he had been pursuing. Finally, there was the purely political explanation. It was contended that Giscard d'Estaing was abandoned either by the centre Left (which was irritated by his lack of reformist policies and was attracted to François Mitterrand especially as he was much more clearly than in the past not the prisoner of the Communists) or by an important segment of the Gaullists (who deserted him for reasons which are explained later in this introduction).

The electors, when questioned about the reasons for Mitterrand's victory by the polling organisation Sofres, quoted in order of preference the following[2]: Mitterrand had the will to introduce great changes into French society (42 per cent); he enjoyed the support of all the parties of the Left (34 per cent); his victory was the only way of getting rid of Giscard d'Estaing (29 per cent); he was the defender of the workers (25 per cent); he was more capable of reducing unemployment (20 per cent). Only 2 per cent thought Mitterrand had won because he was more 'presidential' in stature than Giscard d'Estaing.

In truth, any attempt to explain the May 1981 result must separate the defeat of Giscard d'Estaing from the victory of Mitterrand and analyse the personality, strategy, political organisation, policies, tactics and campaign of each man, against the background of social change and relative economic crisis. Before attempting such an analysis, it is useful to look a little closely at the presidential campaign and the results of the two ballots.[3]

## The Presidential Election Campaign and the Results

The presidential campaign was a very long one. It began tentatively in the spring of 1980, gathered momentum in the early summer (Michel Debré announced his candidacy on 30 June 1980), and was in full swing by the autumn after Marchais (12 October) and Mitterrand (8 November) had officially entered the fray. President Giscard d'Estaing did not declare his candidacy until 2 March 1981, but it was clear to all long before that date that the sitting President wished to renew his mandate. The failure to satisfy the minimum requirements to stand (the gathering of 500 signatures from elected officials in at least thirty *départements* or overseas territories) eliminated a number of hopefuls from the competition: these included not only a number of eccentrics, but also the dissident Communist Roger Garaudy, the Trotskyist Alain Krivine and two candidates of the extreme Right.

'Only' ten candidates eventually fulfilled the necessary requirements. They were Giscard d'Estaing, François Mitterrand, the Gaullist leader Jacques Chirac, the Communist secretary-general Georges Marchais, the Left-wing Radical Michel Crépeau, two Gaullist dissidents (Michel Debré and Marie-France Garaud), two candidates of the extreme Left (Arlette Laguiller of Lutte Ouvrière and Huguette Bouchardeau of the Parti Socialiste Unifié) and Brice Lalonde, the spokesman for the Ecologists.

It was not a particularly inspiring campaign. It was certainly much less exciting than that of 1974, and the themes were very much the same as those developed in the legislative elections of 1978. It was on the whole a rather negative campaign, with the incumbent President receiving the major – and critical – attention for his record, especially on unemployment and inflation. Of the four major candidates, Giscard d'Estaing appeared almost lethargic and aloof, Mitterrand carefully developed his image as the *force tranquille*, Chirac led a dynamic and somewhat populist crusade and Marchais in spite of all his activity (or possibly because of it) merely confirmed that he was not of presidential stature.

However uninspiring, the campaign proper appears to have had an important impact on opinion. In the first place, President Giscard d'Estaing suffered during the early part of the campaign – particularly during the winter months – when the IFOP monthly 'satisfaction level' and the Sofres 'confidence level' opinion polls revealed a high level of dissatisfaction with and a low level of confidence in the President,[4] and when his electoral popularity fell sharply. Almost all the opinion polls – and they were numerous – revealed that the number of those hoping for a Giscard d'Estaing victory and intending to vote for him fell consistently from the late autumn to the early spring, although there was a slight increase at the end of the campaign and *expectations* of his re-election remained above the 50 per cent level. According to IFOP, Giscard d'Estaing lost especially heavily amongst the 25–34-year-olds and the over 65-year-olds (minus 12 per cent), amongst the category of upper management, industrialists and liberal professions (minus 14 per cent), and amongst the 'inactive' (minus 19 per cent). His losses were distributed mainly between Chirac and Mitterrand, although somewhat unevenly (for instance, the over-65s deserted to Mitterrand, whilst the self-employed and the farmers defected to Chirac).[5]

The second important movement of opinion concerned the steady rise in popularity of Jacques Chirac, and the second-ballot voting intentions of Gaullist voters. In August 1980 nearly four-fifths (79 per cent) of the latter were opting for Giscard d'Estaing at the second ballot, but this figure had plummeted to only 54 per cent by January 1981 – the Giscard d'Estaing– Chirac rivalry was clearly making its impact. During the campaign this percentage gradually rose, as the old reflexes of right-wing solidarity began to play, and by the eve of poll had reached 71 per cent. However, a substantial minority of first-ballot Gaullists – 18 per cent – expressed their intention of voting for Mitterrand at the second ballot. The third important shift of opinion involved the emergence of François Mitterrand as the undisputed challenger of Giscard d'Estaing, and the hardening of left-wing unitary sentiment round his candidacy. At the same time, hopes of a victory for Mitterrand – and intentions to vote for him – increased. Both IFOP and Sofres indicated a rapid shift from November 1980 to January 1981, followed by a slower but almost constant evolution in his favour until the last week of the campaign. The IFOP polls plot the trend of opinion very clearly (Table 1).

Table 1   *IFOP Polls: Second-Ballot Voting Intentions (Percentage of Positive Indications)*

|  | *November 1980* | *January 1981* | *February 1981* | *March 1981* | *April 1981* | *May 1981* |
|---|---|---|---|---|---|---|
| Giscard d'Estaing | 60 | 54 | 53 | 51 | 48·5 | 48·5 |
| Mitterrand | 40 | 46 | 47 | 49 | 51·1 | 51·5 |

It is quite possible that Mitterrand had been seriously underrated in pre-November polls as a result of the doubt as to whether he or Michel Rocard would be the Socialist candidate; certainly, the twenty-point lead of Giscard d'Estaing over Mitterrand (60 per cent as against 40 per cent) during January–December 1980 was exceptional in polling records (5–7 per cent was the more normal lead). The first poll to indicate a possible Mitterrand victory, 51 per cent compared with 49 per cent, appeared on 5 January 1981 (by Indice-Opinion, in *Le Quotidien de Paris*), whilst in February a Sofres poll showed a bigger Mitterrand lead: 52 per cent compared with 48 per cent (in *Le Figaro*). Neither of these sponsoring newspapers could be suspected of great affection for the Socialist candidate.

Unitary sentiment on the Left may be seen by looking at the electoral reactions of first-ballot Communist voters: throughout 1980 56–62 per cent of these voters declared their intentions of voting for François Mitterrand at the second ballot. The effect of the polemics between the Socialists and the Communists since the September 1977 breakdown in talks to update their joint programme were thus evident. However, in the months preceding the election there was a sharp rise in pro-Mitterrand sentiment (Table 2).[6] After February 1981, the main movements of

Table 2   *Percentage of First-Ballot Communist Voters Intending to Vote for Mitterrand at the Second Ballot*

| | |
|---|---|
| December 1980 | 56 |
| January 1981 | 61 |
| February 1981 | 66 |
| March 1981 | 73 |
| April 1981 | 84 |

opinion were stabilised, and the first-ballot results produced no major surprises. The official results of the first ballot were announced by the Constitutional Council on 29 April (Table 3). The turnout was quite high by the standards of the Fifth Republic, although it was down on the remarkable 88 per cent vote of the second ballot of the 1974 presidential elections and lower than the mobilisation at the first ballots of 1965 and 1974. The main political tendencies of the results of the first ballot may be summarised as in Table 4, which gives figures for metropolitan France.

*Les petits* – the six minor candidates, Lalonde, Laguiller, Crépeau, Debré, Garaud and Bouchardeau – won 12·46 per cent of the votes – well up on the performance of the smaller candidates in 1974. Lalonde, the leader of the Ecologists, had particular reason for satisfaction.

In terms of the number of votes cast the Left (Mitterrand, Marchais, Laguiller, Crépeau and Bouchardeau) bettered its 1974 performance only slightly, but it did progress. It won an absolute majority of votes in thirty-

Table 3   *Presidential Election: First Ballot*

|  | Voters | Voters (%) | Electors (%) |
|---|---|---|---|
| Giscard d'Estaing | 8,222,432 | 28·31 | 22·58 |
| Mitterrand | 7,505,960 | 25·84 | 20·62 |
| Chirac | 5,225,848 | 17·99 | 14·35 |
| Marchais | 4,456,992 | 15·34 | 12·24 |
| Lalonde | 1,126,254 | 3·87 | 3·09 |
| Laguiller | 668,057 | 2·30 | 1·83 |
| Crépeau | 642,847 | 2·21 | 1·76 |
| Debré | 481,821 | 1·65 | 1·32 |
| Garaud | 386,623 | 1·33 | 1·06 |
| Bouchardeau | 321,353 | 1·10 | 0·88 |
| Electors | 36,398,859 | | |
| Voters | 29,516,082 | | |
| Abstentions | 6,882,777 (18·9%) | | |
| Blank or void | 477,965  (1·31%) | | |

Table 4   *Voting by Major Political Tendencies, 1974–81*

|  | 1974 Presidential | 1978 Legislative | 1979 European | 1981 Presidential |
|---|---|---|---|---|
| Turnout | 84·9 | 83·3 | 61·0 | 81·7 |
| Left | 46·1 | 49·8 | 47·5 | 47·3 |
| Ecologists | 1·3 | 2·2 | 4·4 | 3·9 |
| Centre + Right | 52·6 | 48·0 | 48·1 | 48·8 |

two of the ninety-six metropolitan *départements* (in 1965 Mitterrand as the sole candidate of the Left did so in only two, and in 1974 the Left candidates did so in only eleven). Compared with 1974, the Left progressed in sixty-eight *départements* and lost ground in twenty-eight. It made its major gains where the Left and Right were traditionally evenly balanced (what Jean Charlot calls 'uncertain' constituencies) and where the Socialists dominated the Left and the *Giscardiens* the Right. The Left's bastions remained the industrial north, the Paris region, parts of the Centre and most of the Midi.

The Right (Giscard d'Estaing, Chirac, Debré and Garaud) maintained its performance of 1978 and 1979 but was ominously down on its 1974 position. Together the candidates of the Right won an absolute majority in forty *départements*, twenty-five of them having been on the Right since the time of the Third Republic and a further eight since 1946. The Right did well (although less well than in the past) in its traditional bastions of the west (Brittany and Normandy), the east (Alsace), parts of the Rhône Valley, the Catholic regions of the Massif Central, Paris and parts of the Paris basin.

The socio-economic breakdown of the vote of the four major candidates is given in Appendix 1. Both the IFOP and the Sofres figures are provided, since they give somewhat different information and differ on a number of points. Yet all the opinion-poll data underline the importance of women and of the aged in Giscard d'Estaing's electorate. According to Sofres,[7] Giscard d'Estaing lost particularly heavily (compared with 1974) amongst the farmers: 33 per cent for Giscard d'Estaing and 36 per cent for Chirac, whilst in 1974 Giscard d'Estaing won 49 per cent and Chaban-Delmas, the Gaullist candidate, only 19 per cent. He also lost very heavily amongst the upper social classes (upper management, liberal professions, industrialists and *gros commerçants*): 42 per cent in 1974 and only 24 per cent in 1981, with Chirac winning 36 per cent (compared with 16 per cent for Chaban-Delmas in 1974). Giscard d'Estaing retained his admittedly small support amongst the workers and also amongst the retired. The Sofres figures on working-class voting provide evidence of a major shift of allegiance. The Socialist Mitterrand, with 33 per cent of the vote, beat the Communist Marchais (with only 30 per cent). At the legislative elections of 1978 the Communist Party was ahead of the Socialist Party by 37 per cent to 26 per cent. The PCF's claims to be '*the* party of the working class' – always of dubious electoral validity – could manifestly no longer be sustained. The party also lost, and in dramatic fashion, much of its appeal amongst the young: according to a post-election poll carried out by IFOP, the 18–20-year-olds voted 31 per cent for Mitterrand, 20·5 per cent for Chirac, 14·5 per cent for Giscard d'Estaing and only 11·5 per cent for Marchais.[8]

If the results by candidate are analysed in detail, perhaps the most striking is the disastrous performance of Georges Marchais, the secretary-general of the Communist Party, for the Communists had their worst share

Table 5   *Electoral Performance of the PCF, 1936–81*
*(Percentage of First Ballot)*

| | | |
|---|---|---|
| Legislative elections | 1936 | 15·4 |
| Constitutional elections | 1945 | 26·1 |
| Constitutional elections | 1946 | 25·7 |
| Legislative elections | 1946 | 28·6 |
| Legislative elections | 1951 | 26·9 |
| Legislative elections | 1956 | 25·9 |
| Legislative elections | 1958 | 19·2 |
| Legislative elections | 1962 | 21·8 |
| Legislative elections | 1967 | 22·5 |
| Legislative elections | 1968 | 20·0 |
| Presidential elections | 1969 | 21·5 |
| Legislative elections | 1973 | 21·4 |
| Legislative elections | 1978 | 20·7 |
| European elections | 1979 | 20·6 |
| Presidential elections | 1981 | 15·5 |

of the vote since 1936 – elections in which they made significant progress.[9]
As in 1958, the PCF lost one in four of its previous voters. It should be recalled too, that the party never fully recovered from the 1958 disaster – its best performance thereafter was 22·5 per cent in 1967 (Table 5). In fact, the party's best performance of the Fifth Republic is much worse than its worst performance of the Fourth Republic. Nor could the party draw any comfort from a comparison with Mitterrand's result. Indeed, the figures were damagingly eloquent. The gap between the Communists and the Socialists, which had been inexorably widening since the early 1970s, had become such that the jealously observed *équilibre de la gauche* had tipped dramatically in favour of the latter (Table 6).

In the 1973 elections the PC was still ahead of the PS in 36 of the 96 Metropolitan *départements*, in 1978 in only 23 and in 1981 only four – the Seine-Saint-Denis, the Bouches-du-Rhône, the Corrèze and the Gard. In terms of parliamentary constituencies the PC headed the PS in 194 in 1973, 155 in 1978 and in only 46 in April 1981. Marchais lost ground (compared with the PC in 1978) in 94 of the 96 *départements* (the only exceptions were the Lozère and Corsica), and those losses ranged from 1·0 per cent in the Haute-Saône to 38·6 per cent in the Cher. The Paris region

Table 6   *Electoral Performances of the Left, 1973–81*
*(Percentage of First Ballot)*

| | 1973 | 1978 | 1979 | 1981 |
|---|---|---|---|---|
| Communist Party | 21·4 | 20·6 | 20·6 | 15·5 |
| Socialists and Radical allies | 20·8 | 24·9 | 23·7 | 28·3 |

was a particular black-spot for the party – the slow loss of votes which the party had been suffering since 1967 was sharply accelerated (Table 7).

Table 7 *The PC in the Paris Region (Percentage of First Ballot)*

| 1967 | 29·9 |
| 1968 | 26·5 |
| 1973 | 27·1 |
| 1978 | 23·7 |
| 1979 | 23·0 |
| 1981 | 16·5 |

The losses in the Paris region ranged from 27·5 per cent in the Val-de-Marne to 34·4 per cent in the Seine-Saint-Denis. In Paris itself the party lost two-fifths of its 1978 vote (which was already a relatively poor performance), dropping from 15·6 per cent to a mere 9 per cent. Increasingly the PCF resembles a firmly regionalised party, with significant electoral representation only in parts of the Paris region, in the north, the centre and parts of the Midi. And this 'regionalisation' of electoral support is taking place at a time when the Socialist Party is 'nationalising' its electorate.

Several reasons were put forward to explain the collapse of the PCF vote with most of the missing voters opting for Mitterrand, but in some areas to the extreme Left or the Environmentalists' candidate. These included the personal unattractiveness and the 'unpresidential' nature of Marchais, the party's candidate; the desire on the part of the most pro-left-wing unity elements to vote for Mitterrand, who was the very personification of that unity; and the *voter utile* urge on the part of many PCF voters – to vote at the first ballot for the left-wing candidate seemingly best placed to beat Giscard d'Estaing (this was the favoured argument of the PC leadership). Others saw the PC collapse as a vote of no confidence by many Communist voters in the party's recent sectarian, *ouvriériste* and pro-Soviet policies, whilst others interpreted it as but an acceleration of an electoral decline which had been evident since the mid-1960s. Whatever the reasons for the dramatic collapse of the PCF vote, it was to have important consequences for the outcome of the second ballot. In the first place, it forced a desperate PCF leadership into backing Mitterrand; by being associated with his victory they hoped to save something from the *débâcle*. And more importantly, it reduced the fear of a Communist domination in the event of a left-wing victory – a fear which had always been a key card in the hands of the Right. It was one of the major reasons why the right-wing coalition won the 1978 legislative elections.[10] After the first ballot of 1981, pro-leftist but anti-Communist electors were reassured. It is instructive that the *Le Point* IFOP poll taken after the first ballot indicated that fewer people feared a Mitterrand victory than Giscard d'Estaing's re-election. As Jean Charlot noted, fear had changed camps.[11]

For François Mitterrand, the result was a personal triumph. With 25·8 per cent of the votes, he was only 1·7 per cent behind Giscard d'Estaing in Metropolitan France, and he bettered the performance of the PS–Left-wing Radicals (MRG) alliance of 1978 and 1979 (European elections). Mitterrand and Crépeau together improved upon the PS–MRG 1978 vote in seventy-six of the ninety-six metropolitan *départements*, doing especially well in Communist and Gaullist bastions (notably in the Paris region and in parts of the west). They fared relatively less well compared with 1978 in areas where they had popular sitting Deputies, where Chirac did well and where there was strong traditional rivalry between the Socialists and the Communists: these latter areas included *départements* such as the Nord, the Pas-de-Calais and the Haute-Vienne. Mitterrand increased and further 'nationalised' the electorate of the Socialists: not only did he do better than the best previous Socialist electoral performance (23·4 per cent of the SFIO in October 1945), he also established a substantial Socialist presence in every *département*.

For Chirac the result, although disappointing compared with the heady expectations of his more zealous supporters and poorer than that of the Gaullist party in 1978, was perfectly satisfactory – particularly as he had started the campaign with the polls threatening a mere 8–10 per cent of the vote. He fared better than Chaban-Delmas, the Gaullist candidate in 1974 (15·1 per cent) and better than the Gaullist list in the European elections of 1979 (16·25 per cent). He did especially well in his home region of Limousin (in his home *département* of the Corrèze he won 41·4 per cent of the votes) and the neighbouring Auvergne, and in Paris (with 26·97 per cent), where he has been the highly successful mayor since 1977. In no *département* did he get less than 13 per cent of the vote. If the votes of Michel Debré and Mme Garaud, two dissident Gaullists, are added to those of Chirac, the Gaullist movement emerged well from the first ballot, particularly as it was competing with Giscard d'Estaing who, as incumbent President, attracted the votes of those who favoured established authority (often known – somewhat misleadingly – as the 'legitimist' vote). Chirac's personal position and prestige was unquestionably enhanced by the election: his dynamic campaign (he visited all twenty-two regions and over 100 towns, held fifty-two public meetings and sixty more with various pressure groups) and his good result established his credentials as the future leader of the Right – especially in the light of Giscard d'Estaing's failure.

Giscard d'Estaing's position after the first ballot was far from comfortable. Although he was 2·47 per cent ahead of Mitterrand and won 25 per cent of votes in seventy-four of the ninety-six *départements* of metropolitan France, he was 4·3 per cent down on his 1974 first-ballot result of 32·6 per cent. His performance was not much better than that of

Simone Veil in the 1979 European elections (27·4 per cent of votes). He lost badly in the Paris region (from 33·5 per cent in the 1974 to 24·7 per cent in 1981) and in Brittany, Lower Normandy, Limousin and the Auvergne. Compared with 1974, he lost ground in all types of constituency; and compared with 1978, he fared particularly badly in Giscardian strongholds.[12]

The first-ballot figures when compared with 1974, made grim reading for the Giscard d'Estaing camp. In 1974 the Left, at the first ballot, collected 45·8 per cent of the votes, the Ecologists 1·3 per cent and the Right 52·9 per cent, yet at the second ballot Mitterrand won 49·2 per cent. In 1981 the Left won 46·8 per cent (up 1 per cent), the Ecologists 3·8 per cent (up 2·5 per cent) and the Right 49·3 per cent (down 3·6 per cent).

For Giscard d'Estaing to win, he needed to attract a higher percentage of Chirac's votes than he had of Chaban's votes in 1974 (already calculated at 79 per cent), and the opinion polls were far from reassuring on that score. Furthermore, the leaders of the Gaullist party did little to rally their supporters to the side of the incumbent President: Marie-France Garaud told her first-ballot supporters to vote *blanc* at the second ballot; Michel Debré waited until 5 May before he publicly backed – and then unenthusiastically – Giscard d'Estaing; Jacques Chirac made only two public declarations of support for the President; the Central Committee of the Gaullist party decided, on 29 April, to leave its supporters total freedom of choice. Giscard d'Estaing's only chance lay in Communist abstention but that hope evaporated after Marchais gave his blessing to Mitterrand.

For Mitterrand to win, he needed to hold his own vote; to attract the vote of the rest of the Left; to take some Gaullist votes (it was calculated he had won 11 per cent of Chaban-Delmas's votes in 1974); to win some of the votes of the Ecologists (whose leader gave no recommendation on how to vote at the second ballot); and to pick up the votes of the first-ballot abstainers. He was to do all those things,[13] being helped by the merely lukewarm support given by Chirac to Giscard d'Estaing and by the much less reserved (if still unenthusiastic) support afforded him by the PCF.

The first ballot ended, thus, with the Right having lost votes compared with the 1974 election (which it won by only a whisker), and with that loss largely attributable to Giscard d'Estaing, its standard-bearer for the second ballot, whilst the Left emerged unscathed compared with 1974 and with its representative having scored a personal victory at the first ballot. As Jean Charlot rightly notes, Giscard d'Estaing lost the 1981 presidential election at the first ballot.[14] The results of the second ballot were merely to confirm the lessons of the first (Table 8). The turnout was very high (85·85 per cent), and although lower than the record 87·88 per cent at the second ballot of 1974, clearly indicated the importance the electorate attached to the presidential contest.

Mitterrand's margin of victory was not great, but it was greater than that

Table 8   *Presidential Election: Second Ballot, 1981*

|  | *Votes* | *Percentage of voters* | *Percentage of voters* |
|---|---|---|---|
| Mitterrand | 15,708,262 | 51·75 | 43·15 |
| Giscard d'Estaing | 14,642,306 | 48·24 | 40·22 |
|  |  |  |  |
| Electors |  | 36,398,762 |  |
| Voters |  | 31,249,552 (85·85%) |  |
| Abstentions |  | 5,149,210 (14·4%) |  |
| Blank or void |  | 898,984 (2·46%) |  |

enjoyed by Giscard d'Estaing in 1974. His victory was also the first victory of the Left in a national election during the Fifth Republic, and moreover it was clearer than the figures suggest: he won a majority in sixty-five of the ninety-six Metropolitan *départements* compared with forty-four in 1974 and only twenty-five in 1965. Compared with 1974, he made gains in ninety-one of the ninety-six *départements*, that is, in all types of constituency; but he made his most spectacular gains in those where he had been weakest in 1974. The Catholic west (the *départements* of the Morbihan, Ille-et-Vilaine, Finistère and Mayenne), although still *Giscardien*, saw major Mitterrand progress, accentuating a movement of these areas to the moderate Left already in process since 1967. In the Catholic east he made progress, but less spectacularly than in the west.[15] He consolidated the hold of the Left in the north, the Paris region, the *Midi Rouge* and the *Centre Républicain*; and he made major inroads into parts of the Paris basin and the surrounding provinces – Burgundy, Lower Normandy and Franche-Comté. The 'nationalisation' of the left-wing vote may be seen in the fact that in only four *départements* did Mitterrand not reach 40 per cent (compared with eleven in 1974). Compared with the first ballot, he won 2,073,498 more votes than the combined Left-wing vote; and improved on the performance of the Left in all types of constituency. Only in certain Communist strongholds did he not better the first-ballot performance of the Left. The greatest improvement took place in Gaullist bastions and in areas where the Left and the Right were evenly balanced.[16]

Giscard d'Estaing lost ground, compared with 1974, in all but five of the ninety-six metropolitan *départements*. His vote held up well in those areas where he had been weak in 1974, and he lost disproportionately in those where he had fared particularly well – especially if they were Gaullist.[17] In 1981 he won a majority of the votes in only thirty-one *départements*, compared with fifty-two in 1974. He improved the first-ballot performance of the Right by 301,055 votes; but with a higher turnout, the performance in terms of the percentage of votes was less than impressive. Thus, he progressed in terms of votes in seventy-eight *départements* with a smaller percentage, did worse in sixteen *départements* in terms of votes and the percentage of votes, and in only three *départements* did he do better in both respects. In some *départements* he fell back sharply. These include those areas where Chirac had fared especially well.

A Sofres socio-professional breakdown of the vote shows that Giscard d'Estaing did well amongst the farming community (68 per cent compared with 32 per cent for Mitterrand) and amongst small shopkeepers and self-employed artisans (64 per cent compared with 36 per cent); and he enjoyed a majority (although lower than in 1974) amongst the non-working and the retired (55 per cent compared with 45 per cent) and amongst the category upper managerial/liberal professions/industrialists and *gros commerçants* (55 per cent compared with 45 per cent). Mitterrand enjoyed a substantial advantage amongst the workers (72 per cent compared with 28 per cent – figures very similar to those for 1974) and amongst the lower-managerial and white-collar classes (62 per cent to 38 per cent). It was amongst the latter category that Mitterrand was to make his greatest progress (up 9 per cent on 1974).[18]

Studies of the transfers of votes from the first to the second ballot suggest that most abstentionists and Ecologists voted for Mitterrand (for the latter, the Sofres poll suggests 53 per cent for Mitterrand and 26 per cent for Giscard d'Estaing, with 21 per cent abstaining or giving no reply). Mitterrand also enjoyed the massive support of the first-ballot Communist voters (92 per cent according to Sofres, 88 per cent according to IFOP) – a fact which is all the more remarkable since the most pro-Mitterrand Communists had already voted for him at the first ballot. Communist voter mobilisation was even greater than Socialist voter mobilisation in favour of Mitterrand: according to Sofres, 95 per cent of the 1978 first-ballot voters. On the Right the mobilisation was less effective than usual, although higher than the polls were suggesting. The IFOP opinion polls[19] give the figures shown in Table 9 (they are remarkably close to those given by Sofres).

The result of the election came as a surprise to most – the Paris Bourse, which remained quiet throughout the campaign, reflected the general sentiment that Giscard d'Estaing would be re-elected. The IFOP poll published between the two ballots revealed that 50 per cent of those questioned expected Giscard d'Estaing to win compared with only 22 per cent for Mitterrand (there were 28 per cent of no replies), whilst the post-

Table 9   *Transfer of First-Ballot Gaullist Votes*

|  | 1981 (%) | 1974 (%) |
| --- | --- | --- |
| Giscard d'Estaing | 71·5 | 79·5 |
| Mitterrand | 15·5 | 11·0 |
| Abstained | 13·0 | 9·5 |

election Sofres poll showed that 53 per cent were surprised by the election of Mitterrand (compared with only 22 per cent in 1974 for the election of Giscard d'Estaing). It also indicated that whilst 73 per cent expected the election of Giscard d'Estaing in 1974, only 43 per cent expected that of Mitterrand in 1981. The surprise was possibly due to the experience of 1978, when the poll predictions of a clear left-wing victory proved so wrong.

## The Defeat of Giscard d'Estaing

Why was Giscard d'Estaing beaten? His general record, after all, was far from disastrous – as will be made clear throughout the book. In his farewell speech on television on 19 May 1981 he reiterated the claims underlined in his book *L'Etat de la France* (a 295-page apologia for his *septennat*) and which dominated his election campaign: he had kept France at peace, had defended national independence and given France an honourable place in the counsels of the world; and he had defended basic freedoms, ensured political stability and continuity, had dramatically reduced French dependence on outside sources of energy and had adapted his country to the conditions of the 'new world economy'. In short, he had steered France through 'a difficult, dangerous world, in the throes of an economic, and also moral crisis without precedent in the previous fifty years'. All that was largely true. Moreover, Giscard d'Estaing spoke and acted like a President – he had a stature which was recognised both at home and abroad. And yet he was rejected by the electorate on 10 May 1981.

The reasons for defeat should not be sought in his defence policies, since in the main he maintained those of General de Gaulle, and those policies enjoyed the backing of all the major parties in France. Nor must his defeat be attributed to the failures of his foreign policy – although he certainly alienated the Jewish vote by his pro-Arab (that is, pro-petrol) policies, and he may have enraged or disconcerted many (including Mitterrand and Jacques Chirac, the leader of the Gaullists) by his apparently emollient attitude towards the Soviets over Afghanistan. His European policy which inspired no one did relatively little to antagonise the Gaullists (only his acceptance of direct elections to the European Parliament upset the more biliously nationalist elements in the Gaullist party). In Africa French policy was neither a conspicuous success nor failure, and none of it raised real or lasting controversy.

The reasons for Giscard d'Estaing's electoral failure must be sought in France: elections are invariably won or lost at home, and the French presidential election was no exception. Three interrelated factors appear to have contributed powerfully to the failure of *Giscardisme*: its personal style of government, its economic philosophy and policies; and its political ideology, strategy and tactics. It will be seen that there were contradictions *within* each of these component elements (personal, economic and political) and *between* them. The presidency was flawed by these contradictions which produced inconsistency and incoherence. Too often, the President was unwilling or unable to implement the policies which were dictated by their own premisses. Giscard d'Estaing could analyse a problem, even perceive its solution, but then fail to act effectively. He was hampered by his own growing personal scepticism and pessimism, which were themselves rooted in his perception of the world as dark, troubled, unstable, fragile. His presidency after an early reformist phase became increasingly characterised by its cautious, purely reactive nature. The overall result was not a total failure, and historians are likely to judge the balance-sheet with greater charity than the 1981 electors. But in some respects the presidency was a failure and in many respects a disappointment, and part of the failure and much of the disappointment could have been avoided.

## Giscardisme – the Style

*Giscardisme* was not only a set of ideas (however ill-formulated), it was also a style, personified in the President himself. Giscard d'Estaing had many real qualities, the first being his quick and organised intelligence which was more concrete than speculative, more precise than interesting and often more clear than truly illuminating. His verbal and written style reflected his intelligence: it was neutral, dry, rigorous and didactic, generally lacking literary effects and historical allusions. He was capable of making a decision quickly, and he could display great determination in implementing that decision: his early social reforms, his nuclear energy programme, his vast reform of the telecommunications system provide eloquent illustration. Giscard d'Estaing could also demonstrate audacity in his decisions – as was the case in May 1978 when he sent in French troops to save 2,000 hostages blocked at Kolwezi in Zaire.

When Giscard d'Estaing was elected to the presidency in May 1974 he promised to humanise and modernise the office. And a number of highly symbolic acts indicated his intention of fulfilling his promise. His arrival on foot at the Elysée for the inauguration ceremony and his refusal to wear the official regalia at the ceremony set the early tone. Further such acts followed: in December 1974 he invited four Paris road-sweepers for breakfast at the Elysée (the photographs show them to be as uncomfortable about the occasion as the President); he visited two of the *bidonvilles* in the Paris area (they were to disappear during his presidency); he dined at the homes of several ordinary Frenchmen; in August 1974 he shook hands with the inmates of a Lyons prison; he banned the use of noble titles at the Elysée. He seemed determined to present a new style – almost Kennedy-like – of his office.

Gradually, however, Giscard d'Estaing became 'devoured' by the presidential function,[20] and his much-criticised monarchical practices and pretensions emerged. At the Elysée Palace the easy informality gave way to 'un protocole egotique' (for instance, he had himself served first at table – a reversion to the practice of the *ancien régime*). His safaries in Africa and his hunts in the Sologne were organised in regal fashion. No less offensive to 'republican' sentiment were the activities of his immediate family; his wife behaved as *La Présidente*; his son exploited his position as the *dauphin* to further his own political ends; his daughters were occasionally accorded precedence over foreign dignitaries and accompanied their father on more than one official trip abroad. Such activities were chronicled by the satirical *Canard enchaîné* and the censorious *Le Monde*. They were also published in the many critical books and brochures on Giscard d'Estaing, his family and his presidency. Amongst the most notable were Jean David, *Chroniques pour servir à la déposition du Prince*; Thomas Ferenczi, *Le Prince au miroir*; J.-Ch. Petitfils, *La Démocratie Giscardienne* (possibly the best); Pol Bruno, *La Saga des Giscard*; Roger-Gérard Schwarzenberg, *La Droite absolue*; and J.-P. Jouary, *Giscard et les idées, essais sur la guerre idéologique*.

Moreover, other less attractive personal traits became apparent: a certain lack of courage (his personal 'deep aversion' to the death penalty did not prevent him from allowing the execution of three men during his *septennat*); a penchant for rendering public his every act of private charity; a personal vindictiveness which was revealed in the clumsy and unconvincing prosecution of Jacques Fauvet, editor of *Le Monde* – an act which provoked the anger not only of the Left alone; his apparent lack of concern and compassion (evident in his much-publicised failure to visit Brittany after the *Amoco-Cadiz* shipping disaster or the rue Copernic in Paris after the destruction of the Jewish synagogue). Even his personal integrity was called into question after the *affaire des diamants*, a sordid episode in which it was revealed that he had received diamonds as presents from the highly compromising Central African self-styled Emperor Bokassa. The subsequent inept handling of the affair heightened suspicions rather than allayed fears. Perhaps the most electorally damaging characteristic was his seeming indifference to the problem of the rising tide of unemployment. His language was that of the brilliant *enarque* (the ex-student of the Ecole Nationale d'Administration), of the ex-Minister of Finances (an office he held for many years before becoming President) – analytical, cold, measured and apparently complacent. This complacency – a flaw detected by many – was no less obvious in the political domain. He always underestimated his opponents (notably Mitterrand) and always overestimated his electoral chances. It was not until far too late in the presidential campaign that he sensed the possibility of defeat: because he was President, he thought he could not be beaten – a fact admitted by Jean-François Deniau, who organised his election campaign.[21]

Finally, there was a growing scepticism about Giscard d'Estaing's willingness to carry out his promises: too many presidential promises or projects were never implemented - through lack of courage, lack of conviction, lack of will, or lack of skill. Too frequently, the President's speeches were followed by no action at all, a situation which provoked Pierre Viannson-Ponté's celebrated and cruel taunt that Giscard d'Estaing represented 'the triumph of incantation over action'.[22] The list of broken promises was long and unimpressive. To his failure to implement a number of political reforms (outlined below): the financing of political parties; the reform of the replacement - *suppléant* - system in the National Assembly; the introduction of proportional representation at local level; the limitation on the accumulation of elected offices (*cumul des mandats*); and the reduction of the presidential term of office, must be added others no less important: in the area of regional and local government reform nothing occurred (the Guichard Report of 1976, commissioned by the President, remained a dead-letter); his promise to attack property speculation led to the largely ineffective 1975 Law; his proposed attack on capital gains was converted into an anodyne law by the hostility of his own party coalition; his shelving of the Sudreau Report on workers' rights (which he had commissioned in June 1974); and his unfulfilled promise, announced at a press conference at Dijon in November 1975, to press ahead with the building of the Rhine–Rhône waterway.

By the end of the *septennat* Giscard d'Estaing's personal attributes and style had attracted a great deal of adverse publicity, and it is no exaggeration to claim that his person had engendered a profound aversion in certain circles.[23] Typical of the comments was that of Noël Jean Bergeroux of *Le Monde*, who described Giscard d'Estaing's method of government as 'une association étroite de sensibilité présumée et d'artifice exagéré'.[24]

The change in style was accompanied by a change in tone and approach. Giscard d'Estaing became undeniably more pessimistic, more mistrustful, more sceptical and more conservative.[25] The youthful enthusiasm of 1974 was replaced with a somewhat disabused resignation by 1981. In his speech of 27 May 1974 he could refer to the 'new era of French politics' in tones which invited the pointed comments of the sceptical Right. By May 1981 he could never have made such a speech. His later pessimism was rooted in a sombre reading of the evolution of French society and of the future place of France in the world. It found expression in his dislike of any ambitious or grand project for the country.[26] His mistrust was evident in his increasing political isolation, whilst his scepticism motivated his refusal to consider any alternative economic strategy. His conservatism, which is analysed below, was apparent in the abandonment of the reformist inspiration which marked the early years of the *septennat*. By 1981 Giscard d'Estaing lacked an electorally mobilising theme: in 1974 he had promised 'changement dans la continuité', whereas seven years later he merely offered continuity. He had come to be presented as aloof, patrician and haughty, lacking in compassion and even basic humanity. Perhaps he was aware of this image, for he was to admit in one of his final television appearances in the presidential campaign that 'il faut peut-être un septennat plus humain'. But the 'peut-être' may be as revealing as the admission.

## Giscardisme – the Economic Balance-sheet

There are a number of difficulties in drawing up the balance-sheet of the economic performance of *Giscardisme*.[27] In the first place, economic policies clearly evolved during the presidency. There were, in fact, three distinct phases: the first – 1974–6 or the Chirac period – was characterised by a policy of stop–go; the second – 1976 to the election of 1978 or the first Barre period – was much more liberal and orthodox in inspiration yet hesitant in implementation; and the third – from 1978 to the presidential elections or the second Barre period – was typified by greater resolution in the imposition of liberal practices.

The second problem is to determine how far President Giscard d'Estaing was responsible for France's economic policies during this period. The evidence appears to suggest that the President allowed Prime Minister Barre a degree of freedom which had not been enjoyed by Jacques Chirac, his predecessor. It is also true that France's economic policies were constantly summarised under the description of *Barrisme*. Yet it is equally true that Barre could not have pursued his policies without the full backing (often publicly expressed) of the President. Whatever private differences may have existed between the two men on economic affairs (and hints of such differences were leaked to the press), *Barrisme* came to be seen as the authentic expression of economic *Giscardisme*.

The third major problem in establishing the economic balance-sheet of the presidency relates to finding a satisfactory definition of *Barrisme*. It was never clear how much of the doctrine (if that is the appropriate term) belonged merely to the realms of political rhetoric. And even the rhetoric was ambivalent and contradictory: for instance, the language of effort and sacrifice was preached – France through greater work could overcome and was overcoming her problems – yet there emerged by 1981 a persistently fatalistic message. France could do little, given the appalling constraints imposed by the world economy, an economy dislocated by the chronic instability of the money markets and the 'financial irresponsibility' of the Americans, by the two energy crises of 1973–4 and 1978–9 which led to a quadrupling of France's energy bill, by the marauding activities of the Japanese and by the rivalry of the newly developing countries. Indeed, it was never really clear whether Barre and Giscard d'Estaing had any real directive strategy inspired by a coherent set of doctrines. All too frequently the basic strategy appeared merely to be a series of disjointed responses to day-to-day problems: short-term managerial tactics were rationalised into a medium/long-term strategy. The problem, moreover, was compounded by Barre's avowed eclecticism,[28] and one of his most astute critics could point out that his approach was much more supple than his public posturing suggested.[29] Raymond Barre was certainly more than the 'conjoncturaliste très habile' suggested by some but he was also much less than the unbending apostle of orthodox liberal economic dogma so often depicted in the literature of the Left.[30] Perhaps he can best be described as a pragmatic liberal with a dogmatic style.

The final problem in drawing up Giscard d'Estaing's economic balance-sheet is that of deciding the criteria by which the success should be judged. There are at least two: the extent to which he succeeded in implementing his somewhat attenuated liberalism, and the state of the French economy after seven years of his stewardship. By both criteria the balance-sheet is a mixed one.

Central to the liberal message were three objectives. The first was 'adapting France to the conditions of the new world economy' by the creation of an open economy with its inherent pressures for inducing a more competitive, more flexible, more profit-oriented mode of behaviour. The second objective was to put a brake on state interventionism, especially in favour of the 'lame ducks'. And the third was the declared aim of using macro-economic management to ensure a favourable climate in which firms (the legitimate economic decision-makers) would take the decisions. The three objectives were translated into policies in a number of ways: nationalised industries were forced to adopt a more 'realistic' economic pricing policy; price controls in the private sector were dramatically abolished or considerably eased (in August 1978 the price of bread was decontrolled for the first time since 1791); certain restrictions on capital investment abroad were lifted; and private shareholders were given (albeit limited) access to state industries, banks and insurance companies (thus in 1980 two state-owned banks – the Banque Nationale de Paris and the Société Générale – the insurance group AGF and the Havas advertising empire were allowed to raise money from equity operations on the Paris stock exchange). This policy of 'privatisation' was roundly condemned by the Left.[31] Symptomatic of the government's attitude was its approach to planning. As Jack Hayward points out in Chapter 6, Giscard d'Estaing was less than lukewarm about planning, and his (and Barre's) scepticism was evident in the extremely limited conception of planning which underpinned the eighth national plan.[32] However, accompanying these liberal anti-statist activities were a series of measures which underlined their restricted nature or limited their consequences. Indeed, it could feasibly be argued that during the presidency of Giscard d'Estaing the state became more, not less, interventionist. At least two indices support the argument. First, during 1974–9 the number of civil servants rose by some 300,000 a year (30,000 alone in the ministries of the Economy and of the Budget). By the end of Giscard d'Estaing's presidency one worker in four was employed by the state administration, in local authorities, the public service industries (for example, electricity industry), or the public enterprises (such as Air France, Renault and Seita). The growth of the state may also be seen in the increase in total tax revenue (that is, tax revenues and social security contributions) as a proportion of GDP: it rose from 36·3 to 42·5 per cent – higher than in the UK (35·9 per cent) and Germany (37·2 per cent) and far higher than the USA (30·7 per cent) and Japan (25·9 per cent). Even the Socialists were moved to protest, and Mitterrand rather rashly promised not to increase the proportion during his presidency. Many critics also pointed out that 'privatisation' in one area was matched by nationalisation of a clandestine nature ('by the backdoor') in other areas. Senator Bonnefous was particularly assiduous in unearthing examples of creeping *étatisme*, whilst the much-leaked Jacques Féron report on the public enterprises was to reveal the extent of unofficial nationalisation through the widespread use of state secondary shareholdings.[33]

Giscard d'Estaing's unwillingness or inability to implement his economic liberalism may also be seen in his failure to tackle the problem of the notoriously inefficient distribution networks or to dismantle the network of cartel price-fixing, which was so piously denounced by the Commission de la Concurrence which he had attempted to strengthen. Vulnerable home industries continued to be protected by quotas and tariffs, and the Japanese were kept at bay – at least partially – by voluntary import-restraint agreements and bureaucratic delaying tactics. Massive subsidies and loans were still channelled into private industry, with the state, far from being extricated, becoming more intimately linked into the steel industry (which was nationalised in all but name by 1981) and shipbuilding and textiles. In spite of the rhetoric, subsidies continued to pour into the nationalised industries and were still running at an estimated 20 billion franc a year. Certain French firms wishing to invest abroad found it difficult to do so, and a number of foreign firms wishing to invest in France were refused permission. Not content simply to cushion, protect, or even completely underpin parts of French industry, the state also pursued a policy of 'backing winners', and through the Comité pour l'Orientation et le Développement des Industries Stratégiques actively intervened in the investment programmes of firms engaged in growth areas such as electronics, nuclear power, office technology, aerospace, biotechnics and telecommunications. Other bodies which facilitated state interventionism in the economy – often described as the instruments of *libérodirigisme* – included the Comité Interministériel d'Aménagement des Structures Industrielles (CIASI, created in November 1974), the Fonds Spécial d'Adaptation Industrielle, the Comités Départementaux des Problèmes de Financement des Entreprises (CODEFI), the Comité Interministériel pour le Développement des Investissements et le Soutien de l'Emploi (CIDISE) and the Crédit d'Equipement des Petites et

Moyennes Entreprises (CEPME, a body created at the end of 1980, with a 51 per cent share of the capital belonging to the state and whose task was to organise loans to small- and medium-size businesses). In short, as Diana Green clearly shows in Chapter 5 in this book, the industrial policies of *Giscardisme* represented no dramatic departure *in practice* from those of his predecessors. The strong *dirigiste* tradition continued, distorting the intentions of the economic liberals and making nonsense of some of their pronouncements. Like his predecessors (and his successor), Giscard d'Estaing's economic policies were torn between the conflicting exigencies of ideology, national interest, efficiency and electoral prudence. They were, thus, marked by incoherence and inconsistency.

The management aspect of the balance-sheet provides an equally mixed record. When Barre became Prime Minister in 1976, his declared goal was to 'assainir l'économie': such health depended on a good balance of payments situation, a controlled and moderate growth in the money supply, a stable franc ('la condition principale pour un développement sain'), wage moderation and a balanced budget. The German model was clearly very much in mind.[34] In some respects Barre and Giscard d'Estaing were successful, and in his farewell message to the nation in May 1981 President Giscard d'Estaing claimed that he left France with a stable currency and had limited the budget deficit as well as bringing the social security system back into financial balance (thus saving it). He might have added that the financial position of French industry was better at the end of the *septennat*, with profit margins much healthier in 1981 than in 1974 and, as Prime Minister Barre was to emphasise in his *Report on the Economic and Social State of France on 30 April*, the level of foreign reserves was more than satisfactory. Moreover, as several government spokesmen pointed out, the politically controversial nuclear energy programme had reduced French dependence on outside sources from 70 per cent in 1974 to 50 per cent in 1981 – a remarkable achievement by any standard. Finally, throughout the *septennat* the balance of payments situation was *relatively* good – the damage caused by the first energy crisis was put right, and the deterioration of the last two years was largely due to the second energy crisis. In certain respects, therefore, the balance-sheet was perfectly honourable, and the Bloch-Lainé Commission established by President Mitterrand, was to point to the positive achievements outlined above. Apologists for Giscard d'Estaing such as Michel Drancourt[35] went further and were able to paint a glowing picture of the economic performance of France during the period 1974–81. For instance, with the exception of Japan, France enjoyed the highest growth rate (an average 2·8 per cent during the period 1973–80) of any major industrial country, and in 1981 was preceded by only the USA, Japan, the USSR and Germany in the world production league. If the 5·5–6 per cent growth rates of the early years of the Fifth Republic had not been sustained, this was simply because the state of the world economy had changed.

On the negative side of the balance-sheet must be cited investment performance, inflation and unemployment. The presidency saw the virtual collapse of private investment which, by 1981, was running at less than half the German rate and was even lower than that of Japan and the USA. Without sustained public investment, especially in the telecommunications and electro-nuclear industries, the French economy would have been in a far worse state – a point made repeatedly by the Left. France's average annual inflation rate during Giscard d'Estaing's presidency was 11·2 per cent – again, a record worse than her major competitors (9·3 per cent in the USA, 8·6 per cent in Japan and 4·5 per cent in Germany) if better than two of her other major commercial rivals in the European Community (Italy with 17·8 per cent and the UK with 15·9 per cent). Only once – in 1975 – was the French inflation rate lower than the average of the other major industrial nations (Table 10).[36]

The reasons for failing to solve the inflation problem were multiple: archaic distribution networks were tolerated (often for political reasons), the state (for inherent bureaucratic but also for political reasons) failed to curb its own expenditure and the problems of indexation and restrictive practices – both fraught with political dangers – were left untackled.

On the purchasing-power front the record of the presidency was patchy. Old-age pensions increased in value by 68 per cent, the retirement pensions of self-employed craftsmen and shopkeepers by 42 per cent, the hourly rate of manual workers by 29 per cent (although the number of hours worked dropped), whilst those on the minimum wage (the *smicards*) enjoyed a 28 per cent increase in purchasing power. The groups to suffer most were the managers and the farmers.[37] Only in 1977 and 1979 did this latter group enjoy any progress in living standards: during the presidency this key group in the right-wing electoral coalition suffered an average annual drop of 1·9 per cent in its purchasing power.

As the Bloch-Lainé Commission made clear, the presidency saw a squeezing of wage differentials but the gap between rich and poor remained wide – a point made not only by politicians of the Left, but also by several independent observers.[38] In fact, it is clear that President Giscard d'Estaing, although preoccupied with the plight of the very poor, was far from being an egalitarian.[39] It was equally clear that the politics of his electoral coalition gave him little room for manoeuvre. For political reasons, a tissue of minor privileges, honoured by time and tolerated by the tax system, was allowed to flourish. Tax avoidance – especially amongst

Table 10  *Annual Inflation Rates in Major Industrial Nations, 1974–80*

|         | 1974 | 1975 | 1976 | 1977 | 1978 | 1979 | 1980 |
|---------|------|------|------|------|------|------|------|
| France  | 15·2 | 9·6  | 9·9  | 9·0  | 9·7  | 11·8 | 13·7 |
| Average | 12·7 | 12·3 | 9·6  | 8·8  | 6·1  | 7·5  | 10·6 |

politically friendly groups such as shopkeepers, hoteliers, farmers and certain liberal professions – was dauntingly high: in 1980 it was put at 8–12 per cent of the state budget.

Perhaps the most electorally damaging aspect of the economic balance-sheet was the employment situation. A Sofres poll taken just before the first ballot of the presidential elections showed the overwhelming importance of unemployment as the major theme of the campaign and the conviction on the part of a very big majority that it could be reduced if the problem were properly handled (Table 11).[40]

Table 11    *Preoccupations of French Electors, 1981*

'Which of the following objectives do you consider to be priorities?'

|  | (%) |
| --- | --- |
| Combat unemployment | 90 |
| Combat inflation | 69 |
| Combat social inequalities | 63 |
| Maintain law and order | 56 |
| Defend the interest of your socio-professional group | 55 |
| Improve public services | 50 |
| Ensure oil provisions for France | 47 |
| Ensure defence of country | 44 |
| Modernise the French economy | 40 |
| Protect the environment | 34 |
| Ensure the morality of public life | 34 |
| Reinforce links between France and allies | 23 |
| Help Third World countries | 21 |
| Conduct, in the light of French interests, relations with USSR and Eastern Europe | 18 |

The unemployment rate rose from 2·3 to 7·3 per cent, or from 389,300 to 1,680,000, between May 1974 and May 1981. The army of the unemployed thus quadrupled during the *septennat*.[41] Furthermore, job-seekers were staying longer on the unemployment register: from an average 150 days in 1974 to 242 days in 1981. Particularly affected were women and the young. Several measures were taken to improve the chances and the lot of the unemployed: the Agence Nationale pour l'Emploi was reformed, job-creation schemes were created, unemployment allowances were extended and increased. But the apparently inexorable increase in the number of unemployed was to become the political Achilles heel of the President. The problem might have been less damaging had it not been handled in such conspicuously inept fashion. Even François Ceyrac, the president of the CNPF – the employers' organisation – and a firm supporter of the government, was to admit that the presentation of the problem had been 'too rational and too arid'.[42]

On the whole, the economic performance of the Giscard d'Estaing presidency was quite respectable. But it was to be judged very severely by the electorate in 1981.[43] Many of the President's natural supporters were no less critical: an IFOP poll taken only a few weeks before the presidential election indicated that more than three-quarters (77 per cent) of the managers interviewed thought that Giscard d'Estaing could have done better in the economic domain,[44] whilst a Sofres poll amongst businessmen taken at much the same time (13-30 March) for the influential journal *L'Expansion* revealed that barely a quarter (27 per cent) intended to vote for Giscard d'Estaing (compared with 41 per cent for Chirac), and that over half (53 per cent) thought that the President's economic policies were bad for their firm. The severity of the judgement was probably due to the economic situation in the year leading up to the election: the growth rate was a mere 1 per cent - average by European standards, good compared with Britain but poor by traditional French standards, and the worst performance since the crisis year of 1975; industrial production was falling rapidly; the budgetary deficit was growing; the balance of payments was beginning to cause concern; living standards dropped by an average 0.8 per cent, with farmers being particularly badly hit and people perceiving themselves as even worse off than the figures suggested;[45] prices had risen sharply by an average of 12·5 per cent; the unemployment figures were alarming. In short, there was a very poor performance in the last year, and this had the effect of hiding the general level of achievement of the presidency. When Giscard d'Estaing went into the election campaign, he was very vulnerable on the economic front. His policies were attacked by the Gaullists as *étatique* and as lacking in *volontarisme*, and by the Left as socially unjust. And all his opponents attacked them as being ineffective. Furthermore, as a perceptive American scholar has pointed out, the insensitive and authoritarian methods employed by Barre which involved the exclusion of important social groups from the consultative process impeded the implementation of the policies being pursued and limited their effect: 'societal compliance was necessary for the success of their [Giscard d'Estaing and Barre] policies but certain groups were asked to pay too high a price for policies to which they were not committed.' Part of the price was electoral defeat.[46] There is another way of looking at the contribution of economic factors to Giscard d'Estaing's defeat. President Giscard d'Estaing, as will be made clear later, never enjoyed the *general* level of backing of his two predecessors: he attracted less charismatic support. His reputation rested on the public's perception of his competence, especially in economic matters. When, therefore, that competence was called into question - as it was because of the economic *conjoncture* of 1980-1 - the President was unable to mobilise a sufficient degree of affective or charismatic support to ensure his election.[47] It may be unfair to render Giscard d'Estaing totally responsible for France's post-1974 economic problems, but there is little doubt that his economic policies, and his method of presenting them, were to cost him dear in the presidential elections. Most voters questioned by IFOP between the two ballots were convinced that the result of the elections would be decided on economic grounds,[48] and on the key economic issues most were unimpressed.[49] Perhaps, had the record elsewhere been good, the relative failure of his economic policies might have been forgiven. But, as the next section makes clear, this was far from being the case.

## *Giscardisme* – the Political Balance-sheet

Several attempts have been made to define the politics of *Giscardisme*.[50] For some, *Giscardisme* was but a style, a method of government, a set of reasonably intelligent responses to pressing circumstances. And whilst most would agree that it was more than a mere 'clever presentation of problems', to borrow Michel Debré's biting indictment, they would nevertheless emphasise the absence of any doctrine or coherent set of principles. Explanations of *Giscardisme* varied widely: to parts of the Left it was the political rationalisation of multi-national capitalism or an apologia for state monopoly capitalism; to certain sociologists it was perceived as the expression of techno-bureaucratic elitism; and to the historically minded it evoked a 'political sensibility' – that of the *juste milieu* – which had firm roots in the country's past. Other analyses stressed the ways in which *Giscardisme* differed from other doctrines: it was defined by what it was not. It was not, for example, the liberalism of the traditional Right (although many *Giscardiens* might subscribe to that doctrine or set of doctrines), because of its emphasis on modernity, its uninhibited use of state interventionism (whatever its official statements), its critique of the 'abuses' of old-style liberalism and its occasionally acute awareness of the social consequences of 'unbridled' classical liberalism. *Giscardisme* also differed considerably from Gaullism – in its historical reference-points, its personnel, its organisational ethos, its style and many of its policies.[51] Nor could *Giscardisme* be described as socialist or even social democratic, even though many policies smacked of social democracy and even though some of Giscard d'Estaing's associates did not hesitate to expropriate the label. Giscard d'Estaing explicitly rejected the semi-collectivisation of the economy, the egalitarianism, the regimentation and the stifling of individual initiative which he ascribed to social democracy.

What emerges from Giscard d'Estaing's writings is a prudent, pragmatic, somewhat functional yet socially sensitive reformism – a reformism motivated by the need to adapt, modernise, render more socially harmonious and politically unite the country. Giscard d'Estaing summarised his own basic political philosophy in the preface to the 1977 edition of his *Démocratie française* – the little blue-book of *Giscardisme*:

- at the present stage of its development, French society must be organised by man for man: neither traditonal liberalism nor Marxism, conceived at previous stages in French history, provide satisfactory models to be emulated;

- the salient feature of French society is not its permanent division or the class war. Rather, as with other industrial societies, economic growth has favoured the development of a vast central group which has its own behaviour, life style, education, culture and aspirations, and which is becoming increasingly homogeneous;
- the greater unification of French society must be facilitated by increasing social justice, which involves neither uniformisation nor a levelling-down process;
- the objective of French society is the blossoming of the individual – therefore, a collectivist organisation of society would be both ineffective and against the basic wishes of that society;
- individual autonomy and responsibility are the essential elements of this society which must be based upon a pluralistic conception of society;
- finally, pluralism must relate to all areas – not only political but also economic, in the mass organisations and the mass media.

The *political* strategy of Giscard d'Estaing followed quite logically from the above analysis. It had three major interrelated elements. The first was to facilitate the creation of a centrist political force corresponding to the 'vast central group', the emergence of which was so important in Giscard d'Estaing's analysis of the evolution of French society. As early as 1972 – two years before his election to the presidency – he had made his famous claim that 'la France aspire à être gouvernée au centre'. His task, he thought, would be eased by the disappearance of the evidently artificial divisions in France: indeed, he argued repeatedly that there was a consensus (a key word in the Giscardian vocabulary) on all the major issues. Only the feverish activities of the political parties, intent on promoting antagonism, kept alive the old, artificial divisions. The second main element in Giscard d'Estaing's political strategy was the pursuit of moderate reformist policies – the so-called policy of *changement dans la continuité*. And the third was the creation of a truly pluralistic democracy in all spheres of political life. Centrism, moderate reformism and pluralism were thus the three guiding strategic aims of political *Giscardisme*.

The strategy may have flowed easily and logically from the basic principles, but translating that strategy into a series of coherent tactics was to prove more than difficult. As in the economic field, the gulf between the *discours* and the reality became embarrassingly wide. This may be seen by examining Giscard d'Estaing's attempts to fulfil each of the three strategic aims.

As Ella Searls makes clear in Chapter 2 of this book, President Giscard d'Estaing failed to achieve what his two predecessors had so singularly succeeded in doing and what his successor was to manage – the creation of a political party which dominated the political and parliamentary stage. The majoritarian centrism which Giscard d'Estaing perceived as the dominant political aspiration of the French never found its concrete manifestation in the shape of a dominant political party. The *Giscardiens* – the Independent Republicans – were always only one element (albeit the most powerful) in a heterogeneous, divided, querulous and increasingly uneasy coalition – the Union pour la Démocratie Française (UDF) – which itself was but one component in the general coalition which supported (if that is the appropriate word) the President. The UDF, cobbled together in haste during the 1978 election campaign (that is, four years after his election), comprised the President's own party – the Independent Republicans – the Radicals (themselves weakened since the break away of the Left-wing Radicals) and a motley collection of centrists grouped essentially in the Centre des Démocrates Sociaux, led by Jean Lecanuet. It enjoyed some electoral success: 21·5 per cent of the votes in the 1978 election, and 26·7 per cent in the 1979 European elections – the latter performance making it the most successful electoral force in France. But success was never dominance and, because of that, Giscard d'Estaing was never fully master of the *majorité* – the governing party coalition. Unlike Mitterrand or Chirac, Giscard d'Estaing never created a highly mobilised and enthusiastic party base. His UDF was organisationally weak, divided (particularly over his reformist programme), leaderless and occasionally critical. It never furnished him with the men, the ideas, the activist machine, or the affective support that Mitterrand was to derive from the Socialist Party. It is significant that Giscard d'Estaing ran his presidential election campaign from the Elysée Palace and from his personal headquarters in the rue Marignan, whilst his campaign at local level was often in the hands of local 'apolitical' notables. His disgruntled party coalition was kept very much in the background. He thus failed to mobilise what little structured party support he enjoyed.[52]

The electoral dominance or hegemony of his own UDF essentially depended on either his effectively destroying the Gaullists and supplanting them by the UDF or his bending the Gaullists to his political will. He did neither: he hesitated and then he prevaricated. He did not destroy, dominate or appease the suspicious Gaullists. Indeed, by his clumsy tactics he was to antagonise them, and by so doing pay a heavy electoral price in May 1981.

The Gaullists had always been wary of Giscard d'Estaing. His 'oui-mais' speech of 10 January 1967 in which he revealed his ambivalence towards some of President de Gaulle's policies; his 'exercice solitaire du pouvoir' speech of 17 August 1967 in which he criticised de Gaulle's quixotic and arbitrary style of governing; his ambiguous attitude during the troubled days of May 1968; his hostile stance during the discussion of the budget in December 1968; and his final apostasy at the time of the April 1969 referendum campaign during which he expressed his opposition to

President de Gaulle's proposals, all were to combine to render him suspect in the eyes of the ever-sensitive Gaullists. During the Pompidou presidency Giscard d'Estaing, although Minister of Finances throughout, never ceased to mark his distance from the Gaullists. During his 1974 election campaign he fought the official Gaullist candidate (Chaban-Delmas), divided the Gaullist party and insisted on the need for change. When after this election he appointed the tough-minded Jacques Chirac, the leader of the pro-Giscardian minority within the Gaullist party (he was the leader of the forty-three Gaullist Deputies who supported Giscard d'Estaing and not Chaban-Delmas at the first ballot) to the premiership, Gaullist fears of a Giscard d'Estaing onslaught on their positions and policies were confirmed. Those fears were further heightened when the new President drastically reduced the number of Gaullist ministers and commenced his purge of the Gaullists holding key posts in the administration and in the media. Unfortunately for Giscard d'Estaing, Jacques Chirac was less intent on weakening the Gaullist party and rendering it servile to the President than on forging and strengthening it as an instrument of his own political ambitions.

Relations between President Giscard d'Estaing and his Prime Minister quickly soured, and in August 1976 Chirac resigned (the first genuine resignation of a Prime Minister during the Fifth Republic) in a blaze of acrimonious publicity. Thereafter, between the President of the Republic and the leader of the Gaullist party there deepened a highly personalised mutual enmity. In December 1976 Chirac created the new Gaullist party, the Rassemblement pour la République (RPR) in which he reinforced his personal position and in which anti-Giscard sentiments were never far from the surface and often vociferously proclaimed. Resentment against the President was merely fed by the continued electoral decline of the Gaullists: 25·5 per cent in 1973, 22·5 per cent in 1978 and only 16·3 per cent in the European Parliament elections of 1979. The dominant party of French politics throughout the 1960s and the early 1970s seemed destined to become merely the junior partner in the right-wing ruling coalition.

The period 1976–81 was characterised by growing anti-Giscard d'Estaing sentiment and punctuated by anti-Giscard d'Estaing activity, especially amongst the activists of the Gaullist party. A number of incidents illustrated the tensions and rivalry between Chirac and Giscard d'Estaing: in 1977 Chirac stood against the President's candidate in the Paris local elections – and, to the immense irritation of the *Giscardiens*, won; in the 1978 elections hostility broke out between the two camps over the election to the presidency of the National Assembly – Edgar Faure (Chirac's candidate and the incumbent President) being challenged, and beaten, by Jacques Chaban-Delmas, an anti-Chirac Gaullist and Giscard d'Estaing's candidate; during the 1979 European Parliament elections rival Gaullist and Giscardian candidates exchanged less than fraternal statements; in 1980 during the National Assembly debates on the budget

Prime Minister Barre's economic policies were severely mauled and the budget was passed only after the government resorted to a highly controversial (but perfectly legitimate) constitutional device.

By the 1981 presidential elections the Gaullists had amply demonstrated their opposition to Giscard d'Estaing's economic policies (they favoured a more expansionary policy and had opposed some of his tax-reform proposals), his European policies (notably over the introduction of direct elections to the European Parliament), his foreign policies (especially his attitude towards the Soviets during the Afghanistan crisis) and his practices which strengthened the presidential nature of the regime. It is revealing that President Giscard d'Estaing met his ex-Prime Minister on only six occasions between August 1976 and May 1981 – each occasion was purely formal and demanded by protocol, and he met Bernard Pons, the secretary-general of the Gaullist party, only once during this period.

By the end of his presidency Giscard d'Estaing had neither destroyed the Gaullists (which he might have achieved had he dissolved the National Assembly in 1974 in the wake of his presidential victory), nor had he appeased them by the occasional policy concession, by a more judicious use of his patronage, or by a more placatory attitude towards Jacques Chirac. He succeeded only in irritating them and provoking them into sullen resentment. The result was open opposition from the Gaullists to his candidacy in the presidential elections and Gaullist defections at the second ballot.

There were, in fact, three candidates from the Gaullist movement who stood against Giscard d'Estaing for the presidency. The first, Michel Debré, de Gaulle's first Prime Minister in 1959 and an outspoken opponent of Giscard d'Estaing since 1976, won support from 'historic' and 'legitimist' Gaullist leaders (Pierre Lefranc and Jacques Chaban-Delmas) and from younger militants in the Union des Jeunes pour le Progrès. His campaign was largely directed against the policies of Giscard d'Estaing and, in particular, against his weak, liberal economic measures and their failure to curb unemployment. He called for a stronger state, a 'government of national safety' and a more nationalist foreign policy, especially in EEC matters. Even Debré's verbal criticisms, however, were exceeded by those of the second Gaullist in the presidential race, Mme Marie-France Garaud. This former adviser to President Pompidou and Prime Minister Chirac demonstrated her vitriolic skills in a public 'Open letter to the President of the Republic', published in *Le Monde* on 7 December 1980. In this she attacked Giscard d'Estaing for 'laisser-aller, condescendance', 'désinvolture' and 'censure indirecte' of the media. This proved to be a mild start to an especially critical campaign focused on Giscard d'Estaing's foreign policy failings. Both these Gaullist candidates were important for their criticisms of the President, but neither really represented the activists of the RPR, the Gaullist party.

It was largely in response to demands from his own supporters that Jacques Chirac stood as the official RPR candidate for the presidency. He had been hesitant to enter the race for fear of dividing his own party, but both Debré and Garaud appealed to rather limited groups. After his late and lack-lustre entry into the presidential race, Chirac ran an impressive campaign which led to a first-ballot result better than expected. His vote was higher than that of both Marchais in 1981 and Chaban-Delmas in 1974. An IFOP poll of reactions to the presidential campaign broadcasts[53] showed Chirac to have been the most successful of the major candidates on television. The Chirac campaign insisted on the necessity of reducing unemployment – and the possibility of doing so by changing the government's economic policies. This inevitably reinforced the credibility of Mitterrand's argument that a realistic alternative to Giscard d'Estaing policies was possible.

Giscard d'Estaing failed to give his presidential coalition an appearance of unity between the two ballots. Immediately after the first ballot, Chirac briefly, sadly and critically advised his voters to transfer their support to Giscard d'Estaing at the second ballot. Debré did so even more briefly, whilst Mme Garaud gave no advice except to declare her own intention of spoiling her second ballot paper. In the next few days the incumbent President wrote to the RPR leader, asking for his full support for the second ballot and requesting his personal help at a big election meeting on 3 May at the Porte de Pantin, Paris. Chirac declined this invitation.[54] On 6 May he made a short pro-Giscard d'Estaing speech, and that was the extent of his support. Furthermore, in the two weeks between the polls most RPR activists stayed at home, whilst some RPR leaders (Dechartre and Le Tac are examples) announced that they would vote for Mitterrand. None the less, it should be noted that the Chirac–Giscard d'Estaing rate of transfer of votes between the ballots was not as low as many had predicted (see above).

A pre-election opinion poll study by Roland Cayrol and Jérôme Jaffré showed that whilst the basic political values and ideologies of Giscard d'Estaing and Chirac voters remained very similar, their judgements about the presidency of Giscard d'Estaing and their hopes for the future were very different. Of those voting for Chirac, 49 per cent were 'confident' in Giscard d'Estaing (compared with 95 per cent of Giscard d'Estaing voters), 67 per cent hoped for 'real political change' (42 per cent of Giscard d'Estaing voters), 47 per cent had 'a high opinion' of the Socialist Party (34 per cent of Giscard d'Estaing voters) and 26 per cent would have been satisfied if Mitterrand were elected (14 per cent Giscard d'Estaing voters).[55] In such conditions Giscard d'Estaing was perhaps fortunate to have benefited from such a high transfer rate.

Giscard d'Estaing's inability to widen his centrist alliance to embrace the Gaullists was matched by his incapacity to attract the forces of the non-communist Left – the Movement of Left-wing Radicals (MRG) and the

Socialists (PS). The widening of the centrist alliance to the non-communist Left could have taken place in two ways: by attracting either one or both of the parties into alliance, or by attracting people within both parties into the existing centrist fold. The first alternative was ruled out by two factors. First, the MRG and the PS remained convinced, throughout the presidency, of the need for co-operation – however limited – with the Communist Party. Even after the *rupture* of September 1977 when the parties of the Left failed to agree on an updated joint programme of government (a failure to which Giscard d'Estaing attributed far too much importance), and in spite of the Communist Party's campaign of personal and political vilification, François Mitterrand, the leader of the non-communist Left, remained firmly committed to left-wing unity (see below). The second factor was the 'radicalisation' of the Socialist Party, by far the major party of the non-communist Left, during the 1970s – which widened the political gulf between the Socialists and the President – especially when the latter began to move in a more conservative direction after 1976. Giscard d'Estaing's attempt to tempt individual leftists into the centrist fold was equally unsuccessful. There was the occasional unspectacular conversion: Françoise Giroud, the highly talented journalist who declared her allegiance to Mitterrand during the 1974 election but who served Giscard d'Estaing in junior ministerial capacity; Eric Hinterman, ex-member of the Socialist Party and leader of the small Fédération des Socialistes Démocrates; Pierre Brousse, a Left-leaning Senator; Max Lejeune, ex-Socialist minister. Such people, motivated by anti-communism or personal opportunism, represented a very small minority and carried very little political weight. And often their conversion was of limited duration: Françoise Giroud, Eric Hinterman and Pierre Brousse were all to call for a vote for Mitterrand in 1981. It is arguable that, once again, Giscard d'Estaing willed the end without implementing the means. The means, it has been argued, involved a change in the legislative electoral system to some form of proportional representation: by replacing the existing system which had produced dramatic polarisation by a system of proportional representation the party system would be 'loosened' and realignments facilitated if not ensured. The argument, which met with some approval in Giscardian circles, should be treated with scepticism. A country's party system is shaped by a number of factors, and in France the most single important *institutional* factor inducing polarisation is the presidential system based on direct election, and that system was never the subject of debate during Giscard d'Estaing's presidency. In the event, not even the local electoral system was changed. Yet no tampering with the electoral systems was likely to encourage electoral co-operation between a non-communist Left which was moving further to the Left and the *Giscardiens* whose leader was swinging further to the Right. There was thus a contradiction between the President's centrist political strategy and the policies he pursued: his failure to implement his reformist programme helped to undermine his centrist strategy.

It has been argued that Giscard d'Estaing's conception of *changement* related only to a change of men and not of policies.[56] This seems to overstate the case. As Xavier Gardette shows in Chapter 4, the reformist record is quite a respectable one. In the area of social mores such legislation as the lowering of the voting age to 18 (June 1974), and the liberalisation of the abortion and divorce laws in December 1974 and March 1975 respectively, the extent of the reform was far-reaching. It should also be pointed out that the latter two pieces of legislation were pushed through by the President in the teeth of considerable right-wing opposition. For instance, in the vote on the abortion Bill in November 1974 only 55 of the 173 Gaullist, 17 of the 65 Republican Independent Deputies and 27 of the 52 centrist Deputies voted in favour, and the Bill was carried only because the Deputies of the opposition backed it. On the positive side it should also be pointed out that during the presidency wage differentials between the highest and the lowest paid narrowed, and there was a determined effort to protect and improve upon unemployment benefits, family allowances and old-age pensions (see above). Even towards the end of the *septennat* there were a number of minor reforms, favouring the manual workers, the physically handicapped and the old.

There is no doubt, however, that the reform phase was short-lived, and that it gave way to a much more conservative period, a move that was clearly perceived by the electorate: in a September 1974 Sofres poll fewer than a third of the respondents (31 per cent) placed the President on the Right, compared with over a half (51 per cent) in a similar poll in February 1981. The move to the Right was pronounced not only in the economic domain, with the gradual introduction after 1976 of *Barrisme*. It was no less marked in the political and social field. Major reforms, such as those suggested in the Sudreau Report (commissioned by Giscard d'Estaing himself in the heady days of June 1974) or the Guichard Report on local government or the Mayoux Report on financial decentralisation or the report by 'the three wise men' on the enlargement of the EEC (all three also commissioned by the President), were simply shelved. Others, such as those relating to property speculation (1975), capital gains (1976), or the distribution of shares to employees (1980), were timid in conception, often emasculated in their passage through Parliament and no less frequently diluted in their implementation. The much-promised reform of the tax system never materialised: the capital gains tax of June 1976 proved anodyne indeed; the wealth tax never saw the light of day; the tax system generally continued to be riddled with unjustifiable abuses and its emphasis upon indirect taxes hit the poor disproportionately hard.

In some areas it is even legitimate to talk about a reactionary approach to problems. Security and order replaced reform as the major preoccupations. The activities of Alice Saunier-Seïté, the minister in charge of higher education, were particularly instructive in that respect. Important parts of the 1968 Law which had partially liberalised the structures and decision-making process of the universities were dismantled (notably by the so-called Sauvage Law of 27 June 1980), political friends were placed in the *rectorats* and universities suspected of leftist tendencies were discriminated against. The university world protested with its customary lack of effect, even pro-*Giscardiens* were scandalised by some of the measures and, more especially, by the methods employed to impose them.[57] It was public knowledge that Prime Minister Barre, an ex- (and future) professor of economics, was less than happy about the activities of his troublesome subordinate and intervened increasingly in university affairs to limit the damage.[58]

The area in which the right-wing drift of the presidency was most marked was in that of law and order.[59] If telephone-tapping was curtailed and cinema censorship stopped almost immediately, there were early indications which already pointed to the limits to Giscard d'Estaing's liberalism in this field. The special commission which was established by the Council of Ministers on 31 July 1974 to draw up 'a code of fundamental individual freedoms' was placed under the chairmanship of the Minister of the Interior (that is, a ministry post not reputed in France for its attachment to such freedoms). And it never reported; indeed, it is unclear whether it ever met. More significant were the retention of the repressive *anti-casseurs* law of 8 July 1970, the maintenance of the State Security Court created in January 1963 in the aftermath of Algerian independence and the refusal to abolish the death penalty – or even allow a free vote in Parliament on the issue, the non-ratification of article 25 of the European Convention which gives individuals direct access to the European Court. More alarming was the 1976 law which empowered the police to search vehicles at any moment – a law which was rejected by the Constitutional Council in its judgement of 12 January 1977. But perhaps the measure which most revealed the increasing obsession with the repressive aspects of law and order was the infamous *Sécurité et Liberté* Law of 18 December 1980, which singularly tightened up penalties, restricted the powers of the judiciary and severely limited the rights of the defence.[60] It was pushed through an unhappy Parliament (the legal commission of the National Assembly had to deal with some 200 proposed amendments, sixty of which emanated from the ranks of the Right), and it encountered the bitter and even anguished opposition of large parts of the legal profession (on 27 May 1980 judges and lawyers held protest demonstrations in many of the main towns of France). It was also criticised by several prominent members of the governing coalition. Jacques Chirac (who described the Bill as 'indigne') and Bernard Pons of the Gaullists were joined by Didier Bariani, president of the Radical Party, and Bernard Stasi, vice-president of the Centre des Démocrates Sociaux, in voting against the Bill. The introduction of the computerised identity-card which followed shortly after the passage of the Bill merely confirmed the critics in their fears that Giscard d'Estaing had embarked upon a dangerously repressive path.

The failures to create or facilitate the creation of a majoritarian centrist force and the virtual abandonment of reformism after 1976 were matched by the President's failure to inaugurate 'a truly pluralistic society' in France - the third of his major political ambitions. Yet again, in the early days of the presidency an effort was made to give effect to the promises he had made and the doctrines he had preached. The state-controlled media was reformed with the break-up of ORTF and the granting of autonomy to three separate television networks (the reform is described by Raymond Kuhn in Chapter 7), and the opposition was accorded greater access to the media (it was even after September 1978 given the right to reply to the government - but not to the President - on television). There is no doubt that, compared with the two previous presidencies, the situation was somewhat improved. President Giscard d'Estaing also made a limited attempt to improve the position of Parliament by the introduction of *questions d'actualité* (questions on controversial topical issues), by the commissioning of reports by individual members of Parliament on specific problems (there were fifty-one such *missions*), and, much more significantly, by giving them, by the Law of 26 December 1974, the right to test the constitutionality of any law in the Constitutional Council. This measure was denounced as a *reformette* at the time but it proved to be a useful weapon in the hands of the opposition, since the Council rejected several important pieces of government legislation which had been sent to it by opposition Deputies.

An integral part of Giscard d'Estaing's pluralistic programme was the policy of *décrispation* - the improvement of relations between the governing coalition and the opposition. To that end he made an attempt to give the opposition the chairmanship of one of the six commissions of the National Assembly (the attempt failed because of Gaullist opposition); he appointed the occasional Socialist to the Council of State or to the Economic and Social Council; he asked Robert Fabre, the then leader of the Left-wing Radicals, to report on unemployment; and later appointed Fabre to the post of *médiateur* - the French ombudsman. The President also made several invitations to opposition party leaders to meet him - invitations which were only very rarely accepted. During his official visits to a major town he could be ostentatiously friendly with the mayor, even when he was an opposition leader: this was the case when he visited the towns of Gaston Defferre (Marseilles) and Pierre Mauroy (Lille). But Giscard d'Estaing's pluralistic designs were clearly limited in intention and scope, and many of the practices of the presidency merely underlined this fact.

One of the most striking characteristics of the *septennat* was the increasing power of the presidency - a phenomenon which invited the criticisms not only of the Left, but also of many Gaullists.[61] By 1981 the President of the Republic not only clearly and overtly defined the major policy directives of the government, but also intervened in any area that attracted his attention. He intervened in a number of ways. First, he addressed *lettres directives* to the Prime Minister, the head of the government: there were twenty-five such letters during 1974–80, seventeen relating to specific policy areas and eight on general policy.[62] Secondly, he would bypass the Prime Minister by asking favoured individuals to draw up a report as a basis for future action: thus, Olivier Guichard, ex-Gaullist minister, was requested to report on the reform of local government in November 1975 and Monique Pelletier was asked to look into the drug problem in June 1977. Thirdly, he institutionalised and developed the use of interministerial councils under his chairmanship – arguably the most single important instrument of executive government during his presidency. Fourthly, he exploited his strong and talented Elysée staff to ensure an overall supervision of governmental activities. Howard Machin in Chapter I of this book rightly rejects the oft-repeated charge that the Elysée team had become some form of occult government, but he also stresses the key role it played in decision-making. Finally, Giscard d'Estaing used and occasionally abused the media by over-frequent appearances in which he made it abundantly clear where the source of governmental authority lay.

Giscard d'Estaing was not content to limit his interventions to major policy orientation. He interfered in a host of very specific problems: prison reform, pollution of the beaches and the height of buildings in Paris. The object of presidential interference could border on the derisory: the type of tree to be planted in the Place des Vosges and the rhythm of the Marseillaise. The Elysée was, therefore, clearly reinforced as the major definer and arbitrator of executive policies. The President also became the centre of a vast network of patronage which included the appointments of the Prime Minister and ministers (the latter occasionally against the wish of the former), high-ranking civil servants, university rectors, members of ministerial staffs (*cabinets*) and of the Economic and Social Council.[63] He would even intervene to impose his choice of political candidatures, such as Michel d'Ornano for the mayorship of Paris or Simone Veil as head of the *Giscardien* list for the European elections. It was not only top posts which were the subject of presidential control: Giscard d'Estaing was known to meddle in the choice of minor French embassy officials. He was also keen on placing his men in key posts in the nationalised industries, and the insurance and banking sectors: for instance, Claude-Pierre Brossolette, secretary-general of the Elysée, became the head of Crédit Lyonnais, whilst Jacques Calvet, ex-director of Giscard d'Estaing's private staff (*cabinet*), was awarded the top post in the Banque Nationale de Paris. This 'osmosis' between the political, administrative and business worlds was one of the most salient features of what came to be known as the *Etat-UDF* or the *Etat-Giscard*, and it has been described by several authors including Pierre Birnbaum, who outlines part of the argument in Chapter 3.[64] It is at least debatable whether the result of Giscardisation – an ugly but useful term – was 'the end of the relative autonomy of the state apparatus *vis-à-vis* the financial oligarchy' or the emergence of 'technocratic government' or the creation of an 'autocratic society', all criticisms levelled against the regime. What was undeniable, however, was the unfavourable image which was created: Giscard d'Estaing's France seemed to be run by a narrow and exclusive clique of technocratic managers who, like Giscard d'Estaing himself, were the product of X (Ecole Polytechnique) or ENA (Ecole Nationale d'Administration), who issued from a restricted stratum of society and who were politically insensitive to the aspirations of ordinary Frenchmen. In short, the pluralistic aspirations of the President of the Republic appeared to be in flagrant contradiction with his construction of a narrowly based power structure.

The Giscardisation of the state was also very apparent in the media. The President's policy of placing close associates or political allies in key posts in the media (which included the popular periphery radio stations such as Radio Monte Carlo) and his occasional clumsy meddling in press matters[65] underlined a preference for political expediency over pluralistic principle. As Raymond Kuhn shows in Chapter 7, President Giscard d'Estaing, compared with his two predecessors, merely used different means to achieve basically similar ends.[66] He was certainly as attached to the maintenance of the state monopoly as de Gaulle or Pompidou.

Further evidence of the conflict between declared pluralistic ambitions and much less pluralistic practice is not difficult to find. Yves Mény, in Chapter 8, very clearly indicates the limits to the reforms in the field of regional and local government – both much-vaunted means of diffusing power. The reform which facilitated the means by which those French living abroad could vote (the law of 31 January 1976) was counter-balanced by a scandalous manipulation of such votes in the 1978 elections, a manipulation which was helped by a further law (30 June 1977) which slipped through an unsuspecting Parliament almost unnoticed. The President's promise to help political parties – amongst the major instruments of political pluralism – was never fulfilled, and by the end of his presidency he had even resorted to the Gaullist technique of berating and deriding them. His exclusion of certain politically unacceptable pressure groups from the decision-making process and his favouring of others (sometimes less representative but more politically compliant) was equally revealing.

The President's retention of Raymond Barre as Prime Minister under-lined his limited respect for 'true pluralism'. Barre was greatly admired and respected in certain circles (especially abroad) for his application, intelligence and consistency. He was also a humane, courteous and cultured individual in private life. But his verbal brutality, his hectoring style and political insensitivity in public, coupled with his arrogant and self-satisfied treatment of any opposition however mild and whatever its political complexion as at best ill-informed and stupid and, at worst, treasonable, his insistence that there was 'no other way' than his own, combined to compound the damage already created by other illiberal – and unpluralistic – practices. Barre was, by far, the most unpopular Prime Minister of the Fifth Republic (an unpopularity he publicly savoured, viewing it as proof of the rightness of his policies), and by Christmas 1980 only 27 per cent of those polled by IFOP declared themselves satisfied with the Prime Minister compared with 57 per cent who were dissatisfied.[67] Instead of acting as a screen for the President, shielding him from public disgruntlement, he became an added source of unpopularity: he exacerbated rather than attenuated resentment towards the President. Giscard d'Estaing, by excluding Barre from an active role in the presidential campaign, clearly understood the lesson, but by that time it was too late.[68]

The political balance-sheet of the Giscard presidency was, therefore, not a very positive one. There was a clearly stated series of intentions and ambitions rooted in an analysis of the evolution of French society, and there was an early attempt to give effect to those ambitions and intentions. However, in each of three major strategies which were implied – centrism, reformism and pluralism – there was insufficient will or skill, or both, in implementation. By 1981 his early efforts were derided as *gadgets* or *reformettes*, his declarations in favour of reforming centrism were described as an electoral ploy and his pluralism denounced as a fake. The presidency which commenced with the promise of so much economic, social and political reform ended in an aura of prosaic and prudent conservatism.

The progressive transformation of President Giscard d'Estaing from an enlightened reformer into an apprehensive conservative has been attributed to many factors. Some argue that the later and conservative Giscard d'Estaing was merely the true Giscard d'Estaing – the scion of the upper-class elite which had always dominated French politics. They pointed to the political role of Jacques Bardoux, his maternal grandfather, a parliamentary *notable par excellence* during the Third and Fourth Republics, to his father, the ex-Inspecteur des Finances, and brothers all of whom collected company directorships with alarming ease and frequency. His wife was also from an immensely wealthy industrial and financial dynasty: the only social difference between her and her husband was that her aristocratic credentials were impeccable, more ancient and not at all controversial.[69] The critics also pointed to Giscard d'Estaing's record as the Minister of Finance who had displayed a prudent orthodoxy throughout his long office. Other observers linked his growing conservatism with his increasing personal scepticism and pessimism (see above), whilst others, more charitable, noted that his evolution corresponded to the deteriorating world situation due to the impact of the energy crisis, the disorder in the world monetary system, the insecurity engendered by the rise of terrorism, the Middle East crisis, the Soviet invasion of Afghanistan and the Polish crisis: in such circumstances it was inevitable that France needed security and not change, reassurance and not reformist provocation, prudence and not adventure. There were also those (including, apparently, Giscard d'Estaing himself) who claimed that the President remained an unrepentant reformist but was hampered in his purposes by the hostility of his party coalition and by the reticence of his own electorate – the celebrated *pesanteurs* which constrained his action. It was also claimed that his failure to move France in a centrist direction was equally hindered by the unyielding belligerence of the opposition.[70] Yet the problem goes much deeper. It was clear that there was an extensive consensus amongst the French electors on subjects such as defence, Europe, the place of the family and the nature of the regime, and that consensus was perceived as the basis for political realignment in a centrist direction. But there was dissensus on some subjects. And even an extensive consensus does not necessarily imply the end of polarised politics.[71] Indeed, polarisation is inherent in the presidentialism of the French Fifth Republic, in its electoral arrangements and in its political traditions. It was also unfortunate from Giscard d'Estaing's point of view that constant elections kept the country in a state of permanent political – and generally polarised – activity. The presidential elections of May 1974 (which Giscard d'Estaing won in dramatically polarised circumstances) were followed by the highly politicised – and polarised – local elections to the departmental assemblies (March 1976) and to the municipal councils (March 1977). Both were a resounding success for a united Left, which therefore saw little point in destroying their electoral alliance. The March 1978 general elections saw the unexpected victory of the Right, which had the same effect for the Right. Only the European elections of 1979, which were based on proportional representation, gave a glimpse of the areas of agreement between the *Giscardiens* and the Socialists and the gap between those two and the Gaullists and the Communists. But the European elections were followed by the 'pre-campaign' and then the official campaign for the presidential elections. Whatever the reasons, by May 1981 Giscard d'Estaing had eschewed the strategy elaborated in 1974 and partially implemented in the first two years of his presidency. In pursuing his more conservative, less open and less liberal line he broke many promises and offended many of his party supporters: several, such as Didier Bariani, president of the Radicals, supported Giscard d'Estaing in 1981 but demanded that he change direction. He also misread the temper of the French electors who aspired for the *changement* he had promised in May 1974 and which François Mitterrand was promising with great conviction in May 1981.

The President's political stance is difficult to understand, since opinion not only wanted reform, but applauded his early reformist measures. A Sofres opinion poll taken towards the end of the presidency indicated that a majority of the French were in favour: the reform of the abortion law was favoured by 66 per cent to 24 per cent opposed; 78 per cent backed the liberalisation of the divorce legislation, whilst only 10 per cent were opposed. Only the reduction in the voting age from 21 to 18 was disapproved, by a small margin of 47 to 45 per cent.[72] The same poll revealed that 48 per cent of those questioned thought Giscard d'Estaing had not carried out enough reforms, compared with only 26 per cent who thought he had. The desire for change also emerged from the studies made by the Centre de Recherche et d'étude pour l'observation des conditions de vie, which regularly tests French opinion,[73] and by the Sofres polling organisation. To the question 'On the whole are you for or against far-reaching political change' (*un changement politique profond*), 70 per cent were for (compared with 61 per cent in 1974), 18 per cent against (27 per cent in 1974) and 12 per cent were without opinion on the subject. The same poll, which was taken only two months before the first ballot of the presidential election, indicated that nearly three-quarters (73 per cent) of the electors favoured 'a very or fairly far-reaching transformation' of French society.[74]

Whilst alienating opinion on the centre Left, Giscard d'Estaing also failed to win over the authoritarian or extreme Right, many of whose leaders were attracted to the more muscular message and style of Jacques Chirac or who preached abstention in the election. In contrast with 1974 some royalist groups and elements of Action Française declared their hostility towards him during the 1981 campaign.

When analysing the unwillingness of Giscard d'Estaing to carry out reforms account must be taken not only of the changing domestic and international environment and his own personal evolution. Perhaps of equal importance was his failure fully to appreciate the consequences of the socio-economic transformation of France. He always claimed to have an understanding of *la France profonde*, and it is true that in his writings he displays an awareness of the changes taking place in his country. But the true extent and nature of the changes he failed to grasp. The increasing industrialisation, urbanisation and secularisation of French society with their corresponding impact on the socio-professional structure of the country (fewer farmers and small shopkeepers, many fewer practising Catholics, increasing numbers of wage-earners, a growing number in the tertiary sector, and an expansion in the number of working women) were progressively 'to enlarge the social bases of the Left'.[75] When Mitterrand declared that his victory represented the meeting of 'social' and 'political' France, that is what he had in mind. Such changes, coupled with increasing state intervention and the growth and proliferation of social services, had inevitable consequences for prevailing value patterns and structures. The decline in traditional hierarchical values (often centred on the family) gave rise to new values and aspirations. With four-fifths of the active population classified as wage-earning, the problem of employment becomes fundamental, and demands relating to working conditions, work-hours and the environment were bound to loom large in any set of electoral exigencies. *La France profonde* by May 1981 had become industrial, urban and secular, characterised by greater similarities between groups and often increasing heterogeneity within them. Its demands were often confused and frequently conflicting (for example, individual self-realisation and greater social solidarity) but they were real, and they were being given expression in the policies of that 'cross-roads of contradictions', the Socialist Party headed by François Mitterrand. Giscard d'Estaing analysed his changing country and perceived certain aspirations, but he was blind to others. His tragedy, too, was that he failed to implement even those changes he saw necessary – and which he had promised in his election campaign of May 1974.

## *Giscardisme* – Some Concluding Remarks

President Giscard d'Estaing never enjoyed the popularity of his two predecessors, General de Gaulle and Georges Pompidou. The regular IFOP opinion polls (taken since 1958), which registered the number of voters satisfied and dissatisfied with the President of the Republic, show that presidents de Gaulle and Pompidou enjoyed an average 'satisfaction rate' some 10 per cent higher than that of Giscard d'Estaing (49·2 per cent for the latter, compared with over 58 per cent for the two former). And whereas the popularity of de Gaulle and Pompidou transcended the boundaries of their party coalition, that of Giscard d'Estaing appeared not to do so: he was 'un président sans charisme particulier'.[76]

Moreover, his popularity was extremely volatile: high, for example, at the time of the 1978 elections and low in December 1976 when Jacques Chirac created the RPR. For both previous Presidents of the Republic, the opinion polls registered a general decline in popularity – but not to the same extent, nor from the same base. Indeed, Giscard d'Estaing was the first President to register a negative satisfaction rating. By February 1981 the number of dissatisfied (51 per cent) far outnumbered the satisfied (37 per cent). It was an inauspicious start to the official presidential election campaign. Moreover, his reaction was to reveal one of the weaknesses of the President – his complacency. He believed that he could not be beaten, because he was President of the Republic.

Giscard d'Estaing's election campaign had to be good to redress an intrinsically difficult situation. He and his record (he was the only candidate with a recent record in office to defend) were attacked by *all* other nine candidates – 'le chœur des neuf pleureuses', as he disparagingly described them. Furthermore, his opponents had ample access to the media which, although totally *Giscardien*, were obliged for the first time during the *septennat* to present the President as a simple candidate. There was thus, as in 1965 with President de Gaulle, an *effet démystificateur*.

Giscard d'Estaing's tactics were to present himself as a strong man, a man of experience and of judgement – two qualities so essential in a troubled world – and yet a man, too, sensitive to the need for reform in a rapidly evolving society. In other words, he wished to project himself, with calculated ambiguity, as representing that electorally winning combination of reassurance and reform. It was a combination that had not failed him in 1974, when he conducted a brilliant and successful campaign. But 1981 was not 1974. In 1981 there was a personal and political-reform record to defend.

Giscard d'Estaing's campaign was, moreover, badly handled.[77] He oscillated between being the President of the Republic – aloof, haughty, distant and even disdainful of his adversaries – and being the simple candidate. He was at once the President of all the French and the candidate of less than half of them, and when criticised, he indulged in the tactics of wounded and scandalised nationalism (attacks upon him were also attacks upon France). He was also inconsistent. He attacked Chirac, the Gaullist leader, but embraced some of his ideas during the campaign itself. He denounced the mediocrity of the campaign debate yet resorted occasionally to argument of a highly dubious nature. He displayed a surprising complacency on some occasions and a too-evident apprehension on others. This complacency was almost certainly based on a misreading of the state of the French Left and on the unexpected victory of the Right in 1978. In some respects, too, he seemed out of tune with the desires of the electorate. For instance, it was not until 28 March that the problem of unemployment was raised – and then only with reference to the young. In his television encounter with the Socialist leader on 5 May (an encounter in which he hoped – but failed – clearly to establish his ascendancy over Mitterrand, as in 1974) he emerged as rather defensive, cold, didactic, apprehensive and tired. The hope, the conviction and the enthusiasm of the 1974 campaign was nowhere apparent. Perhaps some of the contradictions of the campaign may be attributed to the conflicting advice he was receiving from the rue Marignan (the official campaign headquarters organised by Deniau), the Elysée and, to a lesser extent, from the political team which included Jean Lecanuet, president of the UDF, and Jacques Blanc, secretary-general of the Republican Party. Since, however, the campaign was a highly personalised one, most of the blame must be placed on the shoulders of Giscard d'Estaing himself.

There are many difficulties in drawing up a balance-sheet of *Giscardisme*, and not the least is to decide in what light it must be judged: in the light of the electoral promises enunciated in May 1974, or of its own rhetoric, philosophical or ideological aspirations, or of its achievements in guiding France through a difficult domestic and international environment? Depending on the starting-point it is possible to reach an overall judgement which is either condemnatory or admiring. A majority of the French electors were to prove critical on 10 May 1981. That electoral

failure must be sought in many factors: they range from the wider factors –
his misreading of the aspirations of a rapidly changing society and his
political mismanagement of the economic crisis – to the narrower ones – his
retention of an immensely unpopular Prime Minister, his provocation of
the Gaullists, his inability to create an effective party machine and his
personal complacency. The various factors have been analysed under the
headings of personal, economic and political. What emerges from the
above analysis is that at all three levels – personal, economic and political –
there were problems and that those problems were rooted in the contradictory and often incoherent set of ends being pursued. Moreover, each
level was to interact with the other in an inhibiting and often conflicting
manner, thus rendering even more incoherent the policies of the presidency. Yet, however severely the balance-sheet of the *septennat* was
judged by the electorate, it must be remembered that until almost the end
the opinion polls suggested that the President would be re-elected and that
even until the very end a majority of the electors expected him to be so.
There is, therefore, another factor which explains the electoral failure of
*Giscardisme* which must now be examined, and that is the emergence of an
attractive and viable alternative in the person, the personnel and policies of
François Mitterrand, his principal adversary.

## The Mitterrand Victory

As already noted, the opinion polls of late autumn and early winter 1980
were indicating both the unpopularity of President Giscard d'Estaing and
the likelihood of his re-election. This apparent paradox was partly
explicable by the absence of a viable alternative to the incumbent. When,
however, François Mitterrand finally entered the fray with the official and
virtually unanimous support of his party, he very quickly established
himself as that alternative. It should be recalled that in October 1980 only
27 per cent of the electors thought Mitterrand would make a good
President,[78] yet between December 1980 and February 1981 Giscard
d'Estaing began to lose ground, Chirac began to improve his position,
Marchais's vote began to stagnate and Mitterrand began to emerge as the
real – and dangerous – challenger to the President.

The emergence of Mitterrand as the major challenger to the President as
expressed in first-ballot preferences was accompanied by (and is perhaps
partially explained by) the increase in the number of voters opting for him
at the second. Yet although the polls were pointing to a Mitterrand
victory, they were also indicating that a majority of the voters expected
Giscard d'Estaing to win: the unpublished IFOP poll taken between the
two ballots showed that whilst 52 per cent hoped for the victory of
Mitterrand, 61 per cent predicted the victory of his opponent.[79] The
general expectation of Giscard d'Estaing's re-election may, paradoxically,

have contributed to his defeat, for some disgruntled centrist voters may have voted for Mitterrand in the mistaken belief that they could punish the incumbent President without running the risk of electing a left-wing President. This had not been the case in 1978 when there was a widespread expectation of a left-wing victory.

The victory of François Mitterrand was that of the man and of the politician who was the leader and principal rejuvenator of the French Socialist Party, the co-ordinator of the non-communist Left and the personification of left-wing unity. It was also the victory of an experienced campaigner who at the critical moment correctly interpreted the mood of the French electorate. The various achievements of his long and varied career contributed to his achievement in May 1981. As an individual politician, Mitterrand demonstrated many qualities and great ability during his thirty years of public life. He was first and foremost a highly talented parliamentarian. His election as Deputy of the *département* of the Nièvre in 1946 at the age of only 30 followed a period as a courageous leader of the Resistance. The Nièvre was to provide him with a firm political base throughout his career: he represented it in the National Assembly, with only a brief interruption at the beginning of the Fifth Republic, he was the chairman of the departmental council (Conseil Général) and was mayor of Château-Chinon, one of the main towns of the *département*. It was at the town hall of Château-Chinon that Mitterrand was to hear the computer predictions and first results of all the elections in which he was involved, including those of May 1981. It was from the same town hall that he was to make his presidential victory speech. In the National Assembly Mitterrand was a formidable figure, the undisputed leader of the opposition to the governments of de Gaulle, Pompidou and Giscard d'Estaing. He was a brilliant, incisive and caustic critic, using irony with frequent and telling effect.

Mitterrand also had a record – if not a reputation – as an able and courageous administrator: in 1953, for example, he resigned from the government because he considered its North African policy to be too repressive. He held ministerial office on no fewer than eleven occasions during the Fourth Republic, his last post being that of Minister of the Interior in 1956. His methods of running the Socialist Party, his skill in maintaining the electoral harmony of the non-communist Left, the pugnacity which he displayed in his relations with the Communist Party and his persistent and even remorseless opposition to the Right, combined to reinforce his earlier reputation as a highly talented, ambitious, tenacious and tough negotiator and organiser. On the negative side Mitterrand was viewed as somewhat Machiavellian and devious – better as a manoeuvrer than as a manager: Rastignac and Florentine were amongst the two most frequent epithets used to describe his character. He was also criticised as lacking judgement, and a number of past incidents (for example, his complete misreading of the situation in 1968) were cited to support this criticism. He was reproached, too, in 1981 with a lack of recent ministerial experience: he was, in Giscard d'Estaing's phrase, merely expert in running the 'Ministry of Words'.

After the 1978 electoral reversal, Mitterrand also gained another reputation – that of the defeated yet dignified, almost disinterested elder statesman. He may have been, in Michel Poniatowski's cruel jibe, an *éternel perdant*, but he was also a man who had established a firm place in French republican and left-wing history. This image as the successor of Jules Ferry, of Jean Jaurès and of Léon Blum was carefully exploited by Mitterrand, but it had a basis in reality. And, aware of this, he appeared to offer himself the luxury of an Olympian – almost *Gaullien* – distance from *la politique politicienne*, from instant politics and politicking. That he was indulging in such politics with constancy and increasing success did little to impair the image. This image was both rooted in and reinforced by his writings. His thoughtful, serious, literary, ironic and readable prose of political life and ideas won his books popular and critical acclaim – an acclaim that completely eluded Giscard d'Estaing who had well-advertised literary pretensions. In short, through his political and literary activities Mitterrand was perceived as an intelligent, articulate, hard-working and tenacious statesman of considerable weight and stature. If obstinacy and ruse were recognised as traits of his personality,[80] so too were a sense of measure, of *calme*, of *Gaullien* distance.

Mitterrand's reputation also rested on his role as the leader and principal inspirer of the rejuvenation of the Socialist Party after 1971. In the late 1960s observers spoke not of the French Socialists, but of the 'non-communist Left', one part of which was the SFIO (*Section Française de l'Internationale Ouvrière*). In steady electoral decline as a result of its ambivalent policies, constant splits and purges, and its failure to recruit new leaders and members, the SFIO was doomed to become a small, marginalised, regional force which, like its Italian cousin, would be completely dominated by its Communist 'brother'.

Mitterrand, who had played a major role since 1965 in attempting to restructure the non-communist Left, was a key figure in engineering the merger of the SFIO with many splinter-groups and political clubs (including his own) which produced the newly named *Parti Socialiste* at the Epinay Congress of 1971. Ably assisted by the congress chairwoman, Nicole Questiaux, and two important SFIO figures (Pierre Mauroy and Gaston Defferre) as well as Jean-Pierre Chevènement, organiser of the Marxist CERES political clubs, Mitterrand succeeded in fusing the various component elements and in taking over the leadership of the new party.

Within a very short time the Socialist Party became a growing, effective force which, if profoundly divided, remained electorally and organisationally united. It adopted a new and much more radical programme after endless and querulous debates, and recruited a new, young and militant membership. It sought and gained allies – the Left-wing Radicals and the Communists, and with them drew up the Joint Programme of Government of 27 June 1972. By late 1972 the Sofres polls were indicating that the Socialist Party of Mitterrand was the most well-liked party in France. In the 1973 legislative elections the party gained votes, seats and new members. The growth continued during and after the 1974 presidential election, and at the *Assises du Socialisme* of September of that year when Michel Rocard led many members of the small PSU (*Parti Socialiste Unifié*) into the Socialist Party. The electoral strength of the party was revealed in the autumn 1974 legislative by-elections, in the 1976 cantonal elections (to the general councils of the ninety-six *départements*) and in the 1977 municipal elections when it became the dominant party of the Left, and the major party in local government. Even in the 1978 legislative elections which were a disappointment to the party, it gained both votes and seats. By late 1980 the PS had become an effective political machine with 160,000 paid-up and enthusiastic members, and with firm parliamentary and local roots.

The PS was, however, never a homogeneous or highly disciplined organisation. The price for uniting the various disparate groups in 1971 had been the creation of a very representative and discussive system of internal party democracy. This system encouraged argumentative factionalism, and at times the party seemed not only divided but chaotic, as rival factors indulged in semantic and quasi-theological debate. Yet the system of internal democracy had its advantages: it enabled the various factions to live together; it distinguished the party from the monolithic and undemocratic Communist Party; it blurred the identity and policies of the party. With leaders as politically diverse as the Social Democratic Gaston Defferre and Pierre Mauroy, the moderate, liberal, modernising Michel Rocard and the Marxist Jean-Pierre Chevènement, the party enjoyed an ambiguous and electorally advantageous identity offering something for many. Throughout Giscard d'Estaing's presidency the PS remained the 'most appreciated' party in France. It also became the most representative party of the electorate as a whole. Its electoral influence was 'nationalised': whilst it lost some ground in its areas of traditional strength, it made gains, often of a spectacular nature, in areas where previously it had been very weak (Table 12).

By 1978 the Socialists together with their Left-wing Radical allies were winning over 20 per cent of the votes in nearly every *département* of metropolitan France. The party was also gaining votes in all the social categories in which it had been weak, and in 1978 more young people, women and practising Catholics voted Socialist than ever before. It thus earned the description of being a *parti à l'image du pays* (Table 13).

If Mitterrand was the leader of this growing political force, he was not the sole or the unchallenged leader. At the 1979 Metz Congress of the party the Mauroy and Rocard factions made an unsuccessful bid to wrest

Table 12 *Examples of Socialist Gains in Areas of Traditional Weakness*

| Département | Percentage of first-ballot votes | | |
| --- | --- | --- | --- |
| | 1968 | 1973 | 1978 |
| Mayenne (west) | 13·9 | 22·8 | 28·2 |
| Meuse (east) | 17·7 | 26·7 | 29·9 |
| Moselle (east) | 5·8 | 16·0 | 23·9 |
| Savoie (south-east) | 10·8 | 23·3 | 32·2 |
| Vienne (centre west) | 11·7 | 21·1 | 29·1 |

Table 13 *PS Representativeness, 1978*

| Profession | PS voters | Total population |
| --- | --- | --- |
| Agriculture | 8·0 | 9·0 |
| Commerce/crafts | 7·0 | 6·5 |
| Lower administrative/clerical | 24·0 | 21·0 |
| Workers | 31·0 | 28·5 |
| Retired/not working | 24·0 | 27·0 |

the leadership from him. And in October 1980 Rocard plunged the PS into the presidential campaign by announcing his intention of standing as candidate if Mitterrand decided not to run. Rocard was probably encouraged by the opinion polls which demonstrated that he was more popular than Mitterrand with 'marginal' and *Giscardien* voters. However, when Mitterrand announced his intention of standing (on 8 November 1980), Rocard at once withdrew from the race; thereafter, whatever their inner sentiments, he and his supporters gave their unstinted and open support to the 'historic leader' of the PS, François Mitterrand. The presence in the Mitterrand campaign of men such as Rocard, as well as the mayors of many major towns, regional and department council presidents, able civil servants and important economists gave his team the image of weight, experience and responsibility. Hence when the PS held its special congress at Créteil on 24–25 January 1981 to give its official and virtually unanimous blessing to Mitterrand's candidacy, it looked like a 'party of government'.[81] It is worth recording that throughout the first-ballot campaign the PS remained more popular than its candidate, and its activist machine, its ambiguous identity and its great popularity were undoubted assets to its founder and presidential candidate.

Another important asset in the 1981 campaign was Mitterrand's perceived role as the co-ordinator of the non-communist Left as a whole and as the organiser of left-wing unity in the 1960s and 1970s. Mitterrand had always been a leading proponent of the need to keep together all the elements of the non-communist Left.

In the wake of the 1965 presidential election, in which he stood as the *candidat unique de la gauche*, he had helped to found and then to lead the Federation of the Democratic and Socialist Left (FGDS). During 1966-9 the Federation ensured electoral and parliamentary collaboration between the Socialists, the Radicals, his own Convention of Republican Institutions (CIR) and a number of small left-wing clubs. After 1971, Mitterrand renewed the alliance with the Radicals although the latter were shortly to split, the Left of the party hiving off to form the Movement of Left-wing Radicals (MRG), which remained in alliance with the Socialists of Mitterrand. In 1974 Mitterrand stood again as the sole candidate of the major parties of the Left, thus strengthening his hold on the leadership of that half of France which identified with the Left, but particularly with the non-communist Left. It is revealing that in the 1981 presidential election the debate amongst the Left-wing Radicals turned on how best to enhance the chances of Mitterrand. Michel Crépeau, who stood as candidate of the MRG, made it clear that his strategy was to extend the appeal of the non-communist Left to the electorally vital Centre, thus improving Mitterrand's second-ballot hopes in that direction.

Of equal significance for Mitterrand's electoral strategy was establishing his role as the reader of the Left as a whole. And that involved forging an electorally paying relationship with the Communists. This he was to accomplish. As already noted, many Communist voters voted for him at the first ballot – and almost all the remaining ones at the second. Yet Mitterrand's maintenance of a satisfactory relationship with the PC was no easy matter. On the one hand, his strategy of left-wing unity was bitterly criticised by many Radicals and also by elements within his own party, some of whom were to desert him because of their anti-communism. Moreover, many who remained within the Socialist Party, such as Michel Rocard and Gaston Defferre, remained deeply – and publicly – sceptical about his alliance with the Communist Party. On the other hand, Mitterrand in his relationship with the Communist Party, was pursuing four basic and inherently conflicting ends: to establish his personal leadership of the Left as a whole, somehow transcending political party lines by appealing to the Communist rank-and-file above the heads of their ever-suspicious party leaders; to forge a binding electoral allliance with the PCF, which meant with the party leadership; to establish the supremacy of the Socialists – his own party – within that alliance; and to pressurise his Communist allies into a less electorally damaging image in order not to frighten potential centrist voters. By 1981 Mitterrand had clearly achieved his first aim of establishing himself as *the* leader of the Left. His presidential campaigns of 1965 and 1974 when he was the *candidat unique de la gauche*, and his persistent, obstinate and even passionate espousal of left-wing unity as the only valid strategy for the non-communist Left, were powerful factors in consolidating his leadership identity. So, too, were his defence of *le peuple communiste* – the ordinary Communist voters – during his 1981 election campaign, his presidential stature and bearing (which starkly contrasted that of Georges Marchais, the Communist leader and candidate), the popularity of his reform proposals (which was particularly striking amongst Communist voters)[82] and his leadership, since the beginning of the Fifth Republic, of the anti-Right campaign.

Mitterrand's second objective, the cementing of an alliance between the Socialist Party and the Communist Party, was nevertheless extremely difficult – and intrinsically so. Both the Socialists and the Communists for most of the Fifth Republic wanted some kind of alliance, but each perceived that alliance as a means of furthering its own particular ends. When those ends were not being achieved or were seen as possibly unrealisable, left-wing unity became expendable. Such unity was dependent upon a fine balance in which each party could discern advantages for itself – and this was the case for only a short period of the Fifth Republic. This imbalance in perceived advantage explains the ever-changing nature of the PS–PC alliance during 1958–81. It oscillated between bitter confrontation (1958–61), suspicion (1968–71) and hostility (1977–81) on the one hand, and growing yet watchful understanding (1961–8) and even confidence and relative harmony (1971–4) on the other. There were the high points, such as the signing of the Joint Programme of Government in June 1972 and the presidential campaign of May 1974. And there were the low points, such as the breakdown of the negotiations to update the Joint Programme in September 1977 and the campaign of mutual recrimination and vilification in the years leading up to the 1981 elections.

The position in April 1981 from Mitterrand's point of view was curiously obscure and unsatisfactory. His party was in alliance with the Communists in the regional, departmental and town councils in which, in spite of the occasional angry squabble, relations between the two *partis-frères* were generally harmonious if distant. But no joint programme bound the two parties, as had been the case during 1972–7, and the parties remained divided over a host of important issues – domestic, European, defence and foreign. The Communists had decided to run a candidate against him, and there was not even an electoral agreement which would ensure the automatic support of the PC for his candidacy at the second ballot. As in 1978, the PCF was to await the results of the first ballot before announcing its second-ballot intentions, and given the violence of the personal and political attacks upon him, it was far from clear what those intentions were. But with many Communist voters opting for him at the first ballot and with the opinion polls indicating that whatever the advice of the party leadership most would vote for him at the second, the party was more or less browbeaten into giving him its official support.

Mitterrand's failure to work out a friendly and harmonious relationship with the PCF was perhaps inevitable, given his publicly expressed desire to dominate that relationship, which was his third end. Indeed, his very success in rejuvenating the Socialist Party coupled with the electoral stagnation of the Communist Party was probably the principal cause of the breakdown of the alliance in September 1977. The figures of the electoral performances of the Left clearly indicate the reasons for Communist concern. The PCF, which had been the biggest party of France until 1958, was no longer even the biggest party of the Left by 1978. Moreover, the competition between the two parties of the Left was not merely electoral. The Communists feared the marauding activities of the Socialists in other areas: the latter were even – the ultimate sin for the PCF – declaring their intention of rivalling the Communists within the working class.

The final aim of Mitterrand in his relationship with the PCF was to render it more discreet and more respectable as an electoral ally. This required constant pressure on the PCF to change its policies and its image. For some time it appeared that he was being highly successful in fulfilling that objective, and by the 1974 presidential campaign the PCF seemed resolutely embarked upon a course of liberalisation and national political integration. But Mitterrand's pressure was but one, and by no means the most important, factor pushing the PCF into change. At the beginning of the Fifth Republic the French PC was the most pro-Soviet in sympathies, the most Stalinist in internal practice and the most illiberal in doctrine of all the Communist parties of Western Europe. It was also a declining, isolated and unpopular force, and after 1958 it lost the political veto power it had frequently and unscrupulously used in the Parliament of the Fourth Republic. The long-term survival of the party appeared to hinge on a change of direction, and this was undertaken from the early 1960s. This change involved three interrelated elements: de-Sovietisation (growing independence *vis-à-vis* the USSR), 'Italianisation' (the liberalisation of many of its policies) and national integration through closer links with the Socialists. The PC's decision to take 'the French road to socialism' was facilitated by a change on the party leadership (Thorez died in 1964 and was succeeded by the more open-minded and tolerant Waldeck-Rochet), by the dramatic changes in the Soviet Union and in the Communist World in general, by the manifest success of the neighbouring PCI and by the new willingness of the Socialists to enter some form of alliance. But the change was hindered by internal opposition from the hardliners, by the need not to disorient party *militants* and by the dilemmas which the new policies posed for the party leadership.

The three ends of the new strategy (de-Sovietisation, 'Italianisation' and national integration) were pursued somewhat inconsistently: 'socialism' and 'democracy' were proclaimed as indissolubly linked but the increasingly criticised 'undemocratic' Soviet bloc could still be described as 'socialist'; Stalinism could be castigated but it still shaped the internal decision-making process of the party; multi-partism was to be tolerated in the transitional phase to socialism but certain Eastern bloc countries were then defined as multi-party. The list of inconsistencies could be prolonged without difficulty. Nor were the three policies ever thoroughly pursued.

For example, there were no criticisms of Soviet foreign policy, whilst the liberalisation of party doctrines did not affect the self-declared vanguard role of the party and its position as the sole repository of scientific truth. Finally, the three policies were pursued somewhat sporadically: there was no gradual unfolding of a coherent strategy, but to all appearances a series of disjointed tactical responses often of an uneasy and contradictory character. The party leadership seemed never fully to grasp the fact that all three policies were inextricably linked, that each was pregnant with consequences for the other two (and for other aspects of party life), and that the partial pursuit of each merely posed new dilemmas. But the PCF continued to be buffeted by the conflicting pressures of internal party politics, of domestic political exigencies and of the requirements of the European and international environment, and this constant buffeting helps to explain the disjointed nature of the party's strategy.[83]

The three years which preceded the presidential elections seemed to mark the failure of Mitterrand's left-wing unity strategy, as the PCF appeared intent on reverting to the ghetto politics of the very early years of the Fifth Republic. The desirability of alliance with the Socialists was openly questioned, and Mitterrand himself and his close lieutenants were subject to hostile comment. A more militant pro-Soviet tone was also adopted: the balance-sheet of the Communist bloc was declared *globalement positif*; Marchais made an ostentatious display of himself at the Moscow Olympics (he also launched a bitter attack on the French Socialists from the Soviet capital); and the Soviet invasion of Afghanistan was justified. The party also resorted to a strident xenophobia, notably in its campaigns against Germany (during the French steel crisis and during the elections to the European Parliament). A belligerent *ouvriérisme* also re-entered the language of the party, and there were one or two spectacular – and highly unpleasant – incidents involving party officials and immigrant workers, notably at Ivry and Montigny-les-Cormeilles. This change of direction may have pleased the party hardliners, but it was to provoke unprecedented dissension amongst the intellectuals and other liberals in the party. It also seemed designed to undermine Mitterrand's electoral strategy and damage his chances. Yet if that was the design, it was singularly unsuccessful, and for two reasons. In the first place, the party was unable to shake the *esprit unitaire* of its own voters or loosen the appeal of Mitterrand as the personification of that *esprit*. Secondly, it performed badly in the elections, being hampered by a poor candidate, by unprecedented dissension in its own ranks, and by incoherent and unpopular policies.

By its attacks upon Mitterrand and by its poor performance it helped to dissipate some of the fear about Mitterrand amongst key centrist voters (who were clearly disgruntled with Giscard d'Estaing), for he could no longer be perceived as the lackey or the prisoner of the Communists. Significantly, the 1981 campaign was marked by the rallying to Mitterrand of a number of centrists who had previously been hostile. Anti-Communists backing Mitterrand in 1981 included Caillavet (Radical Party), Hintermann (Parti Socialiste Démocrate), Jobert (Mouvement des Démocrates) and several left-wing Gaullists, all of whom had backed Giscard d'Estaing in 1974. Thus, by the first ballot of May 1981 Mitterrand had achieved everything he sought in his alliance with the Communist Party: he was undisputed master of the Left; he received its unconditional electoral support at the second ballot; he beat them into a submissive and non-compromising silence. And whilst anchoring his position on the Left he was also able to extend his appeal to the Centre.

Finally, it should be noted that Mitterrand was openly supported at the second ballot by the extreme Left, whose leaders (Krivine, Laguiller and Bouchardeau) emphasised the need to beat Giscard d'Estaing. He was also given the backing of many Ecologists, whose leader Brice Lalonde whilst giving no explicit advice for the second ballot, pointedly reminded his supporters that President Giscard d'Estaing had a record to judge.

This growing coalition of organisations, *militants* and voters around Mitterrand was largely a consequence of his past activities. But it was also, in some measure, the result of his impressive election campaign. Compared with 1974, it was more relaxed, more professional and more effective. A 'communications cell' led by an advertising specialist, Jacques Ségula, supervised advertising, slogans, television appearances and even the nature and style of the campaign.[84] This group also kept a close and critical eye on television and radio news reporting. Mitterrand's campaign was a personal one: he presented his own programme – not that of the united Left (as in 1974) or even that (somewhat more radical) of his own party from which he withdrew as First Secretary. His television appearances were less strained, more competent and more frequent than in 1974 when he had clearly preferred a whirlwind tour of the major cities of France where he entranced his mass audiences with his brilliant oratory – an oratory which fitted ill with the requirements of the television screen. In his television confrontation with Giscard d'Estaing in 1974 he fared badly, and he blamed this on the hostile studio audience, the unfavourable camera shots and the deference of the studio presenters towards his opponent. In 1981 he set the conditions of the debate and emerged with an honourable draw. His campaign was designed to reassure: he was the elder statesman, the man of purpose and determination yet of measure and moderation – the *force tranquille* who promised change, but not of a revolutionary sort. He did not attack the institutions of the Fifth Republic (one of his previous obsessions), but concentrated on those subjects which the opinion polls revealed to be Giscard d'Estaing's weakest points. He and his supporters also organised meetings for and addressed campaign broadcasts towards particular groups of voters – farmers, doctors, small businessmen, young people and even business executives – to explain, cajole, promise and also to deny the threats being made by Giscard d'Estaing. The need to tackle unemployment was perhaps the major theme of his campaign. On one subject he remained profitably ambivalent: whether as President he would appoint Communist ministers. By reiterating his intention of making the appointment of Communists conditional upon a firm PC–PS agreement, he gave hope to Communists and anti-Communists alike.

In general, the opinion polls showed that Mitterrand had run a very good campaign: his main qualities appeared to be that he was in tune with what ordinary voters required, that he would not rule as a solitary despot and that he would carry out major reforms.[85] Such reforms were precisely what a majority of the voters aspired to in 1981 – as they had done in 1974. The difference was that it was now Mitterrand who was perceived as the best instrument for effecting such reforms and that the Communist threat had been dramatically reduced.

The victory of François Mitterrand on 10 May 1981 was the result of many factors. In the first place, Mitterrand was able to exploit the widespread discontent caused by the deepening economic crisis and the changing patterns of social aspirations which were rooted in the rapidly changing socio-professional structures of the country. A second factor was the strong demand for both change and security. In 1974 Giscard d'Estaing was the man perceived as being most able to meet that demand, but in 1981 the record of his *septennat* weighed heavily against him. In May 1981 it was Mitterrand who appeared most likely to meet the demand. Mitterrand was also able in his careful and moderate campaign, to exploit the unpopularity of the incumbent President, some of whose personal qualities, much of his political personnel and policy and most of his economic performance were severely judged, and whose own complacency blinded him to his own vulnerability. A third important factor in explaining the Mitterrand victory was that whilst Mitterrand exploited the position of a growing, dynamic and increasingly popular Socialist Party which gave him its overwhelming support, Giscard d'Estaing never provided himself with such firm and extensive political party backing. Fourthly, François Mitterrand succeeded in building up a personal relationship with the Communist voters in spite of enormous difficulties, whilst Giscard d'Estaing mishandled the much easier task of marshalling Gaullist support. Finally, Giscard d'Estaing had a seven-year record to judge and had made enemies amongst certain groups – the inevitable price of office, particularly in a period of recession. Mitterrand had no record to judge, merely a programme which promised the badly needed and desired reforms, and a personality which exuded reassurance. A combination of reform and reassurance won Giscard d'Estaing the May 1974 election: it was to do the same for Mitterrand in the election of May 1981.

## The Mitterrand Presidency – the Change

The victory of François Mitterrand in May 1981 to the presidency of the Republic was quickly to trigger off further changes – both in the composition of the governing elite and in the policies they proposed to pursue. The programme of the new political masters was an ambitious one, and was designed to constitute a dramatic departure with that of the *ancien régime*. The declared intention was to transform French society, economic relations and political institutional arrangements: in short, to borrow the title of one of the Socialist Party's programmes, it was proposed to 'changer la vie'.

There is little doubt that some of the changes that have been, or are to be introduced are of significance. Yet the extent of the changes and their impact should not be overstated. In the first place, important strands of continuity are easily discernible in both the personnel and policies of the Mitterrand presidency compared with those of the previous presidency. Secondly, there is increasing evidence that the new Socialist leaders are being forced by international and domestic pressures to limit their ambitions. As one Minister of Giscard d'Estaing sourly noted, reality was inducing realism.

The most striking change since May 1981 has been that of the men who now politically govern France. The staff at the Elysée Palace has been totally changed, and as Howard Machin points out in Chapter 1 of this book, its organisation and functioning have been altered. Mitterrand recruited three very diverse elements into his personal staff: a group of personal friends (such as André Rousselet, the ex-managing director of a major taxi company; Régis Debray, the ex-revolutionary who made a name if not a reputation in South America; François de Grossouvre; and Claude Manceron, the historian); a cohort of close political allies (such as Jacques Attali, product of ENA and the Ecole Polytechnique and the author of several books ranging from music to economics; Paul Guimard, a journalist and author; and Jacques Ribs, a lawyer at the Paris bar); finally, a group of politically sympathetic technocrats (such as Jacques Fournier from the Council of State and an expert on social questions; Hubert Vedrine from the French Foreign Office; and François-Xavier Stasse from the Planning Commission). The first secretary-general of the Elysée – an increasingly powerful figure in governmental circles – was Pierre Beregovoy, who was the effective head of the Elysée team and also an influential member of the comité directeur of the Socialist Party, thus providing a link between two of the President's power-bases. Mitterrand has not only changed the men at the Elysée, he has also modified its style of carrying out business: the new President rarely has joint work sessions with the Elysée team, since he prefers a more individual and fragmented – almost *Gaullien* – style of management. Furthermore, in contrast with the Giscard d'Estaing team, that of Mitterrand is more overtly politicised and is characterised by what Jean-Marie Colombani has called 'l'entrée en force du militantisme (socialiste)'.[86]

The second area of personnel change concerns the government. The second government of the Mitterrand presidency (like the first which lasted only a few weeks pending the legislative elections) is headed by Pierre Mauroy, an important local politican (he was president of the Regional Council of the Nord and remains the Mayor of Lille) and an influential figure in the Socialist Party. He has had his political differences with Mitterrand but managed to retain the new President's respect, and he has always enjoyed great popularity in the Socialist Party. In sharp contrast with Raymond Barre, his predecessor, he is conciliatory, jovial, extrovert, overtly political and avuncular – and popular, and is not markedly less able. His government comprises three senators, thirty-one Deputies and, in keeping with the tradition of the Fifth Republic, ten ministers who were recruited from outside Parliament. The Mauroy government has proved itself to be somewhat divided and often openly so. The divisions are scarcely surprising, since the government embraces representatives of Mitterrand's personal and political coalition: personal friends of long-standing such as Charles Hernu (Defence) and Georges Fillioud (Telecommunications); influential members of each of the *courants* of the Socialist Party (including Michel Rocard (Planning), the archrival of Mitterrand within the party, and Jean-Pierre Chevènement, the leader of the CERES faction); and leading figures from the other political parties, including Michel Crépeau who was the leader of the Left-wing Radicals, and Michel Jobert, ex-Foreign Minister under President Pompidou and at present leader of the tiny Mouvement des Démocrates. The government also includes four Communists (Jack Ralite – Health; Anicet Le Pors – Civil Service; Charles Fiterman – Transport; and Marcel Rigout – Adult and Further Education). Thus, for the first time since the Liberation, the Communist Party is represented in the French government. It was a controversial decision and one for which Mitterrand took the full responsibility. The President probably felt it was better to have the Communist Party within the government where it would have to share not only the glory, but also the blame for future policies. Finally, there is a small cohort of non-professional politicians close to the Socialist Party – men such as Claude Cheysson (Foreign Affairs), Jacques Delors (Finance), Robert Badinter (Justice) and Pierre Dreyfus (Industry). The government thus covers the spectrum of the Left – from the very moderate Rocard and Delors to the Communists – and holding them together is one of Mauroy's principal tasks. The team also encompasses the different generations of the Left. If Alain Savary (Education) and Gaston Defferre (Interior), like Mitterrand, held ministerial office under the Fourth Republic after distinguished activity in the Resistance, others such as Nicole Questiaux (National Solidarity), Edith Cresson (Agriculture) and Laurent Fabius (Budget) entered politics only in the 1970s. The change of ministers was accompanied by a major purge of the ministerial private staffs (the *cabinets ministériels*), as each French minister gathered around him a small team of personal friends or politically sympathetic allies, bureaucrats and technocrats.

The third major change in the political personnel of the Republic took place at legislative level – in the National Assembly. One of the first acts of President Mitterrand was to dissolve a politically unsympathetic Chamber, and in the subsequent elections of June 1981 the 'party of the President', the Socialist Party, scored a truly remarkable victory by winning an absolute majority of seats.[87] The electors gave the Socialist Party and its electoral allies 37·6 per cent of the first-ballot votes, and elected 285 pro-governmental Deputies (262 Socialists, 14 Left-wing Radicals and 4 others) to the Assembly. The victory of the Socialist Party was all the more remarkable, since its performance (in first-ballot terms) bettered that of Mitterrand. Moreover, on the Left the Socialist Party clearly established its ascendancy, winning more than twice the votes given to the Communists. With 262 of the 491 seats in the National Assembly, the Socialist Party is reliant neither upon the votes of its immediate Left-wing Radical allies nor upon those of the Communist Party which had its worst general election result since 1936.[88] It won only 16·2 per cent of the votes cast which was a slightly better performance than the disastrous one of Georges Marchais in the presidential elections (15·3 per cent), but it won *fewer* votes in June 1981 in a lower turnout than in the previous May (4,003,025 votes compared with 4,456,922 for Marchais). A comparison with the previous legislative elections – those of 1978 – was far from encouraging for the party leadership: in 1978 it won 20·6 per cent of the votes (5,870,340 votes) and 86 seats, whereas in 1981 it won 16·2 per cent of the votes (on a lower turnout) and it saw its representation in the National Assembly virtually halved to only 44 Deputies. It is small wonder that so many observers of French politics should be turning their attention to the dramatic demise of the Communist Party and its potential impact on the political system.

The opposition parties fared very badly in the June 1981 elections. They emerged as leaderless, disoriented, divided and decidedly weakened. The Giscardian UDF and the Gaullist RPR cobbled together a shaky first-ballot electoral agreement, their quarrels of the presidential campaign temporarily shelved under the pressure of electoral self-interest. Their alliance the Union pour une Nouvelle Majorité (UNM) – together with other right-wing candidates gathered barely 43 per cent of the votes, and their parliamentary representation was decimated: the Gaullists won 83 seats (compared with 153 in 1978), the Giscardians 66 (compared with 125) and other rightists lost 3 of their previous 9 seats. Thus, the previous *majorité* had become an unquestionable *minorité*. The comfort of the new government's parliamentary position was quickly to be revealed in the vote on the first declaration of general policy which was approved by the

National Assembly by 302 votes to 147, whilst in the censure debate of September 1981 the opposition could muster only 154 of the 246 votes necessary for success. The Left are also occupying all the key posts in the six permanent commissions of the Assembly: the chairmanships have gone to four Socialists, a Left-wing Radical and a Communist. The opposition parties refused all offers of a post.

It is only the second time during the Fifth Republic that a party has enjoyed an absolute majority in the Assembly. In 1968 in the *élections de la peur*, following the May events, the Gaullist Party group won 293 of the 487 seats (or 60 per cent). The present Socialist Party group (which includes the Left-wing Radicals) has 285 of the 491 seats (or 58 per cent). There is, however, a difference between the two situations. In 1968 many Gaullist Deputies had been traumatised into a paranoic conservatism by the turbulence of the previous May, and they were both suspicious of and unsympathetic towards President de Gaulle's mildly reformist promises. Many were much more attracted to the cautious pragmatism of Georges Pompidou, the then Prime Minister. The present Socialist Party is very much the *parti du Président*. He helped to found it at the Epinay Congress of 1971, nurture it, unite and bring it to power in 1981. And he never ceased to exploit and dominate it. The ease with which he outmanoeuvred his party opponents was a measure not only of his undoubted tactical skills, but also of the widespread popularity he enjoyed within its ranks. To ensure his continuing domination he has placed his close friends in key positions: Louis Mermaz as president of the National Assembly, Pierre Joxe as chairman of the parliamentary group and Lionel Jospin as first secretary of the party. He has also done nothing to discourage the sectarian marginalisation of the defeated Rocardians within the party. If Mitterrand has a problem with his party, it will not be because it may provide a brake upon his reformism, but because it may find that his reformism is not radical enough. It must be remembered that between Mitterrand's campaign promises (which he has insisted are the sole basis for the government's policies) and the official party programme there exists a wide gulf, and there are perhaps many Socialist Deputies who are keen to bridge it.

The 1981 legislative elections changed not only the political composition of the National Assembly. It also altered its socio-professional composition. It is a much younger Assembly, much less experienced in the conduct of legislative business, ill-versed in the courteous practices of parliamentary life (there have been several turbulent and ill-tempered debates). And it is now dominated by the teaching profession: 59 per cent of the Socialist Deputies and 34 per cent of the total membership of the Assembly belong to the teaching profession. Amongst the PS Deputies there are twenty-five university teachers (compared with twelve elected in 1978), ninety-four secondary-school teachers (twenty-four elected in 1978) and thirteen primary-school teachers (thirteen in 1978). There are also fifty-eight Deputies who come from the ranks of upper management, sixteen doctors, sixteen barristers, and only three shopkeepers, two workers and one farmer.[89] It has been suggested that the *République des fonctionnaires* has now been replaced by the *République des professeurs* since May–June 1981, and it has also been suggested that the new men who dominate French political life are mere 'merchants of words', cut off from the realities of ordinary life. It is true that there are few industrialists, managers, farmers, or (especially) workers in the ranks of the present governing coalition. Yet the accusation levelled against the new Deputies fails to take into account the very wide experience that many have gained at local level. As already noted, the Socialist Party owes part of its remarkable success to the very firm local roots it put down in the 1970s. A majority of the present Socialist Deputies are mayors or town councillors (often of major towns) and/or members of departmental or regional councils,[90] and because of that, are more closely in touch with everyday reality than their critics infer.

The President's men are, therefore, in control both of the executive and the legislative branches of government. But the change in personnel has gone much further. In the top ranks of the administration a fairly radical purge has taken place.[91] The politically sensitive Ministry of the Interior has been particularly affected, since almost all the key posts of *directeur* were quickly purged. The prefectoral administration has undergone its biggest shake-up since the stormy days of the Liberation; within three months of the Mitterrand victory ten prefects were eased out of the administration (they included the immensely able Lucien Lanier, the prefect of Paris region) and within six months of the change at the Elysée two-thirds of the ninety-six French *départements* had been given a new prefect in a gigantic *valse des préfets*. The police forces have also witnessed many changes at the top: the process of change has been far from smooth and has led to public disputes between the brutally insensitive (often justifiably so) Gaston Defferre, Minister of the Interior, and his subordinates in the police. In other parts of the state apparatus overt political sympathisers of the previous ruling coalition have been removed from key posts: these include the director-general of SDECE (the main counter-espionage service), the head of the National Employment Agency, the Planning Commissioner, the head of the service responsible for the sale of French arms abroad, the powerful director-general of telecommunications, the director-general of industry, and several of the immensely influential *directeurs* of the Ministry of Finance. The Ministry of Education was another target of the purges, since the major posts in the central administration changed hands, and during May–June 1981 seventeen of the twenty-seven university rectors (who are the chief regional administrative agents of the ministry) were sacked. Other parts of the state machine to be affected include the Ministry of Research (the shake-up in the Centre National de la Recherche Scientifique led to the resignation of the director-general and most of the *directeurs*), the Ministry of Justice (where several magistrates who had combated some of the projects of the previous presidency have been promoted) and the Ministry of Foreign Affairs (which has seen the appointment of well-known Socialists to top ambassadorial posts and to the top political posts in the central administration). In the nationalised industries and in the para-public sector several appointments have also made clear the new political situation.

Perhaps the most spectacular changes have taken place in the media – a sensitive area where Giscard d'Estaing had so assiduously placed his men. Amongst the heads to roll were those of Yves Cannac, head of Agence Havas, Xavier Gouyon-Beauchamps, head of SOFIRAD (the organisation responsible for managing French state interests in such influential radio stations as Europe I and Radio Monte Carlo), Antoine de Clermont-Tonnerre, head of Societé Française de Production (the main television production unit), the heads of all three television networks, Jacqueline Baudrier, head of Radio France, and other pro-Giscardians who were involved in the news services of the state-run media.

The victory of the Left also had the effect of changing the composition of the Economic and Social Council (the new Prime Minister almost immediately appointed a number of Socialist sympathisers) and of the regional councils (since all Deputies are *ex-officio* members): after the June 1981 elections, the Socialists and their allies won a majority in thirteen of the twenty-two regional councils. Since the Left already controls three-quarters of the major towns of France, its hold over local government became even more marked.

With the Socialists and their political sympathisers firmly in charge of the presidency, the government, the National Assembly, the key posts of the administration and the state-run media, as well as the regions and the main towns, many commentators raised the question whether the *Etat Giscardien* (itself constructed on the ruins of a carefully dismantled *Etat Gaulliste* had not been replaced by the *Etat socialiste*. Furthermore, it was argued, unlike the position of the previous government, the political counter-weights were very weak. The Communists had been forced into respectful and silent submission and were much too preoccupied with internal dissension and electoral decline. The postmortem after the presidential and legislative election promised to be a lengthy one, even if the party leadership emerged unscathed from the 1982 party congress. The right-wing parties were no less divided. If chirac quickly took the Gaullists firmly in hand, his leadership of the Right was hotly disputed by the Giscardians – even though they were in a state of total disarray.

Whatever the truth of the claim about the *Etat socialiste* (and a certain scepticism must be expressed), it was certainly true that after the elections of May and June 1981 President Mitterrand enjoyed a considerable freedom for manoeuvre, and it was scarcely surprising that he and his government were able to push ahead with their fairly radical programme of reform.

## The Ambitions and Early Policies of the Mitterrand Presidency

The ambitions of the Mitterrand presidency were far-reaching and clear. They are spelled out in the election manifesto – 'the charter of governmental action' – in Mitterrand's many subsequent announcements and in the speeches of Pierre Mauroy, his Prime Minister. The latter, in his speech of 8 July 1981 to the National Assembly, referred to the government's programme as 'an original model of society', aimed at creating 'a new citizenship'. To that end, a number of measures have been taken or were envisaged, and they were of an economic, social and institutional nature.

On the economic level there were short-term objectives, medium-term aims and long-term ambitions. The priority – and it was linked both with the objectives and the aims – was to tackle the problem of unemployment. And this involved economic expansion. The problem was highlighted for the government when the politically emotional figure of 2 million unemployed was reached in the spring of 1982. A number of measures were immediately taken after the presidential elections to underline the urgency of the problem: 6·5 million franc were released through the *fonds d'action conjoncturel* for the building and telephone industries; 17 billion franc credit at preferential rates of interests were made available to industry through the locally organised *comités départementaux pour le financement* (Codefis); 7 billion franc were set aside to help the 650,000 school-leavers in search of employment; and jobs in the public sector (both local and national) were created. Longer-term promises designed to ease the unemployment situation included the creation of further public sector jobs (a total of 210,000 in the first two years of the presidency), the lowering of the retirement age to 60 and the reduction of the official working week from forty to thirty-five hours (by May 1982 it had been reduced to thirty-nine). In terms of medium-term macro-economic policy the Socialists substituted a combination of neo-Keynsian reflation and new job-creation measures for the restrictive monetary and budgetary policies of Giscard d'Estaing and Barre. The revised budgetary deficit was equivalent to 3 per cent of GNP – a modest proportion compared with France's neighbours, but high by traditional French standards. Coupled with these short-term measures or medium-term projects is the plan to increase industrial investment and to improve the competitiveness of French industry. The long-term objective of the new Socialist administration is to move from a 'financial strategy' (its description of Giscard d'Estaing's policies) to an 'industrial strategy'.[92] This strategy involves three interlinked ambitions: the first is to 'reindustrialise' France and to combat the trend towards the growth of the tertiary sector; the second is to improve the competitiveness of French industry in order to 'reconquer the domestic market', to improve the balance of payments situation and to limit the 'internationalisation' of the French economy; and the third ambition is the 'de-specialisation' of the French economy, through a policy of increasing vertical integration particularly in the so-called *filières d'avenir*, such as electronics, biotechnology and space technology. The Japanese model is very much in fashion; indeed, it has even been claimed that the overall ambition of the French Socialists is to turn France into 'the Japan of Western Europe'. Certainly, it is a much more research-oriented (by the mid-1980s France will be spending 2·5 per cent of GNP on research, a higher proportion than in the USA or Germany), offensive and voluntarist strategy that is promised.

Three major policy instruments are to be used to assist the relaunching and reshaping of the French economy. The first of these instruments is the extended public sector. By the spring of 1982, in spite of the opposition of the business community, the political parties of the Right and the Senate, the reticence of certain ministers (by no means the least), the minor criticisms of the Council of State and the major criticisms of the Constitutional Council (which insisted on radical – and expensive – changes in the compensation clauses), the government had enacted its main nationalisation proposals, although the detailed provisions were only slowly being implemented. The result of the nationalisation programme was to bring under direct state control the remaining banking and credit institutions. This involved the nationalisation of thirty-six private banks such as the banking giants Paribas and Suez, as well as other important private banks such as Crédit Industriel et Commercial and Crédit Commercial de France. Only foreign banks with French subsidiaries and a number of other smaller credit institutions were excluded. Further Bills have provided for the nationalisation of some of the country's major industrial groups. The very early nationalisation measures covered the armaments and steel industries: Dassault and the armaments division of Matra as well as the two steel giants, Usinor and Sacilor, were quickly brought under state control. In the case of the steel industry formal nationalisation merely regularised the status quo, since the state had effectively taken over the bankrupt industry during Giscard d'Estaing's presidency. Foreign-owned companies or those companies in which foreign holdings were substantial (such as the telecommunications group ITT-France, the pharmaceutical group Roussel-Uclaf or the computer empire Cii-Honeywell Bull) were the subject of detailed and complex negotiations designed to restructure their capital and to ensure continuing co-operation. Moreover, foreign shareholders in the five major diversified industrial groups whose parent companies were amongst the first to be nationalised (Rhône-Poulenc, Saint-Gobain, Thomson-Brandt, Compagnie Générale d'Electricité and Pechiney-Ugine-Kuhlmann) were given the option of retaining some of their shares. The basic purpose of the nationalisation programme is to provide the French state with a major instrument of industrial policy. President Mitterrand in his September 1981 press conference could refer to the nationalised industries as 'the instruments of the next century', whilst Prime Minister Mauroy put the case for nationalisation in the following terms: 'we want the State to acquire, through nationalisation, those industrial poles which seem to us essential for a dynamic investment and employment policy.' The penetration of the state into the industrial structure of the country has been considerably increased. In the competitive industrial sector (which excludes the public utilities) the state's share of turnover will jump from 16 to 30 per cent. In certain key sectors of the economy the state's share of French sales has increased dramatically: from nothing to about 60 per cent in electronics and information processing, from nothing to 75 per cent in synthetic fibres, from 1 to 79 per cent in iron and steel, from 16 to 52 per cent in basic chemicals and from 58 to 74 per cent in armaments. At the symbolic level the nationalisation programme must be seen as an assertion by the Mitterrand presidency of its intention to affect 'a break' (*rupture*) with capitalism, of its attachment to the general interest and of its attempt to combat the 'internationalisation' of the French economy (a point made forcefully by Mitterrand in his first press conference). Finally, nationalisation is designed to provide a more democratic internal decision-making structure in industry and to facilitate decentralised decision-making at regional level.

The second basic instrument in the government's economic and industrial strategy is the national plan. The demise of French planning was attributed to the ill-will of previous right-wing governments, and a reversal of policy was seen to be both economically functional and symbolically dramatic. In December 1981 the new Minister for Planning, Michel Rocard, aided by a new Planning Commissioner, presented a two-year interim plan. This is to be followed by a much more ambitious, more democratic and more decentralised five-year plan – the ninth since the war and designed to cover the period 1984–8.

The third instrument to be used by the Socialists in their quest for a rejuvenated economy is the newly created Conseil Permanent du développement industriel, which has the aim of bringing together private and public industrialists under the chairmanship of the Minister of Industry. Its exact role and powers however remain obscure, and it is unclear how it will fit into the already extremely developed and elaborate network of state-run committees dealing with industrial affairs.

The economic priorities of the Mitterrand presidency underpin its social priorities: the creation of a more equitable society. Certain redistributive measures were implemented very quickly. The *smic* – the minimum wage rate – which affects 800,000 workers was increased, as were old-age pensions (they were raised by 20 per cent almost immediately) and allowances for the handicapped. In the health area prescription charges were abolished, and the active and able Communist Minister of Health has fixed his long-term priorities which include the provision of free hospital care, the phasing out of private medicine from state hospitals, the improvement of general practice and the nationalisation of the three major drug companies. The various social measures are to be paid for by the new wealth tax, an increase in VAT on luxury goods, a more progressive tax system, and increased taxes on banks and petrol companies. A more resolute attack on tax evasion is also to be mounted.

The extension of workers' rights in the factories is but one of the policies designed to forge 'the new citizenship' based on increased participation. The government also wishes to extend participation in housing associations, consumer groups, the universities (the notorious Sauvage Law has been repealed) and school councils, in the social security organisations, and as already noted, in the nationalised industries and the economic planning procedures. The self-declared intention of 'organising new social relations' smacks a great deal of the ideals outlined in the so-called 'New Society' programme of Prime Minister Jacques Chaban-Delmas in 1969 – a programme quietly but resolutely shelved by President Pompidou. One of the principal architects of that programme was Jacques Delors, then a member of Chaban-Delmas's private staff and now a minister in the Mauroy government.

Some of the most radical intentions in the field of citizen participation are in the field of de-centralisation. Brave statements abound about the effort 'to promote the institutional de-colonisation of France' (Michel Rocard) or 'to break the Napoleonic mould' (Gaston Defferre). First, directly elected regional assemblies are to become fully fledged political bodies with significantly extended powers, and executive power will reside with the chairman of the regional council (and not, as was previously the case, with the local prefect) who will convoke the assembly and determine its agenda. Secondly, prefectoral *tutelle* has been eliminated at communal level, and the economic and budgetary powers of the communes will be increased. Thirdly, executive power at the level of the *département* has been transferred from the prefect (who will be renamed, since the name is too evocative of Napoleonic centralisation) to the chairman of the departmental council who becomes the head of all the administrative services transferred from state level. Fourthly, the prefects continue to represent the state at local level, to be responsible for the maintenance of law and order in the *département* and for the legality of local decisions. Furthermore, their powers over the various state field services will be reinforced. Fifthly, the powers of the Trésoriers Payeurs Généraux, the very influential financial local agents of central government, will be curtailed. Sixthly, Corsica has been granted a special statute, with a great deal of local autonomy. Seventhly, an important financial reform will involve the transfer of state fiscal resources to the localities. Finally, the co-ordination of the activities of the four territorial units of government (central state, region, *département* and *commune*) will take place within the framework of the national plan.

By coupling a radical programme of political de-centralisation (devolving power to local elected assemblies) with measures of administrative de-concentration (transferring powers to the prefects) it is hoped that many fewer projects will end up in Paris for approval. More fundamentally, the government wishes 'to transform local political life'. There is certainly no doubt that, *if fully implemented* (and Yves Mény in Chapter 8 is rightly sceptical about the chances), the government's proposals would constitute the most radical local government changes since the early days of the Third Republic.

Economic, social and institutional measures and proposals have been accompanied by others which have given the Fifth Republic a decidedly more liberal hue: the number of immigrants remains severely limited, but the position of those living in France has been regularised, their rights will be protected and even, in some respects, extended; a new statute guaranteeing the autonomy of the television and radio networks has been accepted by Parliament; telephone-tapping will be strictly supervised by a control commission; French citizens have been given the right to go directly to the European Court of Justice; the persecution of, and discrimination against, homosexuals will cease; the death penalty has been abolished; an amnesty was extended to many political prisoners; and political asylum will be assured and extradition made more difficult. Other important liberal measures include the repeal of the so-called *loi anti-casseurs* and later the *loi sécurité et liberté* (the two bitterly contested 'law and order' Acts of previous right-wing administrations), the abolition of the much-hated Court of State Security, the replacement of other special tribunals by more judicial proceedings, the abandonment of the computerised identity-card, the improvement of the legal-aid system and the democratisation of the Conseil Supérieur de la Magistrature.

Finally, at the domestic level, there were two immediate and much-publicised acts which dramatically underlined the change since May and June 1981. They were the abandonment of the nuclear-energy project at Plogoff in Brittany and of the extension of the military camp at Larzac in the Massif Central. Both had triggered off prolonged and often violent confrontation between environmentalists and previous governments of the Right.

In foreign, European and defence policies the change of course has been much less dramatic, but there have been changes of emphasis in the pursuit of largely similar policies. Under Mitterrand and Claude Cheysson, his Foreign Minister, a more determined pro-Third World stance is being adopted: aid is planned to increase and the North–South dialogue will be relaunched. This change, of course, may well involve a clash with the USA, particularly in Latin America, since the new French administration refuses to perceive all conflicts in the Third World as part of the East–West struggle. The reactions of the French to the events in El Salvador (France signed a joint declaration with Mexico, calling for the left-wing opposition, both guerrilla and civilian, to be brought into settlement negotiations) and the French decision to supply arms to the Sandinista government in Nicaragua at the beginning of 1982 clearly revealed Franco-American differences. In their relations with the USSR the French Socialist leaders will continue to pursue a policy of détente, but they have proved themselves much tougher and uncompromising than President Giscard d'Estaing in their approach to the Soviet government over Afghanistan. Over Poland, too, they adopted an outspokenly critical line towards the military coup.

In Africa the new administration was faced with the task of both reassuring France's traditional allies and of responding to the call for a more disinterested policy. It would appear that the kind of military help previously given to Mobutu in Zaire or to General Malloum in Tchad or to combat the Polisario in Mauritania will no longer be offered except in the most exceptional of circumstances. And there will certainly be no repetition of the kind of involvement which characterised French relations with Bokassa, whose grotesque career was furthered and financed by the complacent Giscard d'Estaing. Policy towards South Africa and other authoritarian regimes may be expected to harden in the future. In the Middle East the only major change is in the tone adopted towards Israel, since Mitterrand is clearly intent on improving relations with that country; hence, his much-publicised visit shortly after his election.

Arms sales – an area in which the French have established themselves as one of the world's biggest exporters – were scheduled to be 'moralised', to borrow Mitterrand's own phrase. The Socialist government has stated that present commitments will be honoured, but that henceforth each case will be treated on its merits. A harder line was also envisaged towards countries such as South Africa, Argentina, Uruguay, Bolivia and particularly Chile.

At the European Community level it was hoped to launch a series of initiatives on agriculture (changing the Common Agricultural Policy in a way designed to help the small farmers), industrial development (by a more active use of loans channelled through the European Investment Bank) and regional policies. A more cautious view of the Paris–Bonn axis was initially promised, in favour of a more wide-ranging series of consultations. Furthermore, several attempts have been made to encourage joint political action, notably in trying to pressurise the Americans into a more 'responsible' interest rate policy.

The rapid and sometimes dramatic changes in personnel and policies are beginning to alter several aspects of French political life. And there is no doubt that the tone, style and image of the regime have been modified. But the changes should not mask the considerable, if less publicised, degree of continuity. This continuity has been imposed by both domestic requirements and pressures and by international exigency.

## The Mitterrand Presidency: Continuity, Constraints and Contradictions

The first major area in which continuity is evident is institutional. Looked at closely, the Socialists' plans to liberalise and democratise the decision-making process constitute no radical break with the past. Often in the process of elaboration the plans have been weakened by the conflicting pressures emanating from injured vested interests. Already powerfully placed pressure groups of suspect political persuasion have reasserted their place in the decision-making process, in spite of early Socialist intentions to diminish their power. Significant in this respect is the Socialist government's increasing respect for the FNSEA – the rightist-leaning farmers' union – which by its mobilising tactics has re-established itself as the *interlocuteur privilégié* of the government. Equally significant is the apparent dropping of the promise (or threat) to abolish the notoriously reactionary Ordre des Médecins, the doctors' professional body. Events have also forced the government to reappraise its position *vis-à-vis* other groups: CNPF – the employers' organisation – was certainly strengthened when the government required its co-operation over increasing private investment and over the implementation of the package of austerity measures decided in June 1982.

The dilution of governmental promises may be seen in the new labour code (the so-called Auroux Bill, named after the minister responsible) which made its laborious way through Parliament in the early summer of 1982. In some respects the Bill is potentially radical in consequence, since an estimated third of existing labour-relations legislation will be affected. The employers have exhibited shock at some of the new rules, intemperate language has been employed and major concessions have been sought. Yet by most West European standards many of the new rules appear unexceptionable and innocuous. It should also be noted that the employers' public shock was mingled with private relief, since the major proposals of the Auroux Bill were a diluted version of the minister's own report of 1981 and were far milder than those proposed by the Socialist Party which pressed in vain for some form of recognition for political parties on the shopfloor and which was disgruntled with the minister's refusal to extend the legislation to workers in small firms. Furthermore, the 'workshop councils' advocated by the CFDT and supported by CGT (the two major unions in France) and denounced by the Right as 'soviets' were not imposed by the new law. It should be stressed that some of the new rules merely legalise the practice existing in some of the more enterprising firms, whilst others merely enunciate a series of general principles. There remains, finally, the problem of implementation. The critics have justifiably pointed out there was already an extensive and complex body of legislation which was frequently not applied.

Yves Mény, in Chapter 8 on local government, also makes clear that the much-heralded reforms in this area are less radical than they appear or as they are presented by the government. At the national level, too, the decision-making process has been barely affected. In the National Assembly the government resorted to the system of *ordonnance* (which enables it to bypass Parliament once the latter has voted an enabling Act, which merely spells out the broad objectives of the policy) in order to impose its social policy. It was a practice which the Socialists had found abhorrent when it was employed by previous right-wing administrations. The Socialist government also displayed great impatience when the opposition parties exploited a number of constitutional devices to delay the passage of legislation concerning nationalisation and local government. In short, the executive's treatment of the legislature after May 1981 is strikingly reminiscent of that of the previous presidency.

In another important institutional respect there has been no change: executive power remains clearly focused around the presidency. Meetings of the Council of Ministers may be more relaxed and there has been the occasional genuine debate on certain issues, but there is no doubt who fixes the agenda, directs the discussion and who takes the final decision. The Socialist Party may also play a more active role in influencing governmental policy but the evidence suggests that it has had to swallow some very bitter governmental pills – the traditional fate of left-wing parties in office. It was argued by many (including Mitterrand himself) that a Mitterrand victory would lead to a less presidential style of government. He was, it was contended, essentially a man of the Fourth Republic (it was an argument frequently employed by his political critics). His political experience (eleven times minister during the Fourth Republic), his long parliamentary career, his persistent criticism of the institutions of the Fifth Republic, his emotional reference-points (which included the lives of Jaurès and Blum), his symbolic gestures (his visit to the Panthéon – the burial-place of the heroes of previous Republics – on the day of his inauguration), his style (lyrical, literary, ironic, anti-technocratic, almost archaic), his passion for *la République* – all might have pointed to an antipathy towards the presidential regime he inherited. Yet it was clear from the outset that Mitterrand was intent on exercising presidential powers to the full (*dans leur plénitude*).[93] In his first French newspaper interview he made it clear that he saw his election as investing him with the ultimate political authority. He confessed that 'the [political] institutions were not made with me in mind [*à mon intention*]. But they are well made for me'.[94] And that is the impression he conveys. He looks and acts like a President of the Fifth Republic. If he is more passionate, overtly political, affirmative and *volontariste* than his predecessor, he has the same rather self-assured and statesmanlike approach to his office.

Mitterrand has always made it abundantly clear that his election commitments, and they alone, provide 'the charter for governmental action'. He has reasserted the supremacy of the presidency in foreign and European affairs and in defence matters and, aided only by the appropriate minister, takes all the key decisions in these areas. His visits to Japan, to Israel, to the USA and to French-speaking Africa in his first year of office, his attendance at the European summit meetings and his meetings with individual European heads of government, and his presentation of the French decision to maintain and even develop the nuclear *force de frappe*, all clearly revealed the source of executive authority.

Many other early acts indicated Mitterrand's intention of exercising not only the presidential prerogatives contained in the Constitution, but also those acquired by previous Presidents as the result of misusing and abusing that Constitution. He publicly contradicted his Minister of Justice on two important issues: the abolition of the Court of State Security which the minister wished merely to reform, and the repeal of the *loi sécurité et liberté* which the minister wanted to revise. It was the President who decided that the franc should not be devalued when it was under severe pressure immediately after his election, and it was he who gave the go-ahead for its devaluation in October 1981 and June 1982. It was also Mitterrand who had the final say on which type of banking and credit institution would escape nationalisation, who made it clear that the nuclear power station at Plogoff would be abandoned (he backed Le Pensec, a junior minister, against Pierre Joxe, the Minister of Industry) and who personally intervened in October 1981 to exempt all art-objects from the scope of the new wealth tax which was then going through Parliament, even though the Minister of the Budget, the *rapporteur* and the chairman of the appropriate parliamentary committee had previously declared their opposition to such an exclusion. It was also the President who arbitrated between Prime Minister Mauroy and the Defence Minister Hernu on the abandonment of the military camp at Larzac (a longstanding battlefield for the French environmentalists), who publicly contradicted his minister who had decided on the date for the annual commemoration of the end of the Algerian War who backed the Minister of Culture against the Minister of the Interior over the vexed question of the control of subsidies to local and regional initiatives and who took the final decision in the controversial problem of whether the reduction of the official working week to thirty-nine hours should take place without any corresponding loss of pay. Finally, it was Mitterrand who chose Mauroy as Prime Minister, who influenced the personal and political composition of the government and who intervened in the appointments to certain top posts in the administration.

At his first press conference in September 1981 Mitterrand looked and acted like the undisputed master of the executive. He has made it clear that his task is long-term – *il faut gérer la durée*, he has declared. And it is revealing that his election promise to reduce the presidential term of office to five years has been discreetly yet definitely shelved. And there is no doubt that his power rests on very firm bases: an able, active and politically reliable Prime Minister, a group of close friends and political allies in the Council of Ministers, Parliament and the administration, a powerful and generally grateful Socialist Party, an influential Elysée staff, a legitimacy based on direct election, and precedents which have enhanced the power and prestige of his office. His power also rests upon a popularity which transcends party boundaries and certainly exceeds that enjoyed by his predecessor: a year after his election he would, according to the opinion polls, have been re-elected.[95] Finally, his power rests on his own personality, ability, style and ambition, for he will fully exploit that *Gaullien* mixture of genuine aloofness relieved by unexpected moments of personal charm, of persistent ruse interspersed with ruthlessness, of obstinacy punctuated with tactical concessions, of attachment to high principles spoiled by a penchant for unprincipled manoeuvring, and a combination of rhetorical audacity, sardonic detachment and practical prudence. Already Mitterrand's presidency has been branded as a '*social-monarchie*', whilst the cynical wags who proliferate in Paris have described it as '*Giscardisme* with a human face'. His method of government will be based on the practice of dividing and ruling a fragmented decision-making structure, calling for advice from several and conflicting quarters before deciding: it was a method he employed with such consummate skill when he was first secretary of the Socialist Party. Mitterrand is haunted by the history of the French Left in power: it is a history of either 'brief and glorious moments' such as 1936 or the Liberation, or equally brief but less glorious periods such as 1924 and 1956. He is determined to ensure that the present political power of the Left will be more durable, and a seven-year presidency seems an ideal foundation for that power. Ironically, in a very important sense, the election of Mitterrand to the presidency has helped to consolidate the institutions of the Fifth Republic by legitimising them in the eyes of the Left which had always been suspicious or even hostile. The Socialists may claim that they are inaugurating a new regime but, in truth, they are merely strengthening the existing one.

Institutional stability has been matched by continuity in the personnel of the new presidency. Two ministers – Michel Jobert and Jacques Delors – had been prominent in Gaullist circles: Jobert belonged to Pompidou's staff at the Elysée before becoming his Foreign Minister, whilst Delors played a very active role on the private staff of Prime Minister Chaban-Delmas. The Socialist purge of the state administrative apparatus was legally restricted to a mere 600 top civil service posts which are at the discretion of the government (and which are enumerated in the decree of 21 March 1959). Even for these posts governmental discretion is far from complete: for instance, prefects must on the whole be replaced by other members of the same corps. In other words, the vast majority of civil service posts are protected from direct governmental intervention. Furthermore, to the fury of some Socialists who demanded that more heads should roll, the Socialist government has displayed great moderation in its purge of the state apparatus. Certain 'technical' ministries and the Defence Ministry have been left virtually untouched, whilst several men who enjoyed long and distinguished administrative careers before 10 May 1981 were promoted by the Socialists. André Chadeau who joined Mauroy's private staff before being appointed to head the railways was previously prefect of the Nord and then head of DATAR (a politically sensitive industrial de-centralising agency). Another striking example is Maurice Grimaud, who became head of the Minister of the Interior's private staff and who had been prefect of police in Paris during 1966–71. Other important civil servants were merely shifted (for instance, one of the key *directeurs* of the Ministry of Finance became head of one of the new nationalised industries). And some others retained their posts. The latter include the secretary-general of the government (who is responsible for the administrative co-ordination of the entire governmental programme), the governor of the Bank of France and the head of Air France. In other areas the purge has been more spectacular than substantial. In the prefectoral administration, for example, the 'great purge' involved in the great majority of cases the transfer and not the dismissal of prefects. Even in the politically sensitive media the number of dismissals has been small (far smaller, as Mitterrand insisted, than under previous right-wing administrations),[96] and some of those dismissed have been handsomely compensated: Jacqueline Baudrier left Radio France to become French representative at Unesco.

It is now clear that whilst the top civil service under Giscard d'Estaing was colonised by pro-governmental elements, the process was far from complete. Socialist sympathisers were numerous, and many of the others appointed by Giscard d'Estaing have proved themselves either politically malleable (the so-called *régimistes* – men who will serve any regime provided that it serves them) or politically neutral, considering themselves as 'servants of the state' whatever its political complexion. Amongst the latter must be counted Jean-Yves Haberer, who worked for the Gaullist Michel Debré and for Giscard d'Estaing as *Directeur du Trésor* before being appointed to head the newly nationalised Paribas banking group in February 1982. Of the other men appointed to the top posts in the newly nationalised industries and banks, very few came from an unorthodox or even unusual background and their appointment would have raised no eyebrows under the previous presidency. Managerial experience and competence were invariably more important than political affiliation.

In this so-called *république des professeurs* the students of the Ecole Nationale d'Administration – the bitterly denounced *énarques* of Giscard d'Estaing's presidency – still hold many key positions: the Elysée staff and the Council of Ministers both harbour cohorts of *énarques*.[97] In the

National Assembly the number of *énarques* dropped from thirty-three to twenty-three as the result of the June 1981 elections, although the number of Socialist *énarques* increased from eight to thirteen.[98] A study of the ministerial private staffs[99] undertaken just after the presidential election gives a good indication of the extent of the renewal of the governing personnel of the Fifth Republic. Of the 371 members of the private staffs of the ministers of the last Barre government, 226 were ex-students of ENA or Ecole Polytechnique; whilst of the 360 members of those of the ministers of the Mauroy government, 152 were *énarques* or 'X' (the name given to the students of the Ecole Polytechnique).[100] However, another study has shown that of the 102 key posts in the Mauroy government *cabinets*, 50 are in the hands of the *énarques*.[101] The Barre–Mauroy comparison also reveals that the average age of the two groups is the same (40 years), that there is the same proportion of women (13 per cent in both cases) and that the social background of the *cabinet* members differs very little. The major difference between the two groups lies in the recruitment by Mauroy's ministers of a small group of ex-party and ex-trade union officials – but they remain a very small minority; the great majority still come from the civil service.

The continuity in institutional arrangements and in the personnel of the new presidency has been accompanied by continuity in policies. This is especially true in the areas of defence,[102] foreign and European policies.[103] Already during the 1978 legislative elections, in a speech to the diplomatic press on 2 February, Mitterrand admitted that the basic policies of General de Gaulle would be maintained: 'Mais le Général de Gaulle a existé: cette France a existé: cette France est mon pays. Il a établi des lignes de force dont je dois tenir compte.'

All the evidence suggests that the major lines of Gaullist thinking – French independence within the context of the Atlantic Alliance, the pursuit of national interests and the insistence on a universal mission for France – will be respected. The *force de frappe* may even be developed, and shortly after the election of May 1981 the decision was made to continue the work on the neutron bomb as well as on the new range of M4 multiple-head ballistic missiles destined to replace the ageing Platon range. The length of military service – in spite of election promises – will not be reduced. Mitterrand has also approved the building of the seventh nuclear submarine. In some important respects his defence thinking is closer than that of Giscard d'Estaing to Gaullist orthodoxy. In foreign affairs, too, the main lines of previous policies will be respected. France remains faithful to the Atlantic Alliance and Mitterrand has a good working relationship with Reagan. He has insisted – to the displeasure of his Communist Party allies – that it is reasonable for Western Europe to install tactical nuclear weapons to redress the balance destroyed by the build-up of Russian SS-20 missiles. He also gave Britain very firm support in her dispute with Argentina. French attitudes towards the USSR have generally been tougher since Mitterrand's election, and the President has been outspokenly critical over Soviet policies in Poland and Afghanistan. Mitterrand has also insisted that France will continue to have a world role: there are no *interdits*, as he put it in his press conference of 24 September 1981. France can be expected to be active in Africa, the Middle East and helping to relaunch the North–South dialogue. Relations with the USA have been strained over events in South America but have improved in other respects. Moreover, the constraints of international politics are quickly being appreciated. Mitterrand could make a highly publicised trip to Israel in March 1982 in a badly needed attempt to improve relations with that country, but the message he conveyed to the Israeli Prime Minister and to the Knesset on the Palestinian question differed little from that of Giscard d'Estaing. France was also forthright in its denunciation of the Israeli attack on the Lebanon in June 1982. Pro-Israeli sentiment which is strong in certain French Socialist circles has been tempered by a strong pro-Palestinian streak on the French Left and by the exigencies of oil politics. Similarly, when the new French government's policy of supplying arms to Nicaragua was seen to jeopardise commercial relations with the rest of South America, a rapid diplomatic mission was organised to reassure the Venezualans, the Argentinians and the Brazilians about the limited nature of the arms sales. In Africa, too, French policy is being shaped by the tyranny of facts: authoritarian regimes such as those of Premier Mobutu and Presidents Bongo and Akidgo which are linked to Paris both culturally and commercially (France imports a third of its primary materials from Africa) are still gently courted, and elsewhere continuity is the hallmark of French policy.[104]

In European affairs, despite much rhetoric about 'European initiatives', France continues to defend a resolutely supra-national view of the Community, to maintain a privileged relationship with Bonn and to fight with no less ardour for French national interests: Paris had clashed with Britain over the Community budget, with Italy over the importation of wine and has clearly put a brake (for domestic political reasons) on Spain's accession to the Community. Certain economic policies of France also exude the odour of protectionism: for instance, in spite of preaching the need progressively to broaden public procurement policies, France practises a policy of favouring national firms. The constraints of the European and international environment are also beginning singularly to limit the economic and social ambitions of the Socialists, imposing an involuntary continuity in the policies being pursued by the new presidency.

Within a very short time of assuming office the new Socialist government was confronted with problems arising out of the inter-nationalisation and Europeanisation of the French economy. The 'Paribas affair' was a highly complex and politically explosive operation, involving the shedding of part of the banking empire to foreign interests just before nationalisation. It was to reveal how enmeshed French financial interests had become with those abroad. Indeed, the nationalisation programme generally was highly revealing about the constraints on the government's freedom of manoeuvre. The government, for example, recognised that it had to limit its desire fully to take over the Cii-Honeywell Bull computer group, since the company was linked with an American one which supplied much of the joint company's technical know-how. Separate and very prudent negotiations had, therefore, to take place with the Americans to ensure the continued provision of that know-how. Eventually, Honeywell's stake was reduced from 47 to 20 per cent. Similar arrangements were made with Hoechst over the nationalisation of the West German company's Roussel-Uclaf in France, and with International Telephone and Telegraph in negotiations over the nationalisation of CGCT, ITT's French subsidiary.

Perhaps the most sobering lesson to be learnt by the Socialists has been economic. A year after taking office the government was facing a 14 per cent inflation rate (more than twice the German and American rate), renewed pressure on the franc, a disastrous balance of payments situation, slowly rising unemployment (which passed the 2 million mark), very high interest rates, depleted foreign exchange holdings, a lower than expected growth rate, falling private investment, increasing deficits in the general budget, the unemployment benefit fund (UNEDIC) and the social security fund.[105] France was caught in a vicious circle of inflation, devaluation, a widening trade balance (as more imports were sucked in), high interest rates and low investment. The devaluation of the franc in June 1982 (the second in six months) and the subsequent austerity programme involving a prices and wages freeze were rooted in France's opting for a high-expenditure economy in a low-growth world. The initial policy of reflation through an expanded budget deficit was intended to provoke an increase in investment and exports: neither occurred. If by June 1982 the tight fiscal and monetary policies of Barre had not been reimposed, it was nevertheless clear that much of the alternative economic strategy was in tatters. President Mitterrand in his June 1982 press conference could refer rather primly to the 'second phase of change', but most observers decoded this to mean a slowing down of the process of social reform. All that seems to remain of the initial strategy are a commitment to the national plan; and plans for a massive public investment programme to restructure French industry, using the nationalised sector as the launching-pad, and a determination to pour money into research. The impact of American high interest rates, the relentless pressure from the money markets, the continued competitive pressure from the Japanese, and the financially conservative strategies of Germany and Britain are amongst the international factors which have pressurised the government into a change of economic direction. The consequences for the implementation of its ambitious social programme are also evident, for many of the promised social reforms were posited on the basis of a growing economy.

Pressures within France have also contributed to a change of direction or have slowed down the pace of change. Domestic constraints have been of a legal and of a political nature. At the legal level the Council of State has insisted on several amendments to governmental Bills, whilst the Constitutional Council, to the fury of many left-wingers, threw out the first nationalisation Bill and insisted upon important – and costly – amendments to the compensation clauses. At the political level the government is facing resistance from several sources. The first source is electoral. There have been a number of pointers to the fall in the popularity of the new masters. Although the opinion polls indicate the continuing high level of popularity of the President, they also reveal a drop in that level and an increasing scepticism about the performance of his government. Legislative byelections in January 1982 and elections to the departmental assemblies (*conseils généraux*) in the following March dramatically underlined the fall of electoral support for the Left: the Right won all four seats in January and gained control of fifty-nine (of the ninety-five) departmental assemblies in March. The Right, encouraged by such results, is reorganising itself and is in militant mood after an initial period of dispirited disorientation. In the National Assembly and in the Senate (where it enjoys a majority) the Right has fully exploited the obstructionist potential of parliamentary procedures. Powerfully placed groups have also submitted the government to constant pressure: the doctors have forced an able and determined minister into concessions; the CNPF (the employers' organisation) has squeezed the government into a package of concessions to ease the burden of social charges falling on firms and it has also managed to limit the impact of the Auroux proposals on labour rights; the FNSEA (the farmers' organisation), of overtly right-wing sympathy, has demanded (often violently) and obtained a highly privileged relationship with a government which had previously been extremely reticent; the Confédération Générale des Cadres has launched a militant campaign in defence of its members' interests; the Catholics have pushed the President and the Prime Minister into an emollient stance on the schools issue. Even the trade unions have proved themselves to be far from compliant in their attitude to the government, and several policies (particularly the prices and incomes freeze) have been subjected to vigorous criticism.

The government is also inhibited in the pursuit of its programme by internal dissension. There has been a constant and public controversy between the maximalists who wish to push forward with the reform programme and the minimalists who, alarmed by the cost of the programme, have pleaded for 'a pause'. Traditional departmental conflicts have also emerged: the ministers of the Interior and of Justice have publicly argued over identity controls; the ministers of Education and of Health over the reform of medical studies; and the ministers of Finance and of Social Solidarity on the financing of the social security system.

Perhaps the greatest constraints on Mitterrand's freedom of action lie in the inherent complexity and contradictory nature of the policies being pursued. The complexity most clearly emerged in the nationalisation debates, for the government severely underestimated the extent to which French banking and industrial interests had been integrated into the international networks. It emerged equally in the de-centralisation debates in which certain key problems such as the co-ordination of the four levels of territorial government (state, region, *département* and commune) and their financial powers have yet to be solved.

Contradictions have characterised many government policies. In foreign affairs the France of François Mitterrand may denounce the imperialist designs of the USSR but it has increased its energy dependence on that country by signing a major natural-gas contract – the first Western country to sign a major contract with the Russians since the military crackdown in Warsaw. At the European level pious declarations about new initiatives are accompanied by the customary ferocious defence of national interests. On the domestic front there is a fundamental contradiction between the oft-repeated wish to increase personal freedom and the practice of giving more power to the trade unions which are notoriously unrepresentative in France. And how to square personal freedom with the integration of the Catholic schools into the state system? There is also a contradiction between the government's determination to 'restore Republican institutions' and its continued presidential type of government. Indeed, is there not a conflict between the Socialists' desire to push through a fairly radical reform programme and their wish to de-centralise and diffuse political power? Similarly, is it possible to follow the declared intention of the government of granting 'total autonomy of decision and action' to the extended state banking and industrial sector and, at the same time, ensure firmer control of the economy? It was highly revealing that on the day that the Prime Minister was justifying further nationalisation in terms of greater state control the Finance Minister was denouncing the existing nationalised banks for 'unpatriotic behaviour' over interest rates. It might also be wondered whether the government's top priority – the fight against unemployment – can be reconciled with many of its other priorities. Already the Socialists, who are so intent on protecting national economic independence, have allowed several foreign firms (such as Mitel, the Canadian private telephone-exchange company) to establish factories (and create jobs) in France: some of these firms had been blocked by the previous government. The need to create and protect jobs also explains the government's propping up declining industries, thus diverting precious resources from the technologically advanced industries. The calculation of job losses has also tempered the Socialists' zeal for 'moralising' the sales of arms abroad: as Defence Minister Charles Hernu made clear in the National Assembly in March 1982, principles should not blind the Socialists to the fact that 50,000 people are directly and 300,000 indirectly employed in that flourishing industry. A similar calculation about job losses in the vital building industry through lack of investment may also explain the moderation of the housing reform designed to protect tenants' rights. Finally, it is not always easy to square the government's employment objectives with its initial policies of increasing employers' costs, thus discouraging them from investing and creating jobs. Periods of economic recession are not especially propitious for the pursuit of policies of redistributive economic and social justice.

The basic political problem for Mitterrand is that he is both the 'President of all the French' and 'President of *le peuple de gauche*', and as such the instrument for attacking the privileges of many. How is it possible for the President both to impose social change which involves sacrifices by many and maintain some form of consensus which must underpin that change in any democratic system? How will he retain the loyalty of the mass of the Socialist Party – his major backer? As 'a crossroads of contradictions' it was perfectly placed to become an electorally attractive catch-all party in opposition, but those contradictions – and they are many and profound – become a liability in office.

These various conflicting pressures have led the government into compromises which often please no one (this is evident over Corsica, over workers' and tenants' rights, and the religious schools issue) or into involuntary prudence (as witnessed in the concessions granted to the employers in April 1982 or in the limited nature of the tax reforms). Already promises are being broken: promises such as the reduction of the presidential mandate to five years, the consultation of the local population in the event of the installation of a nuclear power station, the creation of a Basque *département*, the vote for immigrants in local elections, the abolition of the Ordre des Médecins and of VAT on basic necessities.

It would be invidious to catalogue all the other contradictions, compromises, concessions and broken commitments, since any government in a democratic system is locked into a position of satisfying conflicting interests. Yet high hopes were raised by the Socialists in May 1981 after a generation of right-wing governments. The inevitable disillusion may be all the greater.

The present presidency marks, therefore, in some respects a break with the past. There has been a visible if not radical change in the governmental personnel of the country, a change of emphasis in certain major policy areas, a quite radical shift in other areas. The new men at the top have given the regime a more liberal, more humane, concerned and in some senses more voluntaristic and hopeful aspect. Certainly, the technocratic *image* of the Fifth Republic conveyed by the previous presidency has disappeared. But the break with the past is not as radical as government rhetoric would claim or opposition spokesmen fear. The complex, often insoluble, economic, social and political problems confronting the new administration have already slowed down the promised process of change.

The constraints of the international, European and domestic environments are also limiting the Socialists' ambitions. Finally, the aspirations of the new administration will be contained by the political costs of trying to implement the contradictory aims of the governing coalition and of attempting to impose even modified policies on reticent and strategically placed groups. François Mitterrand inherited from his predecessor a long list of problems, broken promises and unsolved contradictions. The early evidence suggests that he may bequeath his successor with a similar record.

**Appendix 1**   *Percentage Breakdown of Votes at the First Ballot, 26 April 1981 (Sofres Post-election Opinion Poll)*

|  | G. Marchais | A. Laguiller | H. Bouchardeau | F. Mitterrand | M. Crépeau | B. Lalonde | V. Giscard d'Estaing | J. Chirac | M. Debré and M.-F. Garaud |
|---|---|---|---|---|---|---|---|---|---|
| Total | 16 | 2 | 1 | 26 | 2 | 4 | 28 | 18 | 3 |
| Men | 17 | 2 | 1 | 29 | 2 | 4 | 23 | 19 | 3 |
| Women | 14 | 2 | 1 | 24 | 2 | 4 | 32 | 18 | 3 |
| *Years of age* | | | | | | | | | |
| 18–24 | 24 | 2 | 4 | 22 | 2 | 11 | 23 | 11 | 1 |
| 25–34 | 23 | 4 | 2 | 27 | 2 | 6 | 16 | 18 | 2 |
| 35–49 | 15 | 2 | 1 | 27 | 2 | 2 | 27 | 20 | 4 |
| 50–64 | 11 | 2 | — | 26 | 3 | 2 | 28 | 24 | 4 |
| 65+ | 7 | 1 | — | 28 | 1 | 1 | 48 | 11 | 3 |
| *Profession* | | | | | | | | | |
| Farmers | 2 | — | — | 23 | 2 | 1 | 33 | 36 | 3 |
| Shopkeepers, small businessmen | 9 | 1 | — | 14 | 3 | 7 | 35 | 29 | 2 |
| Business executives and liberal professions | 7 | — | 2 | 19 | 2 | 4 | 24 | 36 | 6 |
| Clerical and administrative employees | 18 | 2 | 3 | 29 | 4 | 6 | 17 | 18 | 3 |
| Workers | 30 | 3 | 1 | 33 | 1 | 4 | 18 | 10 | — |
| No profession/retired | 12 | 3 | 1 | 25 | 2 | 3 | 35 | 16 | 3 |
| *Monthly take-home pay* | | | | | | | | | |
| Less than 2,000 franc | 11 | 1 | — | 31 | 2 | 5 | 36 | 13 | 1 |
| 2,001–3,000 franc | 18 | 2 | — | 30 | 1 | 2 | 31 | 15 | 1 |
| 3,001–5,000 franc | 19 | 2 | 1 | 28 | 2 | 4 | 26 | 16 | 2 |
| 5,001–7,500 franc | 19 | 3 | 2 | 27 | 2 | 4 | 24 | 13 | 6 |
| More than 7,500 franc | 10 | 2 | 2 | 23 | 4 | 4 | 26 | 25 | 4 |
| *Religion* | | | | | | | | | |
| Regularly practising Catholic | 2 | 1 | — | 12 | 1 | 3 | 50 | 26 | 5 |
| Occasionally practising Catholic | 6 | 3 | 1 | 24 | 2 | 2 | 37 | 23 | 2 |
| Non-practising Catholic | 18 | 2 | 1 | 31 | 3 | 4 | 22 | 17 | 2 |
| No religion | 39 | 3 | 4 | 29 | 1 | 8 | 6 | 7 | 3 |
| *Vote at the second ballot, 1974* | | | | | | | | | |
| François Mitterrand | 32 | 3 | 1 | 51 | 3 | 3 | 3 | 3 | 1 |
| Valéry Giscard d'Estaing | 1 | 2 | — | 9 | 1 | 2 | 49 | 31 | 5 |
| *First ballot of the legislative, 1978* | | | | | | | | | |
| Communist Party | 73 | 3 | 1 | 17 | — | 1 | 3 | 2 | — |
| Socialist and Radical parties | 10 | 3 | 1 | 68 | 4 | 3 | 6 | 4 | 1 |
| UDF | — | 1 | — | 5 | 2 | 3 | 58 | 26 | 5 |
| RPR | — | 2 | — | 6 | — | 2 | 44 | 42 | 4 |

*Source: Le Nouvel Observateur*, 1 June 1981.

**Appendix 2** Social Bases of the Four Main Parties
(Post-election IFOP Poll)

| Age | Communist Party | Socialists and Radicals | UDF | RPR |
|---|---|---|---|---|
| | | (percentage of each category) | | |
| *Men* | | | | |
| 18–34 | 26·0 | 36·0 | 15·0 | 15·0 |
| 35–49 | 21·0 | 29·5 | 20·5 | 25·0 |
| 50–64 | 21·5 | 28·0 | 24·0 | 26·0 |
| 65+ | 6·0 | 31·0 | 40·5 | 21·5 |
| *Women* | | | | |
| 18–34 | 14·0 | 38·0 | 24·0 | 19·0 |
| 35–49 | 13·5 | 37·0 | 27·5 | 18·5 |
| 50–64 | 9·0 | 28·0 | 33·0 | 27·0 |
| 65+ | 5·0 | 17·0 | 57·0 | 18·5 |
| *Profession* | | | | |
| Workers | 28·0 | 37·5 | 18·5 | 13·5 |
| Clerical and administrative | 13·5 | 41·5 | 21·5 | 17·5 |
| No profession | 8·5 | 26·0 | 43·0 | 20·0 |
| Business executives and liberal professions | 6·0 | 24·5 | 29·5 | 32·0 |
| Farmers | 7·5 | 11·5 | 35·0 | 45·0 |
| *New voters* | | | | |
| 18–20 | 11·5 | 48·5 | 14·0 | 24·5 |
| 21–24 | 21·0 | 30·0 | 23·5 | 18·5 |

Source: Le Point, 11 May 1981.

# Notes: Introduction

Some parts of this introduction draw heavily upon two articles: Howard Machin and Vincent Wright, 'Why Mitterrand won. The French presidential elections of April–May 1981', *West European Politics*, January 1982, pp. 5–35; and Vincent Wright, 'The change in France', *Government and Opposition*, Autumn 1981, pp. 414–31.

1 Jacques Capdevielle, Elisabeth Dupoirier, Gérard Grunberg, Etienne Schweisguth, Colette Ysmal, *France de gauche, vote à droite* (Paris: Presses de la Fondation Nationale des Sciences Politiques, 1981).
2 *Le Nouvel Observateur*, 1 June 1981.
3 On the election campaign, see David B. Goldey and Andrew F. Knapp, 'Time for a change: the French elections of 1981. I: The presidency', *Electoral Studies*, April 1982, pp. 3–42. On the results, see the articles by Thierry Pfister, Jean Charlot, Gérard Le Gall and Jean-Luc Parodi in *Revue politique et parlementaire*, May–June 1981, pp. 8–49; Alain Lancelot, 'L'alternance sur l'air de la vie en rose', *Projet*, September–October 1981, pp. 915–39; and Jérome Jaffré, 'De Valéry Giscard d'Estaing à François Mitterrand: France de gauche vote à gauche', *Pouvoirs*, no. 20, 1982, pp. 5–21. For the

detailed results, see *L'Election présidentielle 26 avril–10 mai 1981: la victoire de M. Mitterrand* (*Le Monde*).

4   The February 1981 IFOP poll showed that only 37 per cent of the respondents were satisfied (compared with 51 per cent dissatisfied), whilst the March Sofres poll indicated that those who lacked confidence in the President (55 per cent) far outnumbered those who had confidence in him (41 per cent).

5   On the movement of opinion during the election campaign, see Olivier Duhamel and Jean-Luc Parodi, 'L'évolution des intentions de vote, contribution à l'explication de l'élection présidentielle de 1981', *Pouvoirs*, no. 18, 1981, pp. 159–74; and Jaffré, 'De Valéry Giscard d'Estaing', op. cit., pp. 10–12.

6   Details in Duhamel and Parodi, op. cit., p. 171.

7   See the article by Jacques Julliard, *Le Nouvel Observateur*, 1 June 1981.

8   Jean Charlot, 'Le double enchaînement de la défaite et de la victoire', *Revue politique et parlementaire*, May–June 1981, p. 22.

9   On the PCF's performance, see François Platone and Jean Ranger, 'L'échec du parti communiste français aux élections du printemps 1981', *Revue Française de Science Politique*, October–December 1981, pp. 1015–37.

10  Jean Charlot, 'The majority', in Howard R. Penniman (ed.), *The French National Assembly Elections of 1978* (Washington, DC: American Enterprise Institute, 1980), p. 103.

11  Charlot, 'Le double enchaînement', op. cit., p. 22.

12  Jean Charlot, 'Les 3% qui ont fait l'alternance', *Le Point*, 11 May 1981.

13  Gérard le Gall, 'Du recul de la droite vers l'hégémonie du PS', *Revue politique et parlementaire*, May–June 1981, pp. 39–40.

14  Charlot, 'Le double enchaînement', op. cit., pp. 15–25.

15  For the geographical distribution of the vote, see Hervé Le Bras and Emmanuel Todd, 'Opération Hexagone', *L'Express*, 12–19 May 1981.

16  Charlot, 'Les 3%'.

17  ibid.

18  *Le Nouvel Observateur*, 1 June 1981.

19  Provided in Charlot, 'Le double enchaînement', op. cit., p. 28.

20  See the article by Noël-Jean Bergeroux, *Le Monde*, 20 May 1980.

21  In an article, 'Les cent jours de l'ex-majorité', *Le Monde*, 2 September 1981.

22  *Le Monde*, 5 December 1975.

23  See the review article by Max Gallo, 'La chasse à l'homme', *L'Express*, 21 February 1981.

24  *Le Monde*, 21 May 1981.

25  Thomas Ferenczi, *Le Prince au miroir: essai sur l'ordre giscardien* (Paris: Albin Michel, 1981), p. 16. This is also one of the themes running through J. R. Frears, *France in the Giscard Presidency* (London: Allen & Unwin, 1981), which is a fair and balanced view of the period 1974–81.

26  See his interviews in *Le Figaro*, 28 February 1981, and *Le Point*, 2 May 1981.

27  On the economic balance-sheet, see the report of François Bloch-Lainé, *La France en mai 1981* (Paris: La Documentation française, 1982); two unpublished papers by Diana Green, 'The economic policies of the Barre government', 1980, and by Janice McCormick, 'The limits of liberalism: the failure of the French experiment', 1981; Georges Laverdines, 'Le libéralisme organisé', *Pouvoirs*, no. 9, 1979, pp. 17–26.

28  See his very revealing article, *Revue des Deux-Mondes*, September 1980.

29  Roger Priouret, 'L'Homme qui ne choisit pas', *Le Nouvel Observateur*, 9 March 1981.

30  For a useful summary, see Maurice Roy, 'Barre: échecs visibles, succès cachés', *Le Point*, 12 January 1981.

31  See particularly *L'Agression. L'Etat-Giscard contre le secteur public* (Paris: Club Socialiste du livre, 1980).

32  See also Diana Green, 'The Seventh Plan - the demise of French planning?', *West European Politics*, no. 1, February 1978, pp. 60–76, and her 'The Budget and the

Plan', in Philip G. Cerny and Martin A. Schain (eds), *French Politics and Public Policy* (London: Methuen, 1980), pp. 101-24.

33 On the whole question, see excellent summary by Denis Jeambar, 'La pieuvre étatique', *Le Point*, 16 February 1981.

34 Alain Vernholes, 'Le *barrisme* tel qu'il fut et tel qu'il voulait être', *Le Monde*, 15 May 1981.

35 *La France au grand large* (Paris: Robert Laffont, 1981).

36 Germany, the UK, Italy, Belgium, Holland, the USA, Canada and Japan.

37 Details in 'Actif et passif d'un septennat', in *L'Election présidentielle* (*Le Monde*).

38 For a brief summary of the debate, see the article by Michel Castaing in *Le Monde*, 17 April 1981.

39 This he made clear in his much-quoted interview with *Figaro-Magazine*, 28 February 1981.

40 *Le Figaro*, 19 April 1981.

41 The seasonally adjusted figures give 424,800 in 1974 and 1,561,700 in 1981.

42 *Le Monde*, 3 July 1981.

43 See Sofres poll, *Le Figaro*, 4 March 1981.

44 Claude Sales, 'Cadres: finances à droite, lettres à gauche', *Le Point*, 16 March 1981.

45 *Le Quotidien de Paris*, 22 June 1981.

46 McCormick, op. cit.

47 'Le charisme de Giscard d'Estaing était trop faible pour résister aux perceptions et attitudes de la conjoncture' was one of the main conclusions of the authors of an analysis of the IFOP polls, see *Quoi*, no. 3 (Paris: IFOP, 1981), p. 56.

48 *Le Point*, 2 May 1981.

49 Jérome Jaffré, 'De Valéry Giscard d'Estaing', op. cit., p. 9.

50 Particularly useful is Jean-Christian Petitfils, *La Démocratie giscardienne* (Paris: PUF, 1981); and the special issue of *Pouvoirs*, entitled 'Le Giscardisme', no. 9, 1979.

51 See René Remond, *Les Droites en France* (Paris: Editions Aubier Montagne, 1982), pp. 342-9.

52 On Giscard d'Estaing's failure to create a strong presidential party or coalition, see the debate 'Après l'élection présidentielle', *Projet*, July–August 1981, pp. 786-7.

53 *Le Point*, 14 April 1981.

54 N.-J. Bergeroux, 'Le rendez-vous manqué de M. Giscard d'Estaing', *Le Monde*, 16 July 1981.

55 'Vers l'éclatement de l'électorat majoritaire?', *Le Monde*, 16 April 1981.

56 See the very perceptive, if occasionally polemical, article by Patrick Lehingue, 'Le discours Giscardien', in Jacques Chevallier (ed.) *Discours et Idéologie* (Paris: PUF, 1980), pp. 80-6.

57 See Thierry Pfister, 'Le coup de force d'Alice', *Le Nouvel Observateur*, 26 July 1980; and Jacques Julliard, 'Universités: Alice et ses complices', *Le Nouvel Observateur*, 15 September 1980.

58 Edwy Plenel, 'Les silences de l'ancien ministre', *Le Monde*, 30 May 1981.

59 Lehingue, op. cit., pp. 91-9.

60 For a measured yet critical view of the law, see G. Millet, 'La Loi Sécurité et Liberté', *Projet*, September–October 1980, pp. 941-54.

61 On the evolution of the regime, see Alain Duhamel, *La République giscardienne* (Paris: Grasset, 1980); Petifils, op. cit., pp. 55-75; the round-table debate in *Revue politique et parlementaire*, March-April 1981, pp. 2-95; and several chapters in Roger-Gérard Schwartzenberg, *La Droite absolue* (Paris: Flammarion, 1981).

62 Jean-Claude Picard, 'L'institution gouvernementale de la Cinquième République française à la lumière des lettres directives du Président de la République au Premier Ministre', in Jacques Chevallier (ed.), *L'Institution* (Paris: PUF, 1981), pp. 187-230.

63 For example, see Yves Agnès, 'L'Etat-Giscard', *Le Monde du Dimanche*, 2 March 1980.

64 See also his *Sommets de l'Etat* (Paris: Editions du Seuil, 1977); Schwartzenberg, *La Droite absolue*, pp. 84-100; and Ferenczi, *Le Prince au miroir*, pp. 87-100.

65  Schwartzenberg, *La Droite absolue*, pp. 99–116.
66  See also Sylvie Blum, 'Télévision et libéralisme: la télévision française, d'un ordre à l'autre', *Pouvoirs*, no. 9, 1979, pp. 131–50.
67  André Chambraud, 'Le Politigramme français', *Le Point*, 22 December 1980.
68  The IFOP analysts (in *Quoi*, op. cit.) put the Prime Minister's unpopularity as one of the major causes for the defeat of Giscard d'Estaing.
69  On the Giscard d'Estaing family, see Pol Bruno, *La Saga des Giscard* (Paris: Editions Ramsay, 1980).
70  See Giscard d'Estaing's interview in *L'Express*, 9 May 1977, exactly three years after his election.
71  On the problem of consensus and dissensus in France, see Alain Duhamel, 'Le Consensus français', in *L'Opinion française en 1977* (Paris: Presses de la Fondation Nationale des Sciences Politiques, 1978), and Olivier Duhamel, 'L'étendue des dissensus français', in a special issue of *Pouvoirs*, no. 5, 1978, pp. 87–92, devoted to the problem. See also a revealing series of articles entitled 'Voyages à l'intérieur des partis', *Le Matin*, September 1977.
72  *Le Figaro*, 4 March 1981.
73  See *Le Quotidien*, 19 June 1981.
74  *Le Nouvel Observateur*, 16 March 1981.
75  See the excellent section by R. W. Johnson, in his *The Long March of the French Left* (London: Macmillan, 1981), pp. 71–166.
76  André Chambraud, 'Le Politigramme français', *Le Point*, 22 December 1980.
77  On this section, see Noël Bergeroux, 'A la recherche des causes de l'échec de M. Giscard d'Estaing', *Le Monde*, 16 July 1981.
78  Jérôme Jaffré, 'La France de gauche, vote à gauche', *Pouvoirs*, no. 20, 1980, pp. 6–7.
79  Jean Charlot, 'Le double enchaînement', op. cit., p. 15.
80  See Giscard d'Estaing's comments on Mitterrand in *Le Point*, 2 May 1981.
81  *Le Monde*, 25–26 January 1981.
82  Machin and Wright, op. cit., p. 15.
83  I have tried to develop this point at length in 'Eurocommunism and the French Communist Party during the Fifth Republic', in Howard Machin, *The End of Eurocommunism?* (London: Methuen, 1982).
84  On the campaign, see Claude Estier, *Mitterrand Président* (Paris: Stock, 1981).
85  *Quoi*, op. cit., pp. 46–9.
86  'Un semestre de pouvoir Socialiste', *Le Monde*, 15 November 1981.
87  On the 1981 legislative elections, see Gérard Le Gall, 'Le nouvel ordre électoral', *Revue politique et parlementaire*, July–August 1981, pp. 1–32.
88  See Platone and Ranger, op. cit.; and Jean Baudouin, 'L'échec communiste de juin 1981: recul électoral ou crise hégémonique', *Pouvoirs*, no. 20, 1980, pp. 45–53.
89  On the new Socialist Deputies, see David Hanley, 'Les députés socialistes', *Pouvoirs*, no. 20, 1982, pp. 55–66.
90  Of the 285 members of the Socialist group in the National Assembly, 141 are mayors, 6 are Paris town councillors, 156 are members of a departmental council and 12 preside at departmental councils.
91  On the purge, see Noël-Jean Bergeroux, 'Etat-PS: les nouveaux maîtres', *L'Express*, 15–21 January 1982.
92  I am indebted to Professor Morvan, of the Economics Faculty of the University of Rennes, who is currently an adviser to the present government and who greatly clarified the situation for me.
93  Speech of 13 May 1981.
94  *Le Monde*, 2 July 1981.
95  'La séduction manquée', *L'Express*, 30 April–6 May 1982.
96  Between 21 May–24 September 1981, 'fewer than ten were sacked or had resigned', compared with about sixty in 1968, and the 274 removals, resignations and fifty-five forced retirements after 1974.

97 The ex-ENA ministers include Jobert, Rocard, Nicole Questiaux, Fabius, Joxe, Chevènement, Cheysson and Chandernagor. See *Le Monde*, 8 August 1981.

98 Marianne Amar, 'Les "nouveaux" hommes de l'ombre', *Le Point*, 7 September 1981.

99 ibid.

100 *Le Point*, 22 June 1981.

101 There are somewhat different figures in the article by André Passeron, *Le Monde*, 17 November 1981.

102 Jacques Isnard, 'Défense: le gardien du feu sacré', *Le Monde*, 8 May 1982.

103 See the excellent article by André Fontaine in *Le Monde*, 17 July 1981, and the perceptive editorial by Jean Daniel, *Le Nouvel Observateur*, 28 June 1981.

104 For a very good summary, see Jean-Claude Pomonti, 'La France et l'Afrique', *Le Monde*, 7 April 1982.

105 On the first year's economic performance, see *L'Expansion*, 7-20 June 1982; and Janice McCormick, 'Thorns among the roses: a year of the socialist experiment in France', *West European Politics*, vol. 6, no. 1 (January 1983), pp. 44-62.

# 1

# The President's Men: Advisers and Assistants at the Elysée Palace

*H. MACHIN*

The 1958 Constitution provided for a system of parliamentary government under the leadership of the Prime Minister. The entire administrative system remained under ministerial control and responsibility. The common services and co-ordinating bodies (the Planning Commissariat and the General Secretariat of the government are good examples) were attached to the Prime Minister's office. No provision was made for either a presidential 'executive office' or a *cabinet* of policy advisers, because most of the authors of the Constitution neither desired nor foresaw the active presidential style of General de Gaulle. The first President of the Fifth Republic had no wish to direct or manage the administrative machine, but he did intend to dominate the governmental policy-making process. For this purpose, he assembled at the Elysée Palace a small staff of advisers and assistants to provide him with ideas, research and constant information on the work and achievements of his ministers, but also to 'represent' the presidency in small inter-ministerial committees. The compliance of Prime Minister Debré and the government and a small increase in the budget credits for the presidency to pay a dozen additional salaries were the only necessary conditions, and these were easily obtained. Support staff – typists, secretaries and clerical officers – were 'borrowed' from obliging nearby ministries.

Under the ten years of de Gaulle's presidential rule the Elysée Palace staff remained small and discreet. It received little attention from politicians and political scientists alike. Only Jacques Foccart, one of the five 'barons' of the Gaullist movement and de Gaulle's most trusted specialist on both African and electoral questions, emerged as an influential policy-maker in his own right within this team. After de Gaulle's departure, during the early Pompidou presidency, this quiet, restrained role continued, although Foccart remained as African specialist. The presidential staff did, however, acquire notoriety and attract considerable curiosity during the last two years of President Pompidou's rule. At that time some members of the Elysée staff appeared not only to have a predominant influence over the decisions made by the President, but also to take some decisions on his behalf over and above the heads of ministers. In short, key presidential 'advisers' seemed to many to be the real rulers of France. Furthermore, it was frequently alleged that the controversial political supervision of broadcasting (see Chapter 7 by Raymond Kuhn in this book) was the work of the presidential staff. Hence, the frequent comparisons of this team with Nixon's 'Berlin Wall' White House staff, whilst in reality rather excessive, seemed quite plausible at the time. By early 1974 the advisers and assistants in the Elysée Palace were in considerable disrepute with politicians, press and public.

When he was elected President, Giscard d'Estaing sought to revert to the original Gaullist model of a discreet, self-effacing Elysée staff. He wished to ensure that he alone would make 'presidential' decisions on the basis of full, balanced information and uninfluenced by his *entourage*. He also strove to reassure his Prime Minister and government that his advisers were simply to provide advice – not to spy, cajole, bully, or overrule them. Hence, he reorganised the presidential staff and changed almost all its members. He gave strict instructions to his new team to avoid antagonism of any kind with his government. Whatever Giscard d'Estaing's original wishes or intentions, his staff grew increasingly interventionist and influential during his presidency. In the monarchical metaphors of the later years members of 'the king's household' in the 'château' were again usurping the rightful role of his ministers. The presidency ended as it began. The newly elected Mitterrand again replaced all Giscard d'Estaing's men with his own team of advisers, reorganised the work pattern of the Elysée Palace and ordered his personal staff to leave government to his government. Whether or not President Mitterrand will be more successful than his predecessors in restricting his staff to an 'advisory' role or whether this institution will again be drawn – by both the nature of its work and the President's desire for control of governmental action – into policy-making, remains to be seen.

## The Inheritance

There are about 550 people actually employed in the Elysée Palace and its overspill offices, but only a fraction of these constitute the President's political staff. The majority of the employees are involved in relatively simple subordinate tasks: there are some 200 members of the guard, a considerable domestic staff, and a very large number of secretarial and clerical officers. It is interesting to note that most of the Elysée staff are not formally employed by the presidency at all, but are 'on loan' from the different ministries. De Gaulle devised this system of 'borrowing' civil servants, paid on ministerial budget credits, to disguise the expansion of the presidential office in 1959.[1] It was continued by Pompidou after 1969, and still operates in 1982.

The actual advisory staff of President de Gaulle was a small group of people (never more than forty in number) which de Gaulle organised into four separate units, each with a distinct sphere of competence: the staff of the Military Household, the *cabinet*, the General Secretariat of the Presidency of the Republic and the General Secretariat for French Community and Malagasy Affairs. Each element had its own role to play.

The first element, the staff of the Military Household, was of limited political significance. Much of its work was concerned with security and ceremonial matters, but it was also responsible for the extremely complex system for authorising the launching of France's nuclear weapons (code-named 'Jupiter') and providing for such authorisation whenever and wherever the President was outside the Elysée Palace. The chief of staff and the dozen officers from the three services advised the President on some defence matters, including the appointments to senior military posts. They also helped in the organisation of meetings of the Defence Council. Thus, the staff of the Military Household played both an administrative and an advisory role.

The *cabinet*, a team of six to ten people, had administrative responsibilities which necessitated considerable political sensitivity. The domestic organisation of the Elysée Palace, the arrangements for hospitality to visiting foreign dignitaries (in co-operation with the Quai d'Orsay), the personnel management of the clerical staff and the secretaries, the supervision of the fifty-strong team which dealt with presidential mail, the arranging of interviews with the President, and the detailed preparation of presidential visits to the French provinces: all these were the time-consuming, often routine, but occasionally politically delicate duties of the *directeur de cabinet* and his assistants.

In contrast, the two General Secretariats played much more directly political roles. The Secretariat for French Community and Malagasy Affairs was ostensibly responsible for overseeing relations of all kinds between France and its former colonial territories in Africa. De Gaulle was particularly concerned to maintain French influence after de-colonisation and entrusted this secretariat to Jacques Foccart, who was known for his expertise, his discretion and his loyalty to the General. Foccart remained general secretary (except for the period of Poher's interim presidency in 1969) until Pompidou's death. Under his leadership the secretariat became not only the main advisory body on African policy, but a 'ministry' for African questions, with which French ambassadors and even ministers in African governments might correspond directly. During the Algerian War this secretariat was also often associated with the notorious *barbouzes*, and from this time it remained closely linked to the security and espionage services. Furthermore, de Gaulle usually consulted Foccart about electoral strategy at home. In short, there were good foundations for the construction of a popular myth of this secretariat as a power in its own right and of Foccart as an *eminence grise* of de Gaulle and Pompidou.

At the centre of the presidential machinery constructed by de Gaulle was the General Secretariat of the Presidency of the Republic, the team of advisers and assistants on all matters relating to government, politics and administration. Organised and managed by a general secretary this institution was divided into four parts, each led by a 'technical adviser' (*conseiller technique*) and responsible for a sector of governmental or political activity. The four sectors were: foreign affairs, economic and financial matters, social, scientific and educational questions, and political and judicial problems. Each technical adviser was helped by one or more 'assistants' (*chargés de mission*). The general secretary co-ordinated the work of the whole team and reported on its results each day to the President. Each technical adviser was expected to follow the work of all governmental agencies involved in his sector and to keep the President informed as to how policies were working out in practice and how improvements could be achieved. In short, the secretariat was designed to inform and advise a President outside traditional governmental and parliamentary structures who strove to impose his leadership on the political system.

When Pompidou was elected President of the Republic in 1969, the organisation of the Elysée staff was modified in a number of ways. In the first place, the *cabinet* was merged into the General Secretariat of the Presidency. A second change was the establishment of a public relations unit (of four people) within the secretariat. Of greater importance, however, was the reorganisation of duties within the secretariat. The four sector division was scrapped and instead each adviser or assistant was expected to 'cover' a much smaller, well-defined area of governmental action. This less hierarchical structure might have resulted in less co-ordination (and hence less presidential control) but to meet this problem the new post of assistant general secretary was created. Henceforth the general secretary and this assistant were to work in very close co-operation to ensure that the fifteen or more advisers and the assistants operated as an effective team.

The other important innovation under Pompidou was the creation of a post of 'presidential assistant' (*chargé de mission auprès du Président de la République*) and its attribution to Pierre Juillet. This presidential assistant, formally outside the hierarchy of the secretariat, was ably assisted by an adviser within the secretariat, Marie-France Garaud, who shared and reinforced his conservative influence on the President. The ascendancy of this tandem was striking; Pompidou's decision to ask for the resignation of Chaban-Delmas in July 1972 was described in the press as 'la révolution de Juillet'. The increasing political control of broadcasting after 1972 was attributed to the efforts of this pair. Both appeared as firm supporters, but also manipulators of the rising star, Jacques Chirac, and as stage-managers of the famous forty-three Gaullists who announced their willingness to transfer their loyalties to Giscard d'Estaing even before the first ballot of the 1974 presidential elections. During the months of Pompidou's illness, when the cautious, self-effacing Pierre Messmer was Prime Minister, France appeared to be governed by the independent Elysée *entourage* led by Juillet and Garaud, rather than by the government.[2]

In other respects, however, the Pompidou presidential staff continued very much in the patterns established by de Gaulle. One notable element of continuity was in the nature of the appointments to the staff. Apart from Foccart and two of his team, none of de Gaulle's advisers continued to work for the new President, but Pompidou appointed very similar types of people as advisers and assistants. For the particularly sensitive role of general secretary, de Gaulle chose discreet efficient senior civil servants who avoided controversy and publicity – de Courcel, a diplomat, during 1959–62, Burin des Roziers, also a diplomat, until 1967 and Tricot, from the Council of State, until April 1969. If the first general secretary under Pompidou was a rather more assertive administrator, Michel Jobert (from the Court of Accounts) who left in 1973 to become Foreign Affairs Minister, the second, Balladur (from the Council of State) was in the mould of de Gaulle's men, self-effacing and discreet.

Under Pompidou, as during de Gaulle's presidency, most of the advisers and assistants were top-level civil servants on leave from the *grands corps*: only seven of de Gaulle's total of seventy, and twelve of Pompidou's forty-four advisers, had not held posts in the civil service. Diplomats were particularly favoured (24 per cent of appointments by de Gaulle and 14 per cent of those of Pompidou) as were members of the prefectoral *corps* (11 per cent and 14 per cent for de Gaulle and Pompidou respectively). In general, the advisers were very well educated: 36 per cent of de Gaulle's staff had been at ENA or the Ecole Polytechnique, whilst 54 per cent of Pompidou's team had studied at one (or both) of these prestigious schools. Most members of the staffs of both Presidents were younger than the general secretaries: people were usually appointed in their early forties or late thirties. Neither President appointed many women to their staffs. In short, under de Gaulle and Pompidou, the ideal type of person for the Elysée staff was a well-educated, articulate, discreet, male, top-rank civil servant with considerable knowledge and experience of the administrative machine and with many contacts throughout its structures.[3]

## The Changes in 1974 and 1981

President Giscard d'Estaing attempted to change the structures, the methods and the personnel of the Elysée staff. In the first place, he integrated all the non-military posts into the General Secretariat of the Presidency. Foccart left the Elysée immediately and his Secretariat for French Community and Malagasy Affairs ceased to exist. Henceforth, the general secretary and assistant general secretary were to oversee and co-ordinate all the work of the advisers except that concerning defence questions. Thus, whilst Giscard appointed two 'presidential assistants' (Jean Serisé and Victor Chapot), they were both formally part of the secretariat and worked with the general secretary. This was also the case for the two other 'presidential assistants', Jean Phillippe Lecat and Jean Riolacci, who were appointed in 1976 and 1977 respectively. To reinforce co-ordination at this level brief daily meetings were organised between the general secretary and assistant general secretary, the *chef de cabinet* and the official spokesman, and weekly discussions held with these men and the 'presidential assistants'. In addition, Giscard d'Estaing initially reduced the size of the secretariat to a more cohesive team of fifteen members.[4]

The new President also modified the work methods of the Elysée staff by minimising direct contacts with most of the advisers and avoiding full meetings of the Secretariat except for a short briefing session each Monday morning. Each adviser was given a very clearly defined sphere of competence when he was appointed. Each day he could expect specific requests from the general secretary for information, evaluation or advice for the President, and each evening he would submit brief notes back to the general secretary. This exchange of short, precise memoranda became the main method of communication between the President and his advisers. The entire team would meet once a week in the absence of the President, each Wednesday afternoon, when the general secretary would brief the advisers of the decisions of the Council of Ministers meeting held that morning. Once again, however, little discussion was expected.

The third main change of the new President was the renewal of personnel. In the first place, Giscard d'Estaing appointed a new, smaller team, almost entirely of his own men. Only two men were kept on from the Pompidou staff, René Journiac (formerly the assistant to Foccart) whose expertise on Africa was considered essential, and Gabriel Robin who had served as diplomatic adviser to Pompidou only for his last three months. As his general secretary and assistant general secretary Giscard d'Estaing appointed Claude Pierre-Brossolette and Yves Cannac, close friends and collaborators from the Ministry of Finance. In fact, over half of the presidential advisers in 1974 had worked with the President when he had been Minister of Finances. One other common factor of the Elysée staff was immediately noticed, the preponderance of ENA graduates. Over 50 per cent of Giscard d'Estaing's advisers had passed through the same prestigious civil service recruiting school as the President himself.

A second change, which was not immediately apparent, was that Giscard d'Estaing did not keep a constant stable team of collaborators. There was a high turnover of men and of duties. Only five of the men originally appointed in 1974 were still in the Elysée in late 1980: Polge de Combret (promoted in 1978 from adviser for industry and agriculture to assistant general secretary), Serisé, Fouquet, Rouault and Signorini. In his seven years in office Giscard d'Estaing changed his general secretary as often as de Gaulle had done in ten years: in 1976 Jean François-Poncet replaced Pierre-Brossolette, and was himself replaced in 1978 by Jacques Wahl. There were three assistant general secretaries, two *chefs de cabinet*, four official spokesmen and three chiefs of staff (Guy Méry, Claude Vanbremeersch and Bertrand de Montaudin). Part of this turnover resulted from the growth of the team (from sixteen to twenty-seven) and some changes were forced by outside circumstances (the death of Journiac in an aircrash in February 1980 involved the appointment of Martin Kirsch as his replacement). The President's desire to place trusted collaborators in key positions elsewhere also necessitated the recruitment of replacements: the appointments of François-Poncet to the Ministry of Foreign Affairs, of Lecat as Minister of Culture, Stoleru as Under-secretary for Labour, Cannac as managing director of Agence Havas, Michel Bassi as manager of Radio Monte Carlo and Xavier Gouyou-Beauchamps (after several months' interval in a prefecture) as managing director of SOFIRAD (the state company controlling the 'independent' radio stations) are all examples of this process. Yet another factor affecting this turnover appears to have been the President's dislike of criticism from his collaborators; this was one reason for the replacement of Pierre-Brossolette by François-Poncet in 1976.

The Giscard d'Estaing staff differed from its predecessors in another respect – style. While the social origins and education of the advisers of de Gaulle and Pompidou were far from humble, those of the advisers of Giscard d'Estaing generally mirrored the President's own privileged background, encompassing wealth, excellent schools, socially acceptable marriage and friends. A man such as Serisé (from a humble background) was a notable exception. Journalists noted and caricatured a similar and characteristic manner of speaking and writing, of a 'sporting' stance and an elegance of dress. Perhaps inadvertently, the advisers appeared to resemble their President in seeming distant, superior and condescending in manner.[5]

The style, personnel, methods and organisation established by President Giscard d'Estaing all disappeared when François Mitterrand took office in May 1981. Table 1.1 reveals the main structural differences. President Mitterrand re-established the *cabinet* as a distinct unit (under André Rousselet) and created a small special 'advice cell' led by Jacques Attali, the *conseiller spécial au Président*. These two bodies and the two 'presidential assistants' (Legatte and de Grossouvre) were theoretically outside the general secretariat, but in practice the overall leadership of Pierre Beregovoy, the general secretary, seemed to be accepted by all – at least during the early months of the presidency.

All these collaborators do not act as a 'team', but rather as individuals chosen by and loyal to the President.[6] There are no meetings of the entire staff, but only small group meetings of people working in the same area. The economics advisers hold regular weekly meetings every Wednesday chaired by Jacques Fournier. The other main informal groups are those

Table 1.1  *The Staffs of President Giscard d'Estaing (1980) and President Mitterrand (1981)*

---

**GISCARD D'ESTAING**
*Head of the Military Household*
*Personal Secretary*                         President
Marguerite Villetelle
              *General Secretary* – Jacques Wahl ————————> *Presidential Assistants*
*Assistant General Secretary* – François Polge de        Jean Riolacci (Politics)
                                Combret                  Jean Serisé (Politics)
                                                         Victor Chapot
                                                         Jean-Marie Poirier
                                                         (Spokesman)

*Chef de Cabinet*                    *Technical Advisers*
Michel Mosser                        Patrick Leclercq (Foreign)
                                     Martin Kirsch (Africa)
                                     Henry Jean-Baptiste (Third World)
                                     Bernard Landouzy (DOM-TOM)
                                     Pierre Emeury (Nuclear)
                                     Jean-Pierre Rouault (Economy)
                                     Jean-Claude Trichet (Industry, Research)
                                     Emmanuel Rodocanachi (Agriculture, Commerce)
                                     Alain Lamassoure (Environment, Regions)
                                     Guy de Panafieu (International Economy)
                                     Olivier Fouquet (Justice, Labour, Health)
                                     Charles Debbasch (Education, Youth, Sport)
                                     Jacques Blot (Information, Press)
                                     Jean-Pierre Narnio (Media)
*Assistants*
                        Odile Warin                      Philippe Aucouturier
Eliane Signorini                                         Bernard Rideau
            Jean-David Levitte

**MITTERRAND**
*Head of the Military Household*              *Presidential Assistants*
                                             Paul Legatte (*cabinets, Conseil d'Etat*)
                             President       François de Grossouvre
                                               (Secret services, special tasks)

*General Secretariat*
*General Secretary:* Pierre Beregovoy
*Assistant General Secretary:* J. Fournier                    *Cabinet*
*Adviser to General Secretary:*              *Directeur de Cabinet:* André Rousselet
  M. Charasse (Constitution)                 *Assistant Directeur de Cabinet:*
*Spokesman:* M. Vauzelle                       J. Claude Colliard
*Press Assistant:* Mlle N. Duhamel           *Technical Adviser:* Gilles Ménage
*Technical Advisers*                         *Chef de Cabinet:* Jean Glavany
  Jacques Bonacossa (Commerce)               *Assistant:* Mme L. Soudet
  Antoine Bonnefond (Justice)

Table 1  *(Contd.)*

---

Alain Boublil (Nationalisation)
Pierre Castagnou (Parliament)
Mme Yannick Moreau (National
   Solidarity)
Guy Penne (Africa)
Gérard Renon (Energy)
Charles Salzmann (Computers)
Christian Sautter (International
   Economy)
François Stasse (Economy, Plan)
Hubert Vedrine (Foreign Affairs)

*Assistants*
Robert Chéramy (Education, free-
   time)
Mme Paule Dayan (Parliament)
Regis Debray (Developing Countries)
Paul Guimard (Culture)
Mme Jeannette Laot (Labour)
Claude Manceron (Culture)
Jacques Ribs (Repatriated Citizens)

*Secretaries to President*
Mme P. Decraene
Mlle Marie-Claire Papegay

*Advice Cell*
*Special Adviser to President*
Jacques Attali
*Assistants*
Jean-Louis Bianco
Pierre Morel

---

dealing with the President's speeches and writings, with relations between the government and parliament, with public opinion, with diplomatic questions and with government appointments, but the meetings of these groups are less regular than those of the economists.

In May 1981 it was intended to change the work pattern of the Elysée by asking all technical advisers to operate as non-specialists and to deal with files on very varied subjects. It soon proved to be more practical to return to the 'specialist' system, but there is a slightly different work pattern to that established by Giscard d'Estaing. In the first place, the President not infrequently invites two or three advisers to consider the same problem, or different aspects of the same problem, at the same time. This practice of seeking different views – or at least different 'angles' – on one issue was adopted by Mitterrand when he led the Socialist Party – sometimes to the irritation of his collaborators who found themselves in competition with one another. The President clearly appreciated this method and his Elysée staff had, in general, learned to accept it and work with each other during their years of toil in the Socialist Party. The President also continued another practice he had established whilst leading the Socialists: that of using Jacques Attali as a special adviser on any problem at any time. Whilst Attali was given neither administrative responsibility for the Elysée staff (the *Directeur de Cabinet*, Rousselet has this), nor the leadership of the advisory team (the general secretary, Beregovoy is undisputed in this role) he has a special status, leading his own small 'ideas cell' as 'adviser without portfolio'.

The other significant change of the Mitterrand presidency is that of personnel. Mitterrand did not retain the services of a single adviser or assistant of his predecessor. He appointed his own people and the result was a team very different in style to that of Giscard d'Estaing. In the first place, the Elysée staff chosen by Mitterrand is more varied in age and background. There are several relatively young ENA graduates (Attali – aged 38 in 1981 and graduate of ENA and the Ecole Polytechnique – is the best example of this breed so beloved of Giscard d'Estaing). Other leading members of the staff, however, include Beregovoy (aged 55, a former textile worker, then employee of Gaz de France), de Grossouvre (aged 63, a former doctor, turned gentleman-farmer), Colliard (aged 35, a political-science professor), Rousselet (aged 59, the managing director of a taxi company) and Penne (aged 56, a former professor of dentistry). All the leading members of the different elements of Mitterrand's staff have in common the experience of working with Mitterrand in the Socialist Party for several years. Most – but not all – are used to working with one another and are accustomed to the sometimes irritating habits of their President and the hyper-sensitive fractious attitudes of the Socialist faction leaders who are now ministers or leading Deputies or Senators. Relations within the Elysée Palace are much more informal than in the past, and at the same time, debate and disagreement are more normal and acceptable. Finally, the presidential team no longer acts as if it were under siege. The Socialist Deputies may not be as 'disciplined' as the President and Prime Minister would desire, but the situation is completely different from that under Giscard d'Estaing when the majority of the *majorité* was critical of – if not hostile to – presidential actions of all kinds. This 'openness' has given rise to no indiscretions – at least during the first few months.

In short, both Giscard d'Estaing and Mitterrand imposed their personal choices of men and organisation upon the Elysée Palace staff and some notable changes resulted. These modifications did not, however, redefine the basic role of the institution designed by de Gaulle nor the normal method of specialist advisers 'shadowing' ministers. This continuity of the practice – and the resulting problems – merits closer examination.

## Continuity of Practices and Problems

In spite of his reformist intentions and his wish to destroy the 'kitchen Cabinet' image of the Pompidou presidential staff, Giscard d'Estaing soon realised that he needed his team of advisers to perform similar duties to those of their predecessors. The President's need arose from two sets of factors: the inherent institutional weakness of the presidency, and the particular political circumstances of 1974.

In a sense the French presidency is inherently weak, because the institutional machinery of parliamentary government was not significantly modified by the constitutional changes of 1958 and 1962. Administrative and consultative tasks are carried out by the ministries and the central services and agencies of co-ordination are attached to the Prime Minister's office. The Prime Minister has a most important role; he co-ordinates the work of the ministers, oversees relations between government and Parliament, follows all activities of the government, arbitrates between ministers in budget disputes and is responsible for the activity of the General Secretariat of the Government (which organises the meetings of the Council of Ministers and the programme of government actions). The President's control of decision-making is achieved by his direction of the weekly meetings of the Council of Ministers and his discussions with the Prime Minister and individual ministers, either in private interviews or in the crucial 'limited councils' (*conseils restreints*) at the Elysée Palace. Following the example of de Gaulle and Pompidou, Giscard d'Estaing used the Council of Ministers' meeting each Wednesday as a brief formal meeting for the exchange of information and the official approval of policy choices made elsewhere. He also adopted his predecessor's methods by dealing directly with the general secretary of the government to set the programme for ministerial actions, and by taking over all the foreign policy work of the Prime Minister. Most major policy decisions were made in the meetings between the President and individual ministers or in the 'limited councils'. It was an essential task of the general secretariat team to prepare Giscard d'Estaing with sufficient information, advice and analysis so that he could dominate these meetings. In this respect the President was obliged to rely on his advisers to follow up and evaluate in detail the work of his ministers, and to propose new policies, for he faced basic institutional difficulties as did his two predecessors.

The political situation in 1974 also made Giscard d'Estaing turn increasingly to his advisers for assistance. On the one hand, he had appointed some of his closest collaborators of earlier times to ministries and their involvement in their new functions inevitably deprived him of their advice and support. Michel Poniatowski, for example, at the Ministry of the Interior, just across the road from the Elysée Palace, was no longer available as a councillor. These appointments also lost him valuable links with party opinions in Parliament. On the other hand, the President's relationship with his first Prime Minister, Jacques Chirac, was one of profound mutual distrust. Giscard d'Estaing increasingly suspected Chirac of paying more attention to his political party and his own career than to implementing presidential decisions. It was hardly surprising that the President turned more and more to his advisers and in particular to the general secretary and presidential assistants.

The President's wish to control all aspects of governmental action implied first that his general secretary, together with the assistant general secretary, should continue to play the very important role created by de

Gaulle and extended by Pompidou. This involved the general secretary directly in the decision-making meetings of the government. Each Monday the general secretary and his assistant met the President and the general secretary of the government to prepare the final agenda for the Wednesday meeting of the Council of Ministers and to plan the programme of 'councils' at the Elysée, interministerial committees (chaired by the Prime Minister) and preparatory policy discussions (meetings of members of *cabinets* or ministry directors usually presided by the general secretary at the Elysée) for the following three weeks. The general secretary had then to remind each adviser of the councils, committees, or discussions requiring his presence or the preparation of a brief for the President. Each Wednesday morning the general secretary attended the meeting of the Council of Ministers and later helped the President's official spokesman to prepare a press draft. In the afternoon he would brief the rest of the secretariat on the decisions formally approved that morning. The participation of the general secretary (often with his assistant) was expected at all 'limited councils' at the Elysée, and for these councils, except those concerning economic planning, it was his task – shared with the adviser concerned – to draft the agenda for the meeting. The use of 'limited councils' increased under Giscard d'Estaing until not infrequently the general secretary would be attending two or three a week. Important interministerial committees under the chairmanship of the Prime Minister at the Hôtel Matignon were sometimes considered of sufficient 'presidential' importance to necessitate the presence of the general secretary or his assistant, together with the appropriate presidential adviser, who always attended these meetings. Finally, it was the general secretary who sometimes convoked and chaired preliminary discussions between presidential advisers, ministerial advisers and senior civil servants to explore presidential policy projects. Only at these policy discussions did the general secretary play an important part in proceedings. At the Council of Ministers and at 'limited councils' interventions from the general secretary were relatively rare, and almost always occurred in response to presidential solicitations. The task of the secretary was to listen and note points of interest or ambiguity to draw to the President's attention in a memorandum at a later date: in short, to act as the 'ears' and 'memory' of the President.

The involvement of the general secretary or his assistant in other aspects of the President's political life was also considerable. Giscard d'Estaing had a strong penchant for meeting people – in 1975 he had official discussions with over 200 people (in addition to ministers and visiting foreign dignitaries) and for every such audience he expected a preparatory brief. The general secretary often made the initial arrangements for the meeting (with the *chef de cabinet*) and then requested and checked the necessary brief from the appropriate presidential adviser. Giscard d'Estaing was also a frequent public speaker, and very often it fell to the general secretary, working with an adviser, to draft the 'routine speeches' for provincial visits. Furthermore, whenever major policy speeches or important political announcements were to be made (either by speech, press conference, or a 'directive letter' to the Prime Minister), the general secretary usually worked with the presidential assistants on the first draft of the text.

Finally, the general secretary himself had considerable responsibility in the conduct of foreign affairs. He directly supervised the work of the foreign affairs advisers, read all correspondence from the Foreign Affairs Ministry to the President and kept in frequent contact with the minister himself. Not infrequently, in the absence of the minister, he would be asked to represent the President. François-Poncet was sent to London in 1977 for discussions with Begin, Israel's Prime Minister, and to Tripoli the following year for a meeting with Khadafi. In 1979 Jacques Wahl went on a similar presidential mission for talks with Andreotti (after the Guadeloupe economic summit meeting which the Italians had not attended). Furthermore, the general secretary always participated in the preparations for the President's own visits abroad and accompanied the President on all state visits and at official meetings. In short, the general secretary played a larger and more active role in the conduct of foreign policy than the Prime Minister.

The work of each adviser was very different and much more specific than that of the general secretary or his assistant. Every adviser had a clearly defined sphere of competence and his task consisted of 'covering' everything that happened within that area (a list of the duties of each adviser in 1980 is given in Table 1.1). In practice, this meant that each adviser was in frequent contact with the members of the *cabinet* of the minister(s) concerned and obtained from them information about all the activities of the ministry and the files on all important policy decisions. The adviser was also expected to have his own network of contacts both in the permanent civil service staff and in the client interest groups of the ministry. One unwritten rule for all advisers was to avoid dependence on the minister and his *cabinet* for information. Through daily memoranda each adviser kept the President informed about all major events and decisions in his domain.

In addition to this general supervisory responsibility, each adviser assisted the President by drafting specific briefs for *tête-à-tête* discussions with his individual minister(s) and for 'limited councils', acted as administrative secretary for the meeting and drafted the minutes. Whenever a subject within the adviser's sphere was under discussion at an inter-ministerial committee (at the Hôtel Matignon), he would often attend the meeting with the general secretary. In both council and committee meetings the adviser usually intervened more frequently than the general secretary, but only because his specialist views were more frequently sought by the President or Prime Minister.

Outside these meetings few advisers had many direct discussions with the President. Most advisers would receive presidential requests – for information on specific points, for a brief before a meeting with an important interest-group spokesman, for a draft of a 'routine speech', for ideas to include in a 'directive letter' – in the form of a memorandum passed on by the general secretary at the short meeting of the secretariat each morning. Replies to the President and points or questions which advisers wished to raise also took the form of similar brief memoranda. On rather rare occasions Giscard d'Estaing asked individual advisers to discuss a problem directly with him – or in a small group with a minister and a presidential assistant.

One exception to this rule of written communications was the adviser on African policy, René Journiac (until February 1980). For all questions concerning France's relations with Africa, Journiac acted with almost ministerial authority. He worked directly with the African service of the Quai d'Orsay, communicated directly with French ambassadors in Africa, held discussions with African ambassadors in Paris and even talked on behalf of his President with visiting African ministers or heads of state. Although formally a member of the Secretariat, he did little more than keep the general secretary informed of his work. In fact, he worked very closely with the President himself; all major policy choices were discussed with him, and he usually accompanied Giscard d'Estaing on his visits to Africa. Journiac was often identified as one of the most influential men in the Elysée; amongst his successful initiatives was the toppling of Emperor Bokassa. The basis of his special influence was threefold: he did not work in competition with any minister, he had long experience (with Foccart) and very specialised knowledge and, above all, his policy approach was very close to the ideas of the President.

This harmony of views was the basis of the considerable influence of four other members of the secretariat, the presidential assistants. One should note, however, the pre-eminence of two men, Serisé and Riolacci. The other two presidential assistants played quite specialist roles – Lecat (later Hunt, then Poirier) as official spokesman and Chapot as the expert in 'special operations and discreet contacts' – but neither was consulted for political advice about important problems, which Riolacci and Serisé provided, especially after 1977. In 1974 Giscard d'Estaing had intended to destroy the image of the presidential assistants of Pompidou; hence, he had appointed Serisé to this post to help him in two specific areas – the writing of *Democratie française*, and the study of a few crucial economic problems. In 1976 the defeat of candidates of the governing coalition in local elections and the growing tension with the Prime Minister convinced the President of his need for loyal political specialists of his own. Jean Riolacci (assisted by Philippe Ancouturier) was recruited as electoral adviser. Working on the basis of the reports of the prefects and the *renseignements généraux*, of meetings with politicians (both national and local) of all political parties and of contacts with party officials Riolacci and Aucouturier kept a detailed up-to-date account of the strengths, weaknesses and prospects of the political parties in every constituency in France. Riolacci's knowledge of electoral politics was widely respected and he was one of the rare members of the Elysée who could speak his mind to the President without fear of recrimination. The influence of this assistant was very apparent during the 1978 general elections when he played an important role in organising the Giscardian party, the UDF. When the presidential election campaign began in 1980, again Giscard d'Estaing relied on Riolacci's expertise.

The role of Jean Serisé was rather different but equally important. One part of his work was to maintain contacts with political leaders and especially with those of the UDF. His other responsibility was that of research and policy initiatives for the President's major speeches and press conferences. Both advisers were consulted on all major political decisions by the President. Furthermore, they helped in co-ordinating the political speeches of the President and Prime Minister by holding regular meetings (every ten days) with the political advisers in Prime Minister Barre's *cabinet*. In short, Serisé and Riolacci played increasingly influential political roles; it should be remembered, however, that their political activities were in many ways a necessary response to, and compensation for, the weak, ineffective political and electoral actions of Barre and the UDF.[7]

After May 1981, the relationship between the President and the Prime Minister and 'legitimist' party – now the Socialist Party – changed dramatically. Prime Minister Mauroy is not an 'outsider', but an experienced politician with a long career in the Socialist Party. He has worked for ten years with Mitterrand, almost all, as his second-in-command. He helped Mitterrand take over the PS at Epinay in 1971 and played a leading role in rebuilding the activist party of *militants* of the late 1970s. In short, the problems for President Mitterrand are not those of Giscard d'Estaing: a governing coalition in part disloyal, or hostile, and in part inactive and unorganised under a Prime Minister who seemed to cultivate unpopularity has been replaced by a loyal Socialist majority and a politically skilled premier who is very sensitive to public opinion. The Elysée staff no longer needs to compensate for the inadequacies of the government and its parliamentary supporters, but rather to cool the zeal and check the excesses.

In many respects, however, the practices of presidential government have not been changed by the election of Mitterrand. The Council of Ministers still meets formally each Wednesday, but if Mitterrand allows rather freer and longer discussion than previous Presidents, he has not made it into a collective decision-making body. It remains a mechanism for mutual exchange of information and formal legitimation of decisions made elsewhere. The agenda of the Council and the programme of work of the entire government are still decided by the President in consultation with the Prime Minister and general secretary of the government. Most major decisions result from discussions between President and Prime Minister, President and individual ministers, or in 'limited councils' at the Elysée. Many policy choices are 'prepared' in interministerial committees – small groups of interested ministers chaired by the Prime Minister – and it is here that the presidential advisers (normally Fournier, the assistant general secretary and the relevant technical adviser) 'follow' discussions for the absent President. In contrast to his predecessor, Mitterrand has frequent meetings with his government and Socialist Party leaders, whilst his contacts with many of his Elysée staff are limited to exchanges of brief notes. Some presidential advisers and assistants virtually never see or meet their President.

There is, however, a small group of very close friends and political associates within the presidency with whom Mitterrand has frequent contacts. These include Beregovoy, de Grossouvre, Attali, Penne, Guimard, Fournier, Charasse, Rousselet and Legatte: Beregovoy is a trusted adviser on foreign policy and a leading 'baron' of the presidential party; de Grossouvre deals with the secret services; Attali may advise on any problem but is especially entrusted with economic questions and international trade; Penne seems to have taken over the African 'ministry' created by Foccart and continued by Journiac. Although these advisers sometimes appear as influential *eminences grises*, it seems likely that, in the short run at least, Mitterrand will tolerate few conflicts with his ministers or attempts to usurp the co-ordinating role of his Prime Minister.

## Conclusions

It would be inaccurate to conclude from this study that the general secretariat of the Elysée became the power-house of French politics under Giscard d'Estaing or has become so under Mitterrand. The general secretaries and the presidential assistants have been very influential, the African adviser has had a special position and other individual advisers have determined particular policy choices (Stoleru, for example, decided government policy towards manual labour, and Richard was largely responsible for the establishment of the Guichard Commission on local government reform). It was also often the case that the influence of an adviser was not directly over the options decided by the President, but rather on the proposals of a minister who telephoned for 'unofficial advice' about presidential opinions. There are, however, constant constraints on the influence of the Elysée staff.

The first and major limitation is the personality of the President. Giscard d'Estaing liked to make his own decisions and was angry when he suspected he was being 'pushed' towards a particular choice. He liked to hear advice and opinions from a number of different sources and to make up his own mind. He had frequent contacts with political advisers outside the Elysée – notably with several ministers (d'Ornano, Bonnet, Peyrefitte and Monory, in particular) and with leading UDF politicians (especially Chinaud, Pinton and Blanc). Moreover, he often asked for specialist reports on specific problems from individuals outside the traditional political class. Almost every year a 'wise man' was appointed for an investigation of this kind: in 1975 J.-C. Colli was made 'Monsieur Energies nouvelles'; in 1977 Mme Pelletier, 'Madame Antidrogue'; and in 1978 Tony Roche, 'Monsieur Retraités'. His numerous contacts (noted above) with industrialists, businessmen, researchers, scientists and even artists were also part of his strategy of freeing himself from any monopoly source of information or advice. Mitterrand's style is very different, but he too likes to take his own decisions. The result is his habit of asking several people to advise him on the same subject at the same time.

A second constraint is the need to placate the Prime Minister and ministers by allowing them sufficient freedom of action for political credibility and personal self-esteem. Although highly interventionist by nature, Giscard d'Estaing sometimes held back from making specific demands to members of the government. The ministers were, after all, constitutionally responsible to Parliament, and needed authority for effective control of their bureaucracies and good relations with pressure groups. This was especially the case with Prime Minister Barre, in spite of some disagreements over policy in 1979 and 1980. Mitterrand seems less concerned with details than his predecessor and aware of the great difficulties of holding together a very varied team of ministers representing different factions in the Socialist Party and the reduced but resentful Communist Party.

Another major constraint is the limited resources of the Elysée staff. The total membership of Giscard d'Estaing's secretariat did not exceed thirty. Each minister, in comparison, had a *cabinet* of eight plus all resources of his ministry simply for his one policy area. One presidential adviser – even with an assistant, a secretary and a great deal of help from well-placed friends – could hope to do little more than keep abreast with developments in his field. This, too, did not change in 1981 when Mitterrand took office.

Finally, the role of the President's advisers and assistants is limited by their own abilities, interests and ambitions. Some are exceptionally competent, hard-working and perceptive, but do not wish to play a public role. In the Elysée they may be self-effacing but still hold considerable influence. Others are ambitious and see the Elysée as a stepping-stone to ministerial office. For these men, the presidential staff may be a useful short-cut to a public political career; but their rise to fame and office may cause difficulties or embarrassment for their President. Under Giscard d'Estaing, the domination of the Elysée staff by top-rank civil servants from the same *corps*, the same schools and the same backgrounds as those in the *cabinets* of Prime Minister and ministers and those still serving in the decision-making posts in the administration was not without effect. Giscard d'Estaing clearly preferred a certain civil service conformism in his staff and, moreover, a certain deference to his position. His choice of collaborators who satisfied these requirements – and his dismissals, albeit with 'golden handshakes' of those too critical or outspoken – limited the effectiveness of the secretariat in providing independent, 'different' views of politics and policies. At the same time there is no reason to believe that the *competence* of advisers in their specific areas was any greater than that of their civil service colleagues who remained in their ministries.[8] In short, the role of the presidential staff under Giscard d'Estaing was in many respects similar to that played by the advisers of both his predecessors and his successor. This role is essentially ambiguous. On the one hand, active presidential government means the staff is involved in following the work of the ministers, evaluating their policy proposals and helping the President develop his own ideas on policy, political strategy and the choice of personnel. This implies that enthusiastic, intelligent, dynamic, 'political' abilities are required. On the other hand, the maintenance of the constitutional compromise – the irresponsible presidency and the government responsible to Parliament – means that the Elysée staff must not play a very visible role. Hence, discreet, self-effacing activity is needed and a 'low political profile' must be kept. It is a complex equation, and it does result in some conflicts; the continuity, however, seems to imply some degree of success.

## Notes: Chapter 1

1  See Jean Massot, *La Présidence de la république* (Paris: La Documentation française, 1977), for details of the development of the presidential office. See also on this section: Claude Dulong, *La Vie quotidienne à l'Elysée au temps de Charles de Gaulle* (Paris: Hachette, 1975), and *L' 'Entourage' et de Gaulle* (Paris: Plon, 1979). De Gaulle himself, however, gives very few indications about his staff in his memoirs; see Charles de Gaulle, *Mémoires d'espoir. 1, Le Renouveau, 1958–1962* (Paris: Plon, 1972), pp. 308-9.

2  See chs 7 and 8 of Samy Cohen, *Les Conseillers du Président de Charles de Gaulle à Valéry Giscard d'Estaing* (Paris, PUF, 1980); see also H. de Galard, 'La Révolution de Juillet', *Le Nouvel Observateur*, 10 July 1972, p. 14; and J. Chaban-Delmas, *L'Ardeur* (Paris: Stock, 1975).

3  Statistics from Cohen, *Les Conseillers*, op. cit., pp. 187-8.

4  Information from Samy Cohen, 'Le rôle du secrétaire général de la Présidence de la République', unpublished paper, Paris, 1979.

5  This aspect of the Giscardian 'style' is noted by Cohen, *Les Conseillers*, op. cit.; but also by Pierre Pelissier, *La Vie quotidienne à l'Elysée au temps de Valéry Giscard d'Estaing* (Paris: Hachette, 1977).

6  On the Mitterrand team, see Jean-Marie Colombari, 'Un semestre du pouvoir socialiste: (3) L'entrée en force du militantisme à l'Elysée, *Le Monde*, 15-16 November 1981; 'Elysée: comment fonctionne l'équipe Mitterrand', *Le Nouvel Observateur*, 25-31 July 1981; 'Le Président et ses hommes', *Paris-Match*, 2 October 1981; and 'La social-Monarchie', *Le Point*, 19 October 1981.

7  See 'Ceux qui ont confisqué l'Etat', *L'Humanité*, 21 May 1980; Josette Alia, 'Les hommes du Président', *Le Nouvel Observateur*, 3 July 1978, pp. 31-6; and Robert Schneider, 'Les 30 hommes du Président', *L'Express*, 28 June-4 July 1980, pp. 59-65.

8  See ch. 6, 'De la fonction de conseil', in Guy Thuillier, *Regards sur la haute administration en France* (Paris: Economica, 1979), pp. 44-51.

# 2

# The Giscardians – the Republican Party

*ELLA SEARLS*

## Introduction

The growing link between presidentialism and party politics has been one of the key features of the Fifth Republic. Presidential politics have set the stage for party coalitions, strategies and tactics. Though all parties have awakened to the realities of a presidential system, it is the parties on the Right which have been the most directly influenced. On the one hand Presidents themselves became increasingly dependent on their right-wing coalitions, and on the other both the Gaullist and Giscardian parties were, to some extent, moulded by the exigencies of presidentialism. However, whilst the parties of the right-wing *majorité* had to respond to the needs of Presidents, they undoubtedly also benefited from them. The parties of the Right emerged as a substantial political force, they rose in prestige and status and, most importantly, bathed in the tidal eddies and pools created by presidential electoral success.

Despite General de Gaulle's alleged disdain of party politics, the Gaullist party 'took off' under his presidency and has since remained one of the key parties in the state. As Jean Charlot shows,[1] the initial support for the Gaullists was closely linked to support for the presidency, but gradually the party gained a support-base of its own. Nevertheless, sustaining the President remained until 1974 one of the key functions of the Gaullist party.

Valéry Giscard d'Estaing maintained closer links between the Elysée and 'his' party than former Presidents. However, the relationship was a chequered and changing one. Giscard d'Estaing was the founding father of, and inspiration for, the growth of the Fédération Nationale des Républicains Indépendants (FNRI) and he had an attachment to the Republican Party. The party, for its part, was the political force most closely linked to Giscard d'Estaing. After his accession to power, Giscard d'Estaing continually stressed the need for a party which would 'sustain him in office'. Consequently, the party was continually revitalised and reshaped in order to widen the President's electoral catchment area, to act as a 'pivot within the majority', and to reflect Giscard d'Estaing's 'new-image presidency'. The mantle of presidentialism, however, proved to be difficult for the Republicans to wear, and many of the vestiges of the old Fourth Republic-style politics remained. However, whilst the Republican Party did not become completely harmonised to presidential needs and, arguably, was one of the factors which contributed to Giscard d'Estaing's electoral defeat in 1981, it developed considerably during the Fifth Republic, particularly after Valéry Giscard d'Estaing's accession to power. Independent Republicans held between three and eight ministerial posts in governments during the de Gaulle and Pompidou presidencies, and during Giscard d'Estaing's presidency they initially held about 40 per cent of ministerial posts which rose to more than 50 per cent following the institution of the Barre government in 1976.

The number of Republican Deputies grew from the initial thirty-five in 1962 to sixty following the electoral triumph of the Right in 1968. In 1973 the number dropped to fifty-five, although at this election the Independent Republicans suffered proportionately fewer losses than did the Gaullists. In 1978 the Republican Party won seventy-eight seats, as part of a new presidential alliance, the Union pour la Démocratie Française (UDF). During the 1970s the party consistently held about 10 per cent of local authority seats.

Initially the party had no formal membership, for as Giscard d'Estaing declared, 'We do not seek to be a party. We do not pretend to dictate our law to imaginary militants. We are a meeting place [rencontre] and a movement'.[2] However, after 1970 individual federations were permitted to opt for the institution of membership-cards. The growth in numbers of party members has, on paper, been impressive – the numbers given by the party were 100,000 in 1975. 145,000 in January 1979 and 175,000 in February 1981. However, these figures should be viewed as an exaggeration.

Thus, on all fronts the party's rise was substantial. However, the degree of success and rate of success of the party compared unfavourably with the Gaullist party during its heyday, and gave continual cause for concern within some of the party leadership. The image, structure and power-base were all, to a certain extent, regenerated. In many ways the party has changed from being an old-style 'cadre' party, based around parliamentarians and local notables, who rejected any form of party discipline and organisation, towards a more 'modern' party, based on a coherent party structure, organisation and increased mass support. However, this transformation was neither easy nor complete, and in many senses the Parti Républicain (PR) hovered uncertainly, between the classic 'cadre' party, and a personalised 'catch-all' party based around the leadership of Valéry Giscard d'Estaing.

By tracing the historical development of the party and the position under

Giscard d'Estaing's presidency, this chapter analyses the elements of continuity and change within the party itself. It stresses the dynamic impact of presidentialism on the one hand, and the durability of tradition on the other.

## The Historical Background

Although the FNRI was formed in the early days of the Fifth Republic, by a breakaway group of Deputies from the Centre National des Indépendants et des Paysans (CNIP), it incorporated the liberal Orleanist tradition which dates back to the nineteenth century. The early Independent Republicans, and Valéry Giscard d'Estaing himself, espoused and propounded values which had long been held by the 'moderate' Right - a belief in rationalism, moderation and liberty (with reservations!), the pursuance of the middle way, the desire for order and stability and, in principle at least, the importance of parliamentarianism.

The CNI (which became the CNIP in 1951) itself, led by Duchet, had played not an inconsequential role in the kaleidoscopic politics of the Fourth Republic, having had considerable electoral support and held numerous governmental posts. Its structure was typical of the 'cadre' type, which Duverger describes, as 'the grouping of notabilities for the preparation of elections, conducting campaigns and maintaining contact with the candidates'.[3] Its structure was light and party activity was restricted to a few select people. The factionalism of the party, characteristic of the parties of the Centre and Right during that period, was exacerbated by the problems of de-colonisation.

## 1962–6

The Fifth Republic saw the CNIP divided over its attitude to the regime, and the 1962 referendum over the Constitution brought this split to the fore. The group of CNIP Deputies who formed the core of the new Independent Republican group voted in favour of the Constitution, and the CNIP disintegrated as a parliamentary party after the 1962 legislative elections.[4] The Independent Republicans, who began life as a parliamentary group in November 1962, were bound together by political ambition, circumspect support for the regime (with an ambivalent attitude to the Gaullists) and by Valéry Giscard d'Estaing, then Minister of Finance, who emerged as the leader of the group. There is considerable evidence to suggest that as early as 1963–4 Valéry Giscard d'Estaing was keen to build up the party in order to further his own political ambitions. During this period the Deputies remained little more than a parliamentary group, who individually based their support on local *notables* or on local organisations.

## 1966-9

In January 1966 Giscard d'Estaing was ignominiously dismissed from his post as Finance Minister, and this date marks the beginning of the development of the Independent Republicans as a political *party*. For Giscard d'Estaing saw his departure from office as temporary, and he devoted much of his time and energy to building up the party and its umbrella organisations, as well as continuing to assert himself as a national politician.

The party at this stage was developed on three fronts – first, through the growth of political clubs and other 'supporting' organisations; secondly, within the country, as the basic federal structure was evolved; and finally, the internal structure itself was reformed.[5]

The political clubs, the most important of which was and remains the Clubs Perspectives et Réalités, which preceded the foundation of the FNRI, in many ways reflected the features of the Giscardian elitist approach to politics. On the one hand, the clubs were genuinely based on the idea that France is brimming with thinking, reasoning moderates, who shy away from overt political identification, but who are keen to enter into a 'dialogue' about the state of France. On the other hand, they demonstrated the attempted political channelling of these apolitical resources by Giscardian leaders. The fundamental idea behind the Clubs Perspectives et Réalités, which was evolved by close associates to Valéry Giscard d'Estaing, such as Michel Poniatowski, Xavier de la Fourniére and especially Charles-Noël Hardy, was to provide 'a laboratory for the elaboration of doctrine'. The clubs were also to be a 'breeding-ground for young politicians' and were to provide an infrastructure for the future development of the party. The first club was opened in Paris in May 1965 and by the spring of 1968 there were thirty-eight clubs (with approximately 3,000 'attenders') throughout France.

A founder-member of the clubs claimed that in the early years they functioned as an embryonic political party.[6] They held study days, produced advisory documents and held congresses. A federal structure, headed by a secretary-general gradually evolved, and the clubs proved to be a useful recruiting and socialising organisation for the growing FNRI. At the elite level many of the early activists within the clubs, for example, Chinaud, Dominati and d'Ornano, went on to play key roles within the party. In general the clubs managed to recruit only middle- and lower-middle-class supporters – in particular, young professionals, small businessmen and employers. Their image and approach remained geared to attracting prominent people within the community.

This early period also marked the beginnings of the Young Independent Republican movement (JRI), which was launched in October 1966. By 1969 groups had been formed in most of the major university towns throughout France. The Young Giscardians have always had a vital and close relationship with the party, providing it with assistance and personnel, but they have resisted pressures to become a formal branch of the Republicans.

June 1966 saw the establishment of the Fédération Nationale des Républicains Indépendants as a political party. The party organisation in the country was initiated by the parliamentary group and the leadership and, hence, is an unusual recent example of an 'internally created' party.[7] The regions were chosen as the basic unit for the federations as they were seen to be less traditional and narrow than the *départements* and in Giscard d'Estaing's eyes (at least at that time) were the key to the future economic development of France.

By 1967 six out of the twenty-one regional federations had officially been established and by the beginning of 1969 they numbered sixteen, the remaining five being created by 1973. By this time party organisations were also being formed at departmental level. The growth of these federations was consistent though not startling, and many of the party organisations were inactive between election periods – a feature which was typical of Centre and Right Fourth Republic parties. Initially many of the federations evolved around important parliamentarians, former Deputies, or former ministers from the region. However, Giscard d'Estaing's attempts to fill the regional federations with his own followers and collaborators was more successful after the 1967 elections, which marked the disappearance of many of the old Independents.

During the period 1966-9 the internal structure of the party underwent several modifications. Basically, however, the structure of the party was, and still is, one which gives representation and voice to local and regional elites, and in particular to parliamentarians, but it afforded them little leverage over the leadership, which is normally formed from amongst Giscard d'Estaing's closest colleagues. Consequently, constraints on Giscard d'Estaing's action came from the parliamentary party rather than from the party machine, though since 1974 – and in particular since 1978 – the parliamentary party had also had to tow the executive line.

The structure which was initially evolved for the FNRI in 1967 consisted of a General Assembly,[8] grouping together supporters of the party, who partially elected the more streamlined *comité directeur* – the so-called legislative body of the party. The *bureau politique* or executive committee of the party in principle 'emerged' from the *comité directeur*. However, this experiment was dropped in 1968 in favour of a supposedly more rationalised structure. The basic unit was henceforth to be the *conseil fédéral*, a body of some 500-600 members, grouping together the party elite – Deputies, *suppléants*, Senators, representatives of regional federations, members of economic councils and representatives from the intermediary organs (such as the political clubs and Young Independent Republicans). The *conseil fédéral* elected the President and secretary-general of the party, and its executive committee – the *bureau politique*, which had the facility to enlarge itself into the *comité directeur* when wider problems were being discussed. In practice, power in the party resided in the President (Valéry Giscard d'Estaing) in the secretary-general (Poniatowski) and in the *bureau politique* which, although elected, was staffed by close associates of Giscard d'Estaing.

The period 1966–9 also marked changes in the role which the Independent Republicans played in the political system. Giscard d'Estaing made assertive, though not too assertive, statements against the Gaullist exercise of power, though he was not always backed up by his supporters in Parliament. For the Independent Republican parliamentary group consisted not only of Deputies (such as Marcellin) who were of the old Independent breed and in many senses not Giscardian, but also of former Gaullists (such as Mondon and de Broglie). Valéry Giscard d'Estaing's reservations about the regime were epitomised in his famous 'Yes – but', speech of 10 January 1967. Not all of the party agreed with his attitude, although as Charlot notes, he tended to have greater support amongst the newer and younger Deputies. He again expressed reservations about the regime in his refusal to vote 'yes' in the 1969 referendum, although at this stage most of the party chose to ignore him.[9]

## 1969–74

The presidency of Pompidou marked the beginnings of a new improved era for the Independent Republicans. In many ways the Giscardians were more sympathetic to the Pompidou presidency and Giscard d'Estaing was reappointed as Finance Minister in 1969. The party leadership continued to try to strengthen the party in preparation for the 1973 legislative elections.

Various changes were made in the internal structure of the party – the most significant being the institution of the biannual National Congress, the first being held in Toulouse in 1971, in which the delegates elected the President, secretary-general and various other leading members. Nevertheless the same leadership emerged – as a foregone conclusion Valéry Giscard d'Estaing obtained 961 out of the 973 votes and Poniatowski 875. This set the pattern for future leadership as the National Congress delegates continued to endorse the existing leadership or the 'heirs apparent'. Poniatowski continued to dominate the party even after his appointment as minister, following the 1973 legislative elections, although Giscard d'Estaing himself stepped down from the presidency of the FNRI in 1973, and for a while the post remained vacant. Poniatowski was replaced as secretary-general by d'Ornano in March 1974, who in turn was made minister in 1974 and was, therefore, replaced by Chinaud. However, despite these nominal changes in leadership, Poniatowski remained the key to the party and was instrumental in organising the 1974 presidential election campaign.

## The Impact of Presidentialism

Valéry Giscard d'Estaing assumed the presidency in May 1974 after a close but predictable, second-ballot victory over Mitterrand, the only candidate of the Left. The 1974 presidential election highlighted the potential importance of political parties in the competition. Although the emergence of the presidential candidates within the *majorité* was the result of various manoeuvrings within the political elites, it was clear that presidential candidates, lacking the charismatic draw of de Gaulle or the anointment of Pompidou, needed party organisation (or organisation based on parties) in order to fight their elections. At the same time presidential candidates, particularly on the Right, needed to go beyond and to be above party in order to gain the widest electoral support possible.

Giscard d'Estaing himself organised his electoral campaign around the *comités de soutien* (supporting committees), which were based at both national and local level. The supporting committees, which went wider than the party, drew in local *notables*, representatives and electors who supported Giscard d'Estaing as President, rather than as party leader. However, both FNRI and the Giscardian clubs played a key role both in organising and in manning these committees.

Once the presidential election campaign had been fought and won, Valéry Giscard d'Estaing tried to realise his aim of transforming his party, which he had articulated during the election campaign. Four factors contributed to his desire to reform the party. First, although Valéry Giscard d'Estaing had secured the presidency, the Independent Republicans were still a minority within the governing coalition in the National Assembly. Although ideologically Giscard d'Estaing was not far from the Gaullists, there was considerable tension and rivalry between the two groups and Giscard d'Estaing felt himself to be in a potentially fragile political position. Consequently, he wanted to strengthen his party's power-base in preparation for the 1978 legislative elections. Secondly, there had been much enthusiasm and support in the 'Giscard for President' committees, and Giscard d'Estaing and his collaborators were keen to channel this into the party before it disappeared. Thirdly, the President felt that despite efforts at change, the party was ill-adapted to fulfil its new role as a 'presidential' party. Finally, Giscard d'Estaing found himself at odds with some of the hard-liners in the party whom, he felt, hindered his progress towards an 'advanced liberal democracy' and a Kennedy-style presidency. Consequently, the period leading up to 1977 saw considerable changes in personnel and organisation.

## 1974–7

This period in some senses marked a low ebb for the Giscardians. With Valéry Giscard d'Estaing as President, the party became snuggly installed in the government. However, despite Poniatowski's call for a 'large national party' and the pressure from governmental leaders for the party to become the 'majority within the majority', the party was slow to grow at local level. At central level it was bedevilled by personality clashes, by frequent and unfulfilled plans for reform and by rather unsuccessful recruitment-drives.

Chinaud's stay as secretary-general was short-lived, for conflict with Poniatowski – who eventually became Honorary President in February 1975 – contributed to his removal to the National Assembly, where he became a successful president of the Republican Party group, and after 1978, of the UDF Deputies. He was replaced by Dominati as secretary-general. The highest echelons of the party remained dominated by parliamentarians. During this period there were several attempts at recruiting new personnel. The young Independent Republicans were reformed into the Génération Sociale et Libérale (GSL) in an attempt to revive the movement and bind them more closely to the party. In addition, a new recruiting machine was launched in the shape of the 'Agir pour l'avenir', whose aim was to 'select and form' new candidates.

Despite this change, the FNRI fared poorly in the spring 1977 municipal elections. The demise of the party was symbolised by the defeat of d'Ornano, in the election for the mayorship of Paris, by the triumphant ex-Prime Minister Jacques Chirac. As a result, responsibility for the management and revitalisation of the party machine was transferred by Valéry Giscard d'Estaing to Jean-Pierre Soisson, the Junior Minister for Youth and Sport, who was given *carte blanche* to reform the party, when he became its new secretary-general in April 1977.

## 1977–81

Jean-Pierre Soisson declared that his aim was to transform the Independent Republicans from a cadre party to a party based on activists. Immediately after his appointment, he called an Extraordinary General Assembly of the party at Fréjus, which marks the birth of the Republican Party. The party was to acquire a new name, new personnel and a new image.

A party name is of considerable significance in France, albeit liberal may mean 'conservative', and radical, 'reactionary'. Parties choose and change their names to evoke certain symbols and images in the political conscious-ness of the nation. The naming of the Republican Party was no exception. There was, in fact, considerable controversy over the new name – the eventual compromise was Parti Républicain (et républicain indépendant).[10] The dropping of the word 'Federation' and, more pertinently of 'Independent', was of great significance. It was intended to mark a change in the nature of the party. The title Parti Républicain was simple, catchy and yet evoked the Republic. Jean-Pierre Soisson, almost in the true

Gaullist tradition, declared that the new structure of the party was to 'regroup all citizens who had a strong attachment to the Republican ideal, which had sprung from the Revolution'.

On becoming secretary-general Jean-Pierre Soisson assembled a new team. Almost for the first time in the history of the party Poniatowski was pushed into the background. Soisson brought in a young team which included amongst others, Jacques Douffiagues to deal specifically with the organisation of the party, Alain Griotteray to oversee elections and Bertrand de Maigret who was to be in charge of the National Secretariat. In many ways this team marked a break from the old *notables* vanguard within the party. However, as Colette Ysmal points out,[11] the Republican Party remained a party dominated by its leadership, which was mainly composed of local or central office-holders. Thus the *bureau politique*, and to a certain extent the National Congress itself, consisted of mayors of large towns, Deputies, Senators and Ministers.

Most importantly, the party acquired a new image. Jean-Pierre Soisson established himself as a 'personality leader', encouraging such slogans as 'Allez Jean-Pierre' and 'Avec Soisson'. The Republicans also drew up a party programme, *Le Projet républicain*,[12] which embodied its principles and policies. This new style of politics was indeed a far cry from the FNRI of the late 1960s. The popular image was taken up and developed by Jacques Blanc, who replaced Jean-Pierre Soisson as secretary-general in April 1978, after the latter had been appointed minister in a government reshuffle. Blanc's aim was to create 'un grand puissant parti populaire'. This aim was superficially achieved at the Third Party Congress which was held at the Porte de Pantin, Paris, in October 1979. The congress attracted a large number of activists and had all the trappings of a conservative party trying to popularise itself – fanfares, slogans and a jamboree of prominent people who declared themselves to be supporters of the party.[13] The success of the meeting surprised the political world in France, not least the Republican Party itself!

Therefore, 1977 was a watershed in the development of the Independent Republicans. Thereafter the party grew and was strengthened, but many of the old problems still existed. As a machine for fighting elections, and 'recruiting' and 'training' activists, it made considerable progress. However, as noted above, during the 1977 municipal elections it fell short of Giscard d'Estaing's expectations, and this was one of the main reasons for the setting up in February 1978 of the UDF, an umbrella organisation which federated all the non-Gaullist parties in the *majorité* in preparation for the 1978 legislative elections.

At grass-roots level the party was strengthened, although in some areas it remained dominated by the local *notables* who resisted organisation. A breakdown of membership figures given by the Republican Party reveals that at the end of 1978 the party was predominantly male (66 per cent) and relatively young (69 per cent under 45). The party had a fairly broad membership, drawing activists from across the population. White-collar workers and civil servants were the two largest single groups and together accounted for almost 30 per cent of the membership. Despite efforts of the party to widen recruitment, blue-collar workers accounted for only 8 per cent of the members contrasting with farm workers who accounted for 10 per cent. A wide range of professions and businesses were represented (11 per cent) and the *petite bourgeoisie* (shopkeepers and artisans) accounted for 9 per cent. Retired people made up 8 per cent of the total and teachers 5 per cent. After 1978, the average age of the party became slightly lower, and by 1981 there were more women members, but contrary to the claims of the Republican Party, who were trying to escape from their *bourgeois* image, the growth in the number of working-class supporters was not statistically significant.

By spring 1981 there was a federation of the Parti Républicain in every *département*, and superficially the structure was more democratic. The activists within the federation elected a federal council which, in turn, elected the executive of the local party organisation (consisting of the president, vice-president and various officers). The federations would also, at their discretion, create local committees or socio-professional 'cells'. This elected hierarchy was, however, shadowed by an official hierarchy. The national secretary-general appointed a federation secretary for each *département*, whose function was to work with and 'assist' the party executives. All federation secretaries had voting rights at the National Congress. In practice, the federation secretaries helped to ensure the supervision of the party by the central leadership.

The political clubs continued to play an important and supportive role for the party. In 1981 the Clubs Perspectives et Réalités, which remained the most significant, numbered 300, and they had 50,000 'members'. The clubs resisted integration into the newly formed Parti Républicain, although formally, according to statute 27 of the party, they participated in 'enlivening the party'. The leading personnel continued to have places on the *bureau politique* and there were many informal links between the two. Apart from study documents on specific subjects which appeared following the annual conventions, in 1977 the clubs brought out their blueprint for society – 'Choices for tomorrow' – after the views of all the clubs' supporters had been 'democratically elicited'. The tone of the booklet and the themes which it treated strongly echo those of Valéry Giscard d'Estaing's own work *Démocratie française* and the more liberal policies of the Republican Party. Emphasis was placed on the importance of the family, security and the protection of liberties. The themes of regionalism, economic growth and a strong, wholesome France were expounded at some length.[14]

Since the mid-1970s there were some attempts by the leadership to democratise and open up the clubs to a wider audience. However, as the average club remained essentially a cross between a Rotary Club and a branch of the Fabian Society, leaders did not meet with much success in their half-hearted attempts to attract trade unionists or agricultural workers. A number of specialised clubs were also formed or developed, mainly in Paris – for example, the *Clubs 'Tiers Monde'*, and the *Clubs culture et communication* and the *Club scientifique*.

The *Jeunes Giscardiens* continued to remain a separate yet supportive movement. In October 1977 after considerable contact between Jean-Pierre Soisson and leaders of the GSL movement, the *Jeunes Giscardiens* reformed into a new movement, *Autrement*. Like its predecessor, *Autrement* declined to be formally linked with any political party. It rejected the normal *'politique politicienne'* and stood instead for the 'interests of all youth'. It did not present candidates and had no formal links with the Parti Républicain or with the UDF. However, in practice, the links were strong. Republican Party ministers frequently attended study days or rallies organised by *Autrement*, and at least once a year its collective leadership was received by Valéry Giscard d'Estaing. The movement for its part, whilst expressing its independence, acted indirectly as a recruiting machine for the party, and liaisons with various ministers over public relations.

The years 1977-81 were ones of relative stability for the internal organisation of the party. Structurally a semblance of democracy was achieved but, in reality, the party was dominated not only by the national secretary-general, but by a leadership clique of parliamentarians and ministers. The influence of the former President of the Republic was exerted through the top personnel in the party. There was little impact from the grass-roots within the party, and the party itself had little impact on the government.

The General Assembly was the supreme body of the party. All party members had the right to attend and vote. The Assembly met at least once every three years and its principal powers were to elect the secretary-general, to modify the party statutes and the facility to dissolve the party. The secretary-general, however, had considerable powers over the Assembly – he could determine when it was convened, decide the agenda, choose the various presidents and determine the shape of the working parties and committees. In practice, the General Assembly was hardly a forum for democracy. The 1977 Assembly at Fréjus adopted the new statutes almost without debate and, during this period, ratified rather than chose the secretaries-general.

The party congress met every year, except when a General Assembly was held or when half of the members or the secretary-general called for an extraordinary session. Its representatives consisted of federation presidents and secretaries, representatives from local committees, Republican Party mayors of towns of over 10,000 population, various local councillors, parliamentarians and their *suppléants*. Its composition, therefore, tended to over-represent parliamentarians who, along with members of the government, normally dominated the activities and output of the congresses. In principle, the congress can censure the secretary-general, but in practice this was unlikely to happen.

A slimmed-down form of the national congress, in the shape of the National Council, met every three months (in secret) to implement the decisions taken by the congress and the Assembly and to review the 'general political situation'. In theory it should have served as a link between the highest echelons of the party and the federations, but in practice it was a body which explained the policy of the government to the federations and prepared documents on specialised subjects (for example, energy) for the party leadership.

The highest echelons of the party consisted of the secretary-general, the *Secrétariat National* and the *bureau politique*. Although the Republican Party was not always at one with governmental policy, it appears that both Soisson and Blanc, as secretaries-general, worked relatively closely with Valéry Giscard d'Estaing ('knowing his mind') and the Elysée. In many ways it was this closeness which accounted for the key role which they both played within the party. The role of the secretary-general is to co-ordinate the party and link the party with the outside world. The National Secretariat comprised a group of about twenty prominent people within the party (at present two-thirds are parliamentarians), whose function was to assist the secretary-general in specific policy areas – for example, defence, the environment, or health. In practice most national secretaries were too busy to perform this function effectively and many held the post for reasons of prestige.

Finally, there was the *bureau politique*, or Cabinet of the party, which is in many ways the most important body within the party, although it too was limited to an advisory role; members were appointed by the secretary-general. Historically the *bureau politique* was dominated by ministers and parliamentarians, and ranged from twenty to sixty in number. Since the formation of the Parti Républicain it remained relatively small, in 1980 consisting of twenty members. This included five ministers, the presidents of the parliamentary groups of Republicans (members by right), several other parliamentarians and a representative from the *Clubs Perspectives et Réalités*. The *bureau politique* met weekly to discuss general questions of policy and tactics. Its most useful function appeared to be to allow ministers to take the temperature of the party elite. Ministers for their part used the *bureau politique* as a medium for explaining governmental policy to the party faithful.

## The 1981 Presidential Elections and the Mitterrand Presidency: the Demise of the PR?

It has been shown that the nature of the Republicans as a political party changed considerably since the accession of Giscard d'Estaing to the presidency. The process of modernisation and 'revitalisation' of the party which began rather haltingly in the early 1970s was accelerated. By 1981 the party still contained on the one hand elements of the old elitist, 'cadre'-style party, whilst on the other it had been forced by the needs of presidentialism to take on new and ever-changing roles. The formation of the UDF as a presidential alliance, however, had in some senses taken the presidential wind out of the Republican Party sails.[15]

The 1981 presidential election campaign highlighted the dilemmas, conflicts and problems which the right-wing *majorité* had experienced during the Giscardian *septennat*. Indeed, both the competition on the Right and the organisation and tactics of its campaign contributed to the defeat of Giscard d'Estaing, and the Giscardian camp made a strategic error in underestimating the nature of the Socialist opposition. The rivalry between the Giscardians and the Gaullists was reflected not only in the competition of their respective leaders for the presidency, but also in the often mutually vitriolic nature of the parties' electioneering. The Giscardian campaign, although formally organised around the *comités de soutien* for the presidency, relied on the backbone of the UDF (and more appropriately, at local level, on the *militants* of the constituent parties) for support. However, there was also competition within the UDF over who should control the organisation of the campaign and differences of opinion over how it should be organised.

The defeat of Giscard d'Estaing as President by Mitterrand in May 1981 obviously deflated the Right. In many senses the immediate problem which it posed for the Giscardians at the following month's parliamentary elections was more acute for the UDF than for its constituent parties. The UDF claimed that it had been 'decapitated'; not only had it lost a candidate, but it had also lost its *raison d'être*, that of supporting the policies of Giscard d'Estaing as President, in the political spectrum.[16] Inevitably in this situation, most UDF candidates retrenched and once again emphasised their respective parties' political paths and programmes for the parliamentary elections. The poor performance of the Right, hastily thrown together into the Union pour la nouvelle majorité (UNM) in the legislative elections was almost a foregone conclusion. The number of Gaullist and Giscardian Deputies was reduced drastically to eighty-eight and sixty-two respectively. Within the UDF the Republican Party obtained a mere thirty-two seats; many of its leading Deputies such as Deniau, Poncet, Chinaud and Pelletier lost their seats.

The few months following the elections were a period of reappraisal and self-contemplation both for the UDF and the Republican Party. Events turned full circle for the Giscardians. Giscard d'Estaing as President restored both political and electoral prosperity and success to his party and alliance; in defeat he left them without power or prestige. Further, the UDF and the Republican Party realised the costs of being in many senses little more than a mouthpiece for the decisions of the President. For the

UDF, the impact of opposition led to a reappraisal of their future and of their policies. Inevitably the constituent parties have reasserted their independence and the perennial struggle within the UDF between the 'fusionists' and the 'federalists' has taken on a new flavour. The first few months of opposition posed different problems for the Republican Party. Several groups within it pressed for more internal democracy, a renovation of the party leadership and a new party programme. Leotard and Millon, representing younger elements within the party, put forward plans for revitalising the party structure to give the 'grass-roots' more say in the running of the party.

It appears that Giscard d'Estaing for his part wanted to remain closely connected with both the Republican Party and the UDF. For example, Blanc's new 'team' constituted in October 1981, included several of Giscard d'Estaing's closest confidants. However, at the time of writing not only the exact relationship between Giscard d'Estaing and the Republican Party, but also the future structure and style of the party itself remains uncertain. It is true that the party has many internal problems and is competing within a multi-party right-wing opposition for power and for an electorate. However, the experience of the Gaullists has shown that it is possible for right-wing parties to outlive their charismatic leaders and to survive, and in some respects to strengthen, without the guiding hand of presidentialism.

## Notes: Chapter 2

1  J. Charlot, *The Gaullist Phenomenon* (London: Allen & Unwin, 1971).
2  *Le Monde*, 5 February 1964.
3  M. Duverger, *Political Parties*, 3rd edn (London: Methuen, 1967), p. 64.
4  For a more detailed discussion, see M. Anderson, *Conservative Politics in France* (London: Allen & Unwin, 1974), pp. 249–63.
5  An in-depth analysis of this period is to be found in J. C. Colliard, *Les Républicains indépendants* (Paris: PUF, 1971).
6  Interview.
7  For a discussion of the concept of an internally created party, see J. La Palombara and M. Weiner, 'The origin and development of political parties', in J. La Palombara and M. Weiner (eds), *Political Parties and Political Development* (Princeton, NJ: Princeton University Press, 1966), pp. 8–10.
8  I am indebted to Colliard's work *Les Républicains indépendants*, op. cit., for a background to this section. See also J. C. Colliard, 'Le Giscardisme', paper presented to the European Political Science Consortium workshop, Brussels, April 1979; a shorter version of his paper appears in *Pouvoirs*, no. 9, 1979, pp. 115–29.
9  See J. P. Soisson, *La Victoire sur l'hiver* (Paris: Fayard, 1979).
10  'Républicain indépendant' was very much a subsidiary title and is not normally used even by the PR itself.
11  Colette Ysmal, 'Le difficile chemin du Parti Républicain', *Projet*, September–October 1977.
12  J. P. Soisson (ed.), *Le Projet républicain* (Paris: Flammarion, 1978).
13  The UDF uses these tactics to an even greater extent.

14  See Clubs Perspectives et Realités, *Des choix pour demain, 1978-1983* (Paris: Hachette, 1977).
15  For a discussion of the relationship between the PR and UDF, see unpublished paper by Ella Searls, 'The Giscardiens', presented to a conference, *Contemporary French Political Parties*, organised by the Social Science Research Council in 1981.
16  See *Le Monde*, 12 May 1981, for a discussion of the dilemma of the UDF in the immediate post-election period.

# 3

# The Giscardian Politico-Administrative Elite

*P. BIRNBAUM*

The centralisation of political power in France involved the creation of a highly differentiated state, the general characteristics of which have been described elsewhere.[1] To contend with the violent reaction of a periphery which refused to recognise its legitimacy, the establishment of the central state required strong institutions, an autonomy from competing interests, a withdrawal behind the protection of a specific body of law and, above all, a powerful bureaucracy with an army of state employees who had taken on the role of agents dedicated to the general interest. Although the state has continually been able to strengthen itself throughout French history, it has also had to respond to challenges to its power from two sources. One has come from the upper class which, on several occasions, has resolved to wrest power from the state, transform itself into a ruling class and divest the political Centre of its institutional autonomy. In this sense the July Monarchy (1830–48) represented a negation of the very notion of an independent state. The second challenge has come from the advance of democracy; the extension of the suffrage led to the formation of large mass-based political parties and an appropriation of power largely by the liberal professions. In turn, this provoked a separation of powers previously integrated within the state. This particular challenge occurred under the Third and Fourth Republics. More recently, under Gaullism, the state seemed to have been strengthened; in contrast, the Giscardian period in many ways presented a challenge to the state similar to that of the July Monarchy. The state was absent from the Giscardian discourse of liberalism. The notion of the state as the privileged agent of modernisation, intervening according to its own particular rationality in the social system as a whole, was replaced by that of the market as regulator of social relations. Neither the absolutist state, nor the Gaullist nor Jacobin traditions had any place in *Démocratie française*, where Valéry Giscard d'Estaing reveals his commitment to the idea of a self-regulating civil society. This led to the brief attempt to liberalise social customs (freeing the prices of certain commodities, including bread, the decline of economic planning, an attack on the monopolies of certain public sector firms, the new respectability of economists influenced by Milton Friedmann, and so on). The Bonapartist and Jacobin Right was being replaced by a modernist and Orleanist Right. No longer was social progress to be initiated by the state; instead it would be induced by the allied forces of science and the market.

In the past state activity had largely been the preserve of an autonomous bureaucracy highly conscious of its particular role in society. Gaullism clearly created a 'republic of civil servants'; receiving an excellent technical training at the Ecole Nationale d'Administration (ENA) and assuming a particular social role with a specific set of values: top civil servants infiltrated the government, monopolised ministerial *cabinets*, determined the direction taken by the economy and even imposed their will on the management of large private sector firms. The might of the state seems to have been affirmed by the extent of the power wielded by top civil servants – the custodians of knowledge and spokesmen for the higher rationality. This aspect of the relationship between society and the state was especially undermined during the Giscardian period. Corresponding to the new primacy attributed to the market, the specific role and power attached to high public office diminished. Even the high-ranking officials of the state altered their self-image; they saw themselves as being more and more like managers in the private sector and found it quite acceptable that the latter, at a certain stage in their careers, assumed their own particular role within the state.[2] The co-opting of people from outside the bureaucracy, for example, in the magistrature, placed even further constraints on the institutional autonomy of the state. Finally, there were plans to reduce the number of state employees from 2.5 million to less than half a million (Longuet Report). Thus, the state seemed to be losing its privileged position even if its powers of control and repression were being maintained or increased. As a result of the new pre-eminence of the market, these changes unarguably occurred. In the following pages it is proposed to assess the impact made by these changes on the nature of the political-administrative personnel itself. Was there a decline in the role played by top-level bureaucrats corresponding to the relative eclipse of the state in society as a whole?

It should be stressed from the outset that civil servants are heavily represented among ministerial personnel. This level of representation was maintained during both the Gaullist and Giscardian periods; only during the presidency of Georges Pompidou did it register any significant decline.

As has been shown elsewhere, this osmosis of governmental and administrative personnel is a characteristic especially of those countries with highly differentiated states such as France and Germany; on the other hand, bureaucrats are rarely found in the governments of the UK or the USA.[3] The much greater prominence of civil servants in the governments of the Fifth Republic – a period in which the state reached its zenith – compared with those of the Fourth when parliamentary democracy flourished should be stressed. It should also be noted that, within this category of civil servants, the ratio of teachers to top-level bureaucrats evolved considerably. As Jean-Luc Parodi and Véronique Aubert point out, 'while members of the higher echelons of the civil service account for 18 per cent of Deputies and 33 per cent of ministers, civil servants whose careers began in the Fourth Republic contribute 39 per cent and 73 per cent respectively to these two categories under the Fifth'.[4] This underlines the predominance of civil servants under the Fifth Republic (Table 3.1).

This much is well known. What is less well appreciated is the difference in this respect between the Gaullist/Giscardian administrations and those of Pompidou. This poses a theoretical problem. In spite of the diminished role of the state in the Giscardian ethos, the Giscardian elite remained just as prominent among ministerial personnel. After becoming a party in power, the Giscardians attributed increasing importance to the top levels of the civil service. During the Fourth Republic and at the beginning of the Fifth, before Giscard d'Estaing broke away from Antoine Pinay,[5] the Independants were still much a party of provincial notables; the ministers representing them in government were nearly all landowners, lawyers and notables from regional areas. They adapted themselves remarkably well to executive office and went just as far as the Gaullist movement in promoting the technocratic character of their leading personnel. Under Gaullism, there were few Giscardian top civil servants in ministerial positions. But following their accession to power, their presence at this level increased considerably. More generally, if the classification 'top civil servants' is taken to include the category 'teachers' (almost all of whom in parties of the Right during the Fifth Republic have been university teachers of a technocratic type, teaching for the most part in faculties of law, economics and medicine), out of sixteen civil servant ministers in 1958 (69·5 per cent of the total number of government members), twelve were top civil servants; in 1976 out of twenty-two civil servant ministers (64 per cent of the total number of ministers), eighteen were top civil servants (Table 3.2).

By way of comparison, in the Fourth Republic, in the Mollet government, which had the highest proportion of civil servants in relation to all other governments (41 per cent of its ministers), there were only four top civil servants, ten secondary school teachers, four primary school teachers and none from the university sector. Finally, it should be noted that an increasingly important proportion of ministers were beginning their careers in a ministerial private office (*cabinet*), indicating the growing predominance of executive over parliamentary office; during 1959–74, 36 per cent of all ministers began their political careers in a ministerial *cabinet*; in 1979 they represented 41 per cent of the total.

As far as the nature of its government personnel was concerned, the

Table 3.1  The Professional Backgrounds of Members of the Eight Governments of the Fifth Republic (Percentage Representation of Various Groups)

| | de Gaulle 1958 | Debré 1959 | Pompidou 1962 | Pompidou 1966 | Couve de Murville 1968 | Chaban-Delmas 1969 | Messmer 1973 | Chirac 1976 | Barre 1976 | Average |
|---|---|---|---|---|---|---|---|---|---|---|
| Civil servants | 69·5 | 52 | 43·3 | 50 | 58 | 43·5 | 66 | 62 | 64 | 55·0 |
| Businessmen | 4·3 | 16 | 16·6 | 25 | 13 | 12·8 | 10·5 | 5·4 | 8·3 | 11·4 |
| Lawyers | 8·7 | 8 | 16·6 | 14·8 | 13 | 15·4 | 2·6 | 5·4 | 2·8 | 9·9 |
| Journalists | 8·7 | 8 | 13·3 | 3·5 | 6·4 | 7·7 | — | 8·1 | 8·3 | 6·8 |
| Political party officials | — | 4 | — | — | 3·2 | 5·1 | 8 | 2·7 | — | 4·2 |
| Farmers | — | 4 | 6·6 | — | — | — | 2·6 | 2·7 | — | 2·0 |
| Doctors | — | — | — | — | — | 5·1 | — | 2·7 | — | 1·3 |
| Shopkeepers | 4·3 | 4 | — | 3·5 | 3·2 | 5·1 | 2·6 | 2·7 | 2·8 | 2·7 |
| Men of letters | 4·3 | 4 | 3·3 | 3·5 | 3·2 | — | 2·6 | — | — | 2·0 |
| Miscellaneous (including chemists, vets, technicians) | — | — | — | — | — | 5·7 | 5·2 | 8·1 | 5·6 | 3·5 |

Source: Francis de Baecque and J. L. Quermonne, 'L'interpénétration des personnels politiques et administratifs', Administration et politique sous la Ve République (Paris: Presses de la Fondation Nationale des Sciences Politiques, December 1981), p. 28.

Table 3.2  An Analysis of Civil Servants in Government (Fifth Republic)

| | de Gaulle | Debré | Pompidou, I | Pompidou, II | Couve de Murville | Chaban-Delmas | Messmer | Chirac | Barre |
|---|---|---|---|---|---|---|---|---|---|
| Total | 16 | 13 | 12 | 14 | 18 | 17 | 25 | 22 | 22 |
| Non-members of Parliament | 8 | 7 | 6 | 6 | 6 | – | 1 | 6 | 9 |
| High public office | 11 | 9 | 9 | 10 | 12 | 15 | 19 | 15 | 17 |
| Technical corps | 3 | 2 | – | – | – | – | – | – | 22 |
| Other civil servants | – | – | – | – | 1 | – | 1 | 5 | 1 |
| Teachers | 5 | 4 | 3 | 4 | 5 | 2 | 5 | 2 | 4 |
| Teachers – from higher education | 1 | 3 | 3 | 4 | 3 | 1 | 1 | – | 1 |

Source: From Francis de Baecque, 'L'interpénétration des personnels politique et administratif', op. cit., p. 21.

Giscardian period was still part of the Republic of civil servants. In contrast, the presidency of Georges Pompidou marked a significant departure from this norm (in 1962, for example, 25 per cent of the government's members were industrialists; in 1958 they represented only 4 per cent and in the Chirac government of 1974 only 5·4 per cent). Although Giscardian and Gaullist ideologies and practices differed fundamentally, the personnel involved were, on the contrary, strikingly similar. Looking at the composition of those ministerial *cabinets* which have contributed so much to the strengthening of state autonomy, there also appears to have been a great similarity between the *cabinets* of General de Gaulle and Michel Debré and those of Valéry Giscard d'Estaing or Jacques Chirac: top civil servants accounted for nearly three-quarters of the members of these *cabinets*, whilst in contrast to the *cabinets* of Georges Pompidou, private sector representation was practically non-existent (Table 3.3).

Similarly, the representation of top civil servants from ENA remained very high, reaching its highest in the *cabinet* of Valéry Giscard d'Estaing (53 per cent). A government which implemented liberal policies was less concerned to assert the pre-eminence of the state than preceding governments and which, in contrast, attached a much greater importance to the market, was also that in which former students of ENA, created by General de Gaulle and Michel Debré to further ensure the independence of the state, were most prominent. In January 1980 former *énarques*

Table 3.3  *The Backgrounds of* Cabinet *Members*

| | High administrative public office | Economic sector | | | Others |
| --- | --- | --- | --- | --- | --- |
| | | public | private | total | |
| General de Gaulle (President) | 76 | 7·4 | 1·6 | 9 | 15 |
| M. Debré (Prime Minister) | 69 | 0 | 0 | 0 | 31 |
| M. Couve de Murville (Prime Minister) | 76 | 4 | 0 | 4 | 20 |
| M. G. Pompidou (Prime Minister) | 66 | 10 | 7·5 | 17·5 | 16·5 |
| M. G. Pompidou (President) | 58 | 10 | 10 | 20 | 22 |
| M. J. Chaban-Delmas (Prime Minister) | 70 | 14 | 0 | 14 | 16 |
| M. P. Messmer (Prime Minister) | 77 | 6·7 | 2·3 | 9 | 14 |
| M. V. Giscard d'Estaing (President) | 71 | 11 | 0 | 11 | 18 |
| M. J. Chirac (Prime Minister) | 68 | 8 | 0 | 8 | 24 |

*Source:* Bertrand Badie and Pierre Birnbaum, 'L'autonomie des institutions politico-administratives. Le rôle des cabinets des présidents de la République et des Premiers Ministres sous la Cinquième République', *Revue Française de Science Politique*, April 1976, p. 289.

(students of ENA) accounted for 40 per cent of the 230 official members of ministerial *cabinets*; in strategic decision-making centres the percentage was even higher: 60 per cent at the Elysée and 55 per cent at Matignon.[6] Ministerial *cabinets* were, therefore, literally invaded by *énarques*, especially those who graduated at the top of their year and went directly into the *grands corps* of the state: by May 1981 more than 40 per cent of ministerial personnel came from the Conseil d'Etat, the Inspection des Finances and the Cour des Comptes. In contrast, lower-ranking civil serv? its who were also at ENA but not among the top students of their year and who are, furthermore, far more numerous than members of the *grands corps*, formed only a quarter of private ministerial staffs.[7] So ministerial *cabinets* remained the locus of interpenetration between government personnel and the *énarque* elite from the *grands corps*.[8] Even if the role of the state was fundamentally changed under Giscard d'Estaing, the nature of the political-administrative elite remained surprisingly constant.

Furthermore, top civil servants, mainly from the Ecole Nationale d'Administration, moved from the public to the private sector much more than in the Gaullist period. During 1964–74 the rate of *pantouflage** in the higher civil service increased from 20 to 28 per cent.[9] In the banking sector, for example, the chairmen of Crédit Lyonnais, the Banque Nationale de Paris, Crédit Industriel et Commercial, Crédit du Nord, the Société Lyonnaise de Dépôt et de Crédit Industriel, as well as the governors of the Banque de France and Crédit Foncier, all came from ENA. *Enarques* were also to be found on the boards of the Chase Manhattan Bank, the Morgan Guaranty Trust, the Banque de Paris et des Pays Bas, the Banque Rothschild and the head of the Assurances Nationales, the Assurances Régionales de France, Air Liquide, Rhône–Poulenc, Creusot–Loire and Dassault, and so on. ENA was becoming a type of management school. This point can be concluded with the hypothesis that if the state during the Giscardian period was no longer the privileged actor it once was, the political-bureaucratic elite at its peaks was identical to that which dominated it under Gaullism; and in addition it also succeeded, through the process of *pantouflage*, in improving its contacts with private or public banking and industrial sectors, encouraging, as a result, an interpenetration of elites which, rather than strengthening the state, reinforced the cohesion of the ruling class.[10]

If we now consider the total number of Deputies in Parliament in 1977, a relatively rapid growth in the number coming from high public office can be observed. It is true that, just as in the Fourth Republic, the liberal professions were still the best represented group in the Assembly whilst, on the other hand, they practically disappeared from the government itself;

---

* The process whereby top-level bureaucrats transfer to equally high positions in the private sector.

but, that said, they continued to reflect the decline that Parliament experienced to the profit of executive power. But since top civil servants began to take positions at the summits of the state they also tried to discover a new source of legitimacy for their power by entering electoral politics. In 1951 only 2·7 per cent of all Deputies were also civil servants. In 1962 they accounted for 9 per cent and in 1978 for 13 per cent. This evolution particularly concerned the parties of the right-wing governing coalition to which members of the *grands corps* more readily attached themselves.[11] The members of the diplomatic corps in parliament, for example, all belonged to the Giscardian majority, as did most *inspecteurs des finances* and those from the Cour des Comptes. Only members of the Conseil d'Etat and the prefectoral corps were distributed in a more even manner between the Left and the Right.[12]

A comparison of the Giscardians (UDF) with the Gaullist party (RPR) reveals the degree of change experienced by the Independent Republicans (IR). Previously from the milieu of provincial *notables*, like ministers of the IR, the greatest proportion of their Deputies now came from the higher civil service. In 1978 top civil servants accounted for 26 per cent of UDF Deputies (if teachers from tertiary education are added to the 15 per cent of Deputies who came from the *grands corps* and the 66 per cent from upper management levels in the public sector); this was similarly the case for 24 per cent of RPR Deputies. In this respect, both of these parties which experienced executive power bore a close resemblance to each other. In contrast, no top civil servants were to be found among Communist Party Deputies in this period, and in the Socialist Party they accounted for only 20 per cent of all Deputies. In moving progressively closer to executive power the Socialist Party has equally promoted top civil servants, even if primary and secondary school teachers still constituted its largest single group in parliament (32 per cent of PS Deputies); in contrast, the latter accounted for only 5 per cent of the RPR's parliamentary group and 5 per cent of that of the UDF. So, whilst the civil service was certainly well represented in Parliament, its distribution among the parties was highly uneven. If we compare the Independent Republicans once again with members of the RPR, neither had any Deputies of working-class origin (and this applies equally to the Socialist Party), be it industrial, agricultural, or service sector. In the Communist Party, if professional political personnel – officials and members of the party machine – are excluded, only 13 per cent of its Deputies could be described as workers. Both the RPR and IR had an identical proportion of Deputies from the business world or the liberal professions. The only real difference was the slightly stronger representation of the middle classes in the RPR (reflecting its more populist orientation) and the still slightly greater number of landowners in the IR (remembering, however, that in 1958 20 per cent of IR members were farmers). In spite of these slight differences arising from dissimilar historical backgrounds, Giscardian Deputies had become less and less distinguishable from Gaullist Deputies. The approach to executive power therefore imposed its own particular logic on all levels of government.[13]

The increasingly apparent convergence of these two political parties is further indicated by the fact that an almost identical proportion of UDF and RPR Deputies elected in 1978 came directly from ministerial *cabinets* – the key centres of decision-making power. In 1978 26 per cent of newly elected UDF Deputies and 29 per cent of RPR Deputies came from ministerial *cabinets*. This also provides further evidence about a new type of career-path which no longer began at the local government level (mayor, councillor, and so on) before proceeding to the national level (Deputy, Senator, or minister) (Table 3.4).

The nationalisation of political life indicated the new predominance of the executive to the detriment of legislative power, allowing an access to ministerial *cabinets* for certain top civil servants – belonging more often than not to right-wing rather than left-wing parties – who can then stand for Parliament in safe constituencies where they are certain of being elected Deputy.

There has been a tendency to exaggerate the importance of this second type of career-path; the direct transfer from high public office to the position of Deputy should not mask the fact that sometimes the newly elected Deputy was actually born in the region of his constituency. At the beginning of the sixth legislature, for example, 60 per cent of UDF Deputies, 64·5 per cent of PS Deputies and 68·5 per cent of PC Deputies were born in the regions where they eventually became Deputies after pursuing quite different careers. The proportion is almost identical for each political group even if the left-wing parties are more locally oriented and are traditionally better established at the local level. The parties of the Right, on the other hand, had the advantage during the Giscardian period of holding executive power. But note also that out of sixty-two top civil servant Deputies in the sixth legislature, twenty-four were born in the region of their new electoral constituency; this was similarly the case for sixteen of the thirty-seven *énarques*. These proportions are certainly much lower than those applying to the total number of Deputies where, once again, one finds the distinction between teacher and civil servant which partially obscures the distinction between Left and Right; out of 100 teachers, sixty-seven were born in the region of their constituency (a proportion of 60 per cent compared with less than 50 per cent for top-level bureaucrats).[14] Beyond these differences, which are very important in assessing the relative influence of two processes – the localisation of national politics and the nationalisation of local politics[15] – it should be noted that even top civil servants, who belonged in large part to right-wing parties, sometimes maintained personal links with the regions of their new constituencies even if they had not been especially evident during the course of their earlier careers. From a more general point of view, 63·5 per cent of the Deputies of the sixth legislature were autochthones and 71·3

Table 3.4  New Deputies in 1978: Professional Background

| | Percentage of each category in active population | UDF | | RPR | | Socialist Party | | Communist Party | | Total | |
|---|---|---|---|---|---|---|---|---|---|---|---|
| | | Candidates (%) | Elected (%) | Candidates (%) | Elected (%) | Candidates (%) | Elected (%) | Candidates (%) | Elected (%) | Candidates (%) | Elected (%) |
| Businessmen/industrialists and big shopkeepers | 1.1 | 16.5 | 13 | 12.2 | 11 | 3.4 | 5 | 0.2 | – | 5 | 9 |
| Liberal professions | 0.8 | 24 | 31 | 21.8 | 31 | 11.5 | 20.5 | 1.9 | 8 | 15 | 24 |
| lawyers | | 7.3 | 10 | 4.7 | 9 | 3.4 | 8 | 0.2 | – | 4 | 7 |
| doctors | | 9.6 | 15 | 10.6 | 14.5 | 5.4 | 8 | 1.3 | 2.5 | 6 | 10 |
| Upper management, private sector | 3.5 | 18 | 7 | 21 | 9 | 13.5 | 4.5 | 2.6 | – | 5 | 6 |
| Chartered engineers | | 9.6 | 2 | 5 | 4 | 4.3 | 3 | 1.9 | – | 3 | 2.5 |
| Grand corps: | 0.1 | 4.3 | 15 | 6.6 | 15 | 2 | 6 | – | – | 2 | 10 |
| Upper management, public sector | | | | | | | 6 | – | – | 3 | 3 |
| Secondary and higher education | 1.3 | 6.6 | 6 | 3.8 | 4 | 2.5 | 28 | 17.3 | 9 | 12 | 14 |
| Total: upper classes | 8 | 79 | 73 | 75.6 | 79 | 33.9 | 70 | 22 | 17 | 42 | 66 |
| Artisans, small shopkeepers | 6.7 | 3.5 | 2 | 3 | 1.5 | 1 | 1 | 1 | 1 | 4 | 1 |
| Middle management | 10.2 | 11.5 | 3.5 | 14 | 5.5 | 17.7 | 10 | 19.5 | 10.5 | 18 | 9 |
| Primary school teachers | 2.5 | | | 1 | 1 | 5.9 | 12 | 10.2 | 10.5 | 5 | 5 |
| White-collar workers | 13.2 | 1.6 | – | 2.2 | – | 4.1 | 1 | 11.3 | 8 | 11 | 2 |
| Total: middle classes | 38.6 | 16.6 | 5.5 | 20.2 | 8 | 28.7 | 23 | 42 | 30 | 38 | 17 |
| Workers | 37.7 | 0.3 | – | – | – | 1.1 | 1.1 | 33 | 13 | 8 | 2 |
| Agricultural workers | 1.7 | | | | | | | | | – | – |
| Service personnel | 5.7 | | | | | | | | | | |
| Total: working classes | 45 | 0.3 | – | – | – | 1.1 | 1.1 | 33 | 13 | 8 | 2 |
| Farmers | 7.6 | 4 | 8 | 3.5 | 3 | 0.02 | 7 | 2.3 | 1 | 2 | 4 |
| Miscellaneous | 0.5 | 2 | 3 | 0.5 | 3.5 | 2.3 | | 0.6 | 38 | 9 | 12 |
| Grand total: 100   N = | 21,974,260 | 380 | 120 | 407 | 145 | 444 | 112 | 472 | 86 | 4,266 | 476 |

Note: Table constituted by Véronique Aubert.

per cent of them (if not necessarily autochthonous) had followed the classic career-path from local to national politics, a proportion which is not very different from that of certain legislatures in the Fourth Republic. It should be mentioned once again that among those who became Deputies after following the reverse career-path (from national to local level), quite a large number became Deputies either by direct appointment or from political inheritance (from the same family: son, brother, cousin, son-in-law, spouse, grandson, and so on),[16] which further confirms the persistence of the most classic career pattern.

If the argument about the reversed career-path – symbolic of the predominance of the state over society – should not be exaggerated, neither should it be totally rejected. By taking it into account one can better understand why those Deputies who took this path to legislative positions maintained such close links with executive power; on the other hand, one can also understand why the local presence of left-wing Deputies, especially those in the Socialist Party, should be more established than that of right-wing Deputies. Of all Socialist Deputies elected in 1978, 52 per cent had previously been mayors, compared with only 38 per cent of new Gaullist Deputies and 40 per cent of new Giscardian Deputies (see Table 3.5). Also 58 per cent of those Socialist Deputies elected in 1978 held two elective offices simultaneously, compared with 34 per cent in the case of the PCF, 35 per cent for the RPR and 39 per cent for the UDF.[17] Like the PCF in this respect, the RPR seems to be a party where career patterns are determined at the political centre (the state or the higher echelons of the party machine; in 1978 73 per cent of newly elected Communists were party officials). In contrast, the UDF, which succeeded to the place of the moderate Right of the Fourth Republic and the beginning of the Fifth, retained a more entrenched position at the local level (47 per cent of new UDF Deputies were *conseillers généraux*, compared with only 38 per cent in the case of the RPR) and in the Giscardian period enjoyed a privileged access to a state whose pre-eminence was contested, at least theoretically, in its discourse. This allowed its Deputies to follow both the classic and the reverse career-paths to political power. The new Socialist political elite, with the added advantage of an even more firmly entrenched local position and access since 10 May 1981 to a state whose pre-eminence, in a Jacobin sense, it wishes to maintain will similarly benefit from these two bases of power.

In conclusion, although the upper class attempted to transform itself into a ruling class during the Giscardian period by attributing a lesser importance to the state in both its discourse and in practice, the Giscardian political-administrative elite displayed characteristics identical to those of the Gaullist political-administrative elite which had tried, on the contrary, to govern society with the aid of the state. The conclusion must be that elites dispose of a surprising degree of autonomy by virtue of their own specific roles in society; the nature of their power is not simply derived, as

| | UDF (N = 53) (no.) | (%) | RPR (N = 34) (no.) | (%) | MRG (N = 4) (no.) | (%) | PS (N = 44) (no.) | (%) | PC (N = 34) (no.) | (%) |
|---|---|---|---|---|---|---|---|---|---|---|
| **Period of entry to political life:** | | | | | | | | | | |
| III Republic | — | — | — | — | — | — | — | — | 2 | 6 |
| Resistance | — | — | 1 | 3 | — | — | 2 | 4 | 4 | 12 |
| IV Republic | 8 | 15 | 2 | 6 | — | — | 2 | 4 | 13 | 39 |
| V Republic | 45 | 85 | 31 | 91 | 4 | 100 | 40 | 91 | 15 | 44 |
| **Party activities:** | | | | | | | | | | |
| Activists | 4 | 7 | 2 | 6 | 1 | 25 | 10 | 23 | 9 | 26 |
| Officials | 20 | 38 | 9 | 26 | 1 | 25 | 27 | 61 | 25 | 73 |
| **Non-elected candidates:** | | | | | | | | | | |
| Local | 4 | 7 | — | — | — | — | — | — | — | — |
| National | 7 | 13 | 4 | 12 | 1 | 25 | 6 | 14 | 5 | 15 |
| **Former office-holders:** | | | | | | | | | | |
| Local | 5 | 9 | 1 | 3 | — | — | — | — | — | — |
| Deputies | 4 | 7 | 5 | 15 | — | — | 1 | 2 | 6 | 18 |
| Senators | — | — | 1 | 3 | — | — | — | — | — | — |
| Regional Council | — | — | — | — | — | — | 5 | 11 | — | — |
| **Local offices held in 1978:** | | | | | | | | | | |
| Local Councillor | 13 | 25 | 4 | 12 | 1 | 25 | 13 | 29 | 11 | 32 |
| Mayor | 21 | 40 | 13 | 38 | 1 | 25 | 23 | 52 | 10 | 29 |
| Departmental Councillor | 25 | 47 | 13 | 38 | 2 | 50 | 24 | 54 | 20 | 59 |
| Chairman, Departmental Council | — | — | — | — | — | — | — | — | — | — |
| Regional council | 7 | 13 | 1 | 3 | — | — | 1 | 2 | 3 | 9 |
| **National political position in 1978:** | | | | | | | | | | |
| Replacement Deputy (*suppléant*) | 6 | 11 | 4 | 12 | — | — | 4 | 9 | 2 | 6 |
| Senator | 1 | 2 | 0 | — | — | — | — | — | 1 | 3 |
| **National functions:** | | | | | | | | | | |
| Former government member | 2 | 4 | 2 | 6 | — | — | — | — | — | — |
| Junior Ministers | — | — | — | — | — | — | — | — | — | — |
| Ministers | 1 | 2 | — | — | — | — | — | — | — | — |
| Ministerial *cabinet* | 14 | 26 | 10 | 29 | — | — | — | — | 1 | 3 |

*Note:* Table constituted by Véronique Aubert.

has previously been thought, from the relative strength of the state. It remains to be seen, in a future scenario, whether the democratic upheaval of May 1981 will provoke the formation of a new species of political-administrative elite and whether or not this would pose any degree of challenge to the power of the state itself.

## Notes: Chapter 3

1  Pierre Birnbaum, *The Summits of the State* (Chicago: Chicago University Press, 1982); B. Badie and P. Birnbaum, *The Sociology of the State* (Chicago: Chicago University Press, 1982); and P. Birnbaum, 'The state in contemporary France', in R. Scase (ed.), *The State in Western Europe* (London: Croom Helm, 1980), pp. 94–114.

2  Pierre Grémion, 'La concertation', in M. Crozier (ed.), *Où va l'Administration française?* (Paris: Editions d'Organisation, 1974), pp. 165-86; J. C. Thoenig, 'La stratification', in ibid., pp. 29-54; and J. Chevallier, 'Un nouveau sens de l'Etat et du service public', in *L'Administration et la politique en France* (Paris: Presses de la Fondation Nationale des Sciences Politiques, 1979), pp. 163-204.

3  Pierre Birnbaum, 'Institutionalisation of power and integration of ruling elites: a comparative analysis', *European Journal of Political Research*, vol. 6 (March 1978), pp. 105-15.

4  Véronique Aubert and Jean-Luc Parodi, 'Le personnel politique français', *Projet*, July-August 1980, p. 792.

5  Jean-Claude Colliard, *Les Républicains indépendants* (Paris: PUF, 1971).

6  Bertrand Badie and Pierre Birnbaum, 'L'autonomie des institutions politico-administratives. Le rôle des cabinets des Présidents de la République et des Premiers Ministres sous la Vè République', *Revue française de science politique*, April 1976, pp. 286-309.

7  José Freches, *L'ENA. Voyage au centre de l'etat* (Paris: Conti-Fayolle, 1981), pp. 36-7. See also Ezra Suleiman, *Les Hauts Fonctionnaires et la politique* (Paris: Editions du Seuil, 1976).

8  Jean-Luc Bodiguel, *Les Anciens Elèves de l'ENA* (Paris: Presses de la Fondation Nationale des Sciences Politiques, 1978). See also Jean-Luc Quermonne, 'Politisation de l'administration où fonctionnarisation de la politique?', in *L'Administration et la politique en France*, op. cit., pp. 329-60, and *Le gouvernement de la France sous la Vè République* (Paris: Dalloz, 1980).

9  P. Birnbaum, *et al.*, *La classe dirigeante française* (Paris: PUF, 1978), p. 64; Freches, op. cit.

10  A. Darbel and D. Schnapper, *Les agents du systeme administratif* (Paris: Mouton, 1979).

11  A. de Stéfano, *La participation des fonctionnaires civils à la vie politique* (Paris: Librairie Générale de Droit et de Jurisprudence, 1979).

12  Guy Drouot, 'Les fonctionnaires députés sous la Vè République', thesis, Aix-en-Provence-Marseille, 1975.

13  See Aubert and Parodi, op. cit.; and D. Gaxie, 'Les logiques de recrutement politique', *Revue Française de Science Politique*, February 1980, pp. 5-45.

14  J. C. Cardy, 'Les députés français élus en 1978', thesis, University of Paris I, 1981, T 2.

15  See Marcel Merle and Albert Mabileau (eds), *Les Facteurs locaux de la vie politique nationale* (Paris: Pedone, 1972); and Pierre Birnbaum, 'Office holders in the local politics of the French Fifth Republic', in J. Lagroye and V. Wright (eds), *Local Government in Britain and France* (London: Allen & Unwin, 1979), pp. 114-26.

16  Cardy, op. cit., p. 463 ff.

17  Michel Reydellet, 'Le cumul des mandats', *Revue de Droit Public et de Science Politique*, no. 3, 1979, pp. 713-19; Aubert and Parodi, op. cit., p. 798.

# 4

# The Social Policies of Giscard d'Estaing

## X. GARDETTE

When Giscard d'Estaing took office in 1974, some doubt could indeed be cast on his ability to pursue a meaningful social policy. An aristocrat born, he had never really behaved like a potential socialist when he was Minister of Finance; nor had he truly belonged to the Gaullist ranks, which had evinced some genuine good-will in the social field. Giscard d'Estaing's only credentials were his claim to be an 'advanced liberal'.

## Women and Families

The first sign of that advanced liberalism in the field of social policy was the Veil Act of 17 January 1975, named after the popular Simone Veil, then Minister of Health. This Act made abortion legal, although strong safeguards were set against abortion on demand: a maximum of ten weeks' pregnancy, an interview with two general practitioners and a state of personal distress (a clause now flexibly interpreted). The Veil Act excused GPs from performing abortions on grounds of conscience. Reimbursement of the cost of the operation by the French National Health Service was not available.

Linked with abortion, access to contraception was also made easier. The Contraception Act of December 1974 and decrees which followed in 1975 made prescriptions for the 'pill' valid for one year and exempted teenagers from parental approval when buying their contraceptives at their local chemist's.

Divorce also benefited from Giscard d'Estaing's liberal convictions. The Divorce Act of 11 July 1975 made divorce by mutual consent available, sparing spouses the painful exercise of proving misconduct.

But at the same time, the family had to be supported. One-parent families were guaranteed a minimum income. Husbands were given the opportunity to benefit from maternity leave, as well as their wives. Largely less symbolic was the rationalisation and improvement of maternity grants for the third child and beyond. The decision to increase part-time work opportunities through legislation was made in 1980, starting with the civil service, and although the application of this measure was delayed this would attain full effect by 1982. A minimum family income was guaranteed from 1981 onwards to families with three children or more. Health Service protection for mothers staying at home with a large family was granted in 1981. Despite Giscard d'Estaing's promise in 1975, free access to public playgrounds for children is still not in sight, after more than a century of strict containment. Perhaps the most costly of all?

## Health and Welfare

The French Health Service works differently from that of Britain: 95 per cent of GPs belong to the private sector, are free to take on as many patients as they like and to charge whatever they think appropriate. However, the great majority have chosen to sign an agreement with the state Health Service. 'Approved' GPs undertake not to charge more than the official fee and, in turn, patients are reimbursed from the Health Service (usually 75 per cent of the total fee). Prescriptions are also partly refundable.

In December 1978 and July 1979 the Council of Ministers took a number of measures aimed at restoring the Health Service's financial position, then running deep into the red. In order to boost the inflow of receipts a provisional increase of 1 per cent of health contributions was decided, affecting the majority of the working population. It ceased to be levied on 1 February 1981, two months before the presidential elections. Pensions contributions went up as well; old-age pensioners were asked to pay health contributions for the first time, and a budget contribution (that is, the tax-payer or inflation) also came to the rescue.

On the expenditure side the management of public hospitals was to be more closely monitored, and reforms were introduced to achieve savings. Some medicines were labelled 'luxury' and as a result withdrawn from the list of refundable prescriptions (for example, laxatives). A number of benefits were reduced, or their access made more strictly conditional (for example, spa treatments). Doctors' unions also asked their members to voluntarily soft-pedal on prescriptions: a new approved fee was set at only 50 franc for an ordinary appointment, but despite moaning and groaning, very few GPs contracted out for fear of losing tax and pension privileges attached to the Health Service agreement.

## Producers and Consumers

One of the ways of bestowing upon the French 'the ownership of France', to use Giscard d'Estaing's own words, could be to turn wage-earners into shareholders. In this spirit a number of measures were put on the statute-book in May and October 1980. The distribution of shares among the workforce by companies was made easier, 65 per cent of the new shares being financed by the government. However, nothing was made compulsory, and no more than 3 per cent of the company's capital could change hands in that way. A new type of company in the form of the Société d'Actionnariat Salarié (SAS) was also created, so that employees of such companies could share in the ownership of capital investments. Middle-range executives were given a seat in boardrooms.

Probably more genuine was Giscard d'Estaing's concern for the less gratifying jobs in industry: in 1974 his close friend and adviser, Lionel Stoleru, was appointed Junior Minister for Manual Work with the mission to 'promote this type of work which ought to acquire greater status and attract more young people in the seven years to come if the French economy is to remain sound'. Payment of wages on a monthly basis was extended to new categories of workers: this meant, in practice, longer holidays and better protection against sickness and redundancies.

In 1976 the new system of 'compulsory time off' was introduced: any overtime work done over and above forty-four hours a week has now to be offset by a shorter working week soon after. In the same spirit of reducing physical strain retirement for manual workers was made possible at 55 years of age, on a pension equal to 77 per cent of the last monthly wage.

Producers are also consumers, and Giscard d'Estaing's intentions in that respect were similarly symbolised with the appointment in 1976 of Mme Scrivener as Junior Minister for Consumer Affairs. Protective legislation on door-to-door sales, HP commitments and mortgages now followed. Five minutes a week on television were set aside for a consumer programme, and the National Institute for Consumers, which was created in 1968, was placed under the authority of Mme Scrivener and launched a monthly magazine, *50,000,000 Consumers*.

## Housing and Mortgages

In 1975 Raymond Barre, then Minister of Foreign Trade, produced a report on housing which had been commissioned by Giscard d'Estaing. Following this report, the old system of subsidies known as 'subsidies to builders' was replaced in 1977 by 'subsidies to individuals' (APL). APL helped low-income households intending to rent either a council flat, or government-approved private accommodation, or flats in modernised buildings. At the end of 1980 130,000 households were being helped in this way. With tenants in need now being subsidised, rent controls could be abolished in July 1979, being progressively carried out for various types of accommodation.

In line with its ownership policy the government launched a scheme as an 'access to private ownership' – not out of place in a country where tenancy has been for long far more widespread than in Britain. 'Home-ownership loans' (PAPs) were now granted by state agencies to those working- or middle-class households who were either building their own house or wanted to buy and modernise accommodation over twenty years old. APL subsidies also played a major part in that field and, at the end of 1980, were helping 23,000 households to buy their house or flat.

## Unemployment Benefits

Unemployment increased from 1·8 to 7·5 per cent of the working population during 1974–81. In January 1975, at a time when bankruptcies were multiplying, workers who were 'made redundant on economic grounds' (a status legally defined) were granted 90 per cent of their former salary during a whole year, tax-free. However, this concerned only a minority of people and as time went by seemed increasingly unfair to the others. In January 1979 the government and the main unions agreed on a new and more rapidly regressive scheme of benefits, at the same time reducing redtape and extending minimum protection to all wage-earners who could testify to at least three months' work during the previous twelve months.

As in Britain, specific schemes were aimed at school-leavers, labelled 'youth employment pacts' and starting in 1977. The third – due to run until 1982 – was extended to unmarried women and elderly workers chronically unemployed. The pacts aimed at giving employers incentives to recruit a fresh workforce: partial or total rebate on the employers' share of National Insurance contributions, partial payment by the government of apprentices' salaries, a lump-sum for craftsmen taking on their first employee and tax rebates for companies going over the bar of ten people employed (thereby offsetting an automatic increase in National Insurance contribution).

In addition, government money was made available for the training and retraining of the workforce both inside and outside companies. As in other countries, subsidies were offered to companies willing to settle in particularly hard-hit regions, such as the Vosges where the textile industry was closing plants, or northern Lorraine where 21,000 redundancies were announced in the steel industry soon after the 1978 general elections.

How, then, does Giscard d'Estaing's social policy compare with what had been achieved under de Gaulle's and Pompidou's presidencies?

## Relegated Issues

In May 1974 high on the agenda was the general question of women's status and rights. Women had massively entered the labour market during the Fourth and Fifth Republics, accounting for 80 per cent of the growth in working population since 1954. In the civil service during Pompidou's presidency women had breached male bastions such as the Council of State in 1969, with the appointment of the first woman councillor, and the powerful Finance Inspectorate in 1974. Role-crossing within the family was gaining widespread support, if not practice, amongst the middle class.

'Equal opportunity' legislation started under Pompidou (Equal Salaries Act, December 1972) and was extended by Giscard d'Estaing (Appointments Act, July 1975). A promotion and conditions of work Bill was to be examined during the autumn 1981 parliamentary session. Of course, this is a long-term effort, and 'equal opportunity' will probably become a reality in France in more than a generation.

Of more immediate urgency when Giscard d'Estaing took office was the long-outstanding problem of abortion that Pompidou had been unable – or unwilling – to tackle. Abortion was still a crime under the 1920 Act, passed in the aftermath of the First World War. But since 1969 it had been defiantly practised by militant groups such as the Movement for the Freedom of Abortion and Contraception (MLAC), and had been brilliantly debated in the courts with great publicity.

On contraception, the first and only step had been made under de Gaulle with the Neuwirth Act of 1967, which merely acknowledged the existence of family-planning centres set up by militants and doctors. The French Socialist Party estimates that reforms on abortion and contraception, if one accepts the lowering of the age of majority to 18, was Giscard d'Estaing's only significant move in the social field. Today, after the Veil Act, backstreet abortions have virtually disappeared: there were 350,000 in 1970. Eighteen abortions for 100 births are performed on average, roughly amounting to the British figure.

Pompidou had been more instrumental over the conditions of the elderly, whose economic position had been seriously eroded under de Gaulle. Since 1969, the year Pompidou took office, pensions had been progressively increased, but when Giscard d'Estaing entered the Elysée Palace in 1974, one-third of old-age pensioners were still living on one-half or less of the statutory minimum salary (SMIC).

Giscard d'Estaing maintained Pompidou's financial effort. After 1974 the statutory minimum pension improved faster than SMIC and by 1981 was 63 per cent higher in real terms. But it was still rather low by European standards, and 2 million old-age pensioners had no other resources to live on.

On housing, Giscard d'Estaing had a number of reasons to depart from what had been done under de Gaulle and Pompidou. First, the existing system of 'subsidies to builders' had more or less achieved its original aims: reconstruction had been carried out, the population boom of the 1950s and 1960s had been accommodated and by 1974 the rented housing stock had reached an acceptable level. Secondly, that system had come under criticism because it had in fact favoured the middle class, not the working class which should have been the prime beneficiary. Thirdly, existing rent controls were not totally consistent with Giscard d'Estaing's 'liberal' designs as reflected in the 1975 Barre Report on housing. The report was in favour of a market economy in the housing field, and led to the 1977 reform.

The 'policy of private ownership' also advocated had, in fact, started out under de Gaulle with house-sharing schemes (*Epargne-logement*), and continued under Pompidou with the *Chalandonettes* (named after the then Minister of Infrastructure). The extension of that policy was a response to a growing desire amongst the French, and was perceived, incidentally, as a means to foster the 'Anglo-Saxon' political moderation that Giscard d'Estaing would love his fellow-citizens to adopt. Today, three-quarters of the APL beneficiaries belong to the working or lower-middle class. But still only 22 per cent of the total number of households are owner-occupied.

Another problem which seemed to have lost its edge by 1981 – but for how long? – was the recurring question of the welfare services financial deficit. It was under de Gaulle in 1967 that the emergency brake was applied: the accounts were put back into the black by means of unpopular ordinances, which the unions said contributed to the May 1968 upheaval.

The welfare services muddled through under Pompidou's mandate, but by 1975 spending started running at a much faster rate than the growth in the national income, and got totally out of hand by the end of 1978. This was mainly due to increases in health spending which, in turn, could be explained by GPs' generous prescriptions; by the packaging of tablets and phials in full boxes whatever the need; and by the growth in unemployment, reducing the amount of health contributions actually paid in. As a top civil servant put it, the French had had a tendency to see social questions as health problems, and to think that 'tranquillisers could solve income disparities, bad working conditions, the shortcomings of marriage, of domestic life, and the pressure of state gigantism'. The set of measures taken in 1979 provided the welfare services with a sounder financial basis than they had enjoyed since 1967.

## Persistent Issues

A reduction in income differentials was again advocated in 1975, this time in the Méraud Report on social inequalities, which was part of the preparatory work on the seventh economic plan (the eighth plan, published in 1980, was much more elusive on the subject).

If one is to believe the official Statistical Services, the gap between high and low *average* salaries – after having grown slightly under Pompidou – was marginally reduced under Giscard d'Estaing until 1980. The increase in social contributions which followed the 1979 health measures, and which affected more the upper end of the income scale, had played a great part in this evolution. But the increase dropped in February 1981. Also, as one of *Le Monde*'s economists, Gilbert Mathieu, has pointed out, the gap between the lower paid and the average worker had widened since Giscard d'Estaing took office, due to a SMIC policy carried out more according to the letter than the spirit of the 1970 Act.

As far as non-salary incomes were concerned, Giscard d'Estaing made an attempt in 1976 to introduce in France a capital gains tax to which the country had been allergic for decades. It ended in Parliament a total disaster, the Act which came out of the confusion stripped of any muscle.

Profit-sharing was an equally lingering question. One of de Gaulle's battle-cries 'la participation', as far as profit is concerned, had never really gone beyond the 1967 ordinances. Small- and medium-sized companies were not covered by the scheme, and money was 'frozen' for five years every year before it could be distributed to the workforce.

Pompidou had never been very enthusiastic about that particular 'grand design' of the founder of the Fifth Republic, and things were quiet on this front until 1975 when the Sudreau Report was published. Sudreau, in his report on company reform commissioned by Giscard d'Estaing, suggested an extension of the 1967 ordinances to all companies, and cash to be made readily available to the beneficiaries at the end of each year. However, nothing ever happened during Giscard d'Estaing's presidency.

Of another aspect of *la participation*, workers' shareholding, there has been a continuous effort since the birth of the Fifth Republic in producing rather complicated pieces of legislation but which have fallen short of the mark: at the end of 1980 most of the workforce of the 11,711 companies concerned had hardly been turned into business associates scrutinising the books; they had sold the few shares that they had been given as soon as that had been possible under the law.

After the 1959, 1970 and 1973 workers' shareholding Acts, Giscard d'Estaing's own 1980 contribution could again be dismissed by a Socialist MP as 'derisory legislation with derisory effects'. That contribution also fell short of the Sudreau proposals on decision-sharing inspired by the German system of *Mitbestimmung*. Company reforms remains a pending question.

'Contractual policy' is another example of schemes which started before Giscard d'Estaing took office and were not allowed to develop during the last presidency. The policy was initiated by Chaban-Delmas in 1970, when the latter was Pompidou's Prime Minister. 'Contracts of progress' were signed with most of the unions represented in public companies (railways and electricity). These agreements were established for several years, and linked pay rises to productivity gains and GNP rate of growth.

Quite an unusual type of agreement and quite separate from the collective bargaining legal framework, these 'contracts' were meant to show the way towards a new relationship between industry and the unions, and towards social peace: a sort of no-strike commitment was actually written into the electricity contract, as a trade-off for guarantees on wages. That type of long-term commitment did not fit easily into the frame of Giscard d'Estaing's 'liberalism', and the economic slump arrived in time to help put an end to what remained a short-lived story.

On family policy, Giscard d'Estaing came back in 1977 to the spirit which had prevailed under de Gaulle before 1967. Before that date, family benefits were organised more in order to encourage births than to remedy social inequalities (they had also been regularly falling in real terms). After 1967 and during Pompidou's mandate the redistributive aspect had been emphasised, although the fecundity rate was still consistently falling.

In 1975 for the first time since the 1930s the number of newborn babies fell short of what was needed to ensure population renewal at its present figure, and the warning bell began to ring. As a result, after 1977, access to maternity and family benefits was made less conditional on resources than before. The latest measure in that field, which took the form of an extra tax rebate three months before the presidential elections, favoured three-children families with high incomes.

The fecundity rate went up slightly in 1980, but it is impossible to say whether this precludes a long-term bottoming out, and it is difficult to distinguish between the result of governmental policy and deeper factors at work.

## Some New Issues

If one excepts the important 1971 legislation on industrial training, the 'promotion of manual work' had hardly been a concern before 1974. Giscard d'Estaing made it a new issue, arguing that growth and employment had suffered in the past from the excessive prestige attached in France to white-collar work (everyone wanted to become a *cadre*). This had been reflected in the numbers turned out in the 'wrong fields' by the education system, and by wage differentials on the labour market: in 1969, the year Pompidou took office, the average French blue-collar worker was paid a third less than his German counterpart and the white-collar worker 8 per cent more.

As a result of the measures taken by Stoleru and of the propaganda and warnings of unemployment consistently injected into the media since 1974, there was a certain shift amongst the young towards technical training: 40 per cent more apprentices and 35 per cent more A levels in technology in 1980, compared to 1974, for a school-age population only growing marginally.

The purchasing power of an hour's work in those six years also increased by 26 per cent for manual workers, compared to 11·4 per cent for white-collar workers. But these are average figures: traditionally low-paid sectors like textiles, or unqualified jobs, were no better bargains in 1981 than they were under de Gaulle or Pompidou.

Immigration also became a new issue after 1974, in so far as the economic slump and growing unemployment made Algerians, Portuguese, Africans, blacks and West Indians rather less wanted. From 1974 onwards regulations and controls became tighter. The net inflow of immigrants, which had run between +90,000 and +180,000 a year during 1964–73, was stopped in 1976. Voluntary return was officially encouraged, reversing the policy which had been carried out in the 1960s.

But despite the financial inducement and the one-way air-fare, courtesy of the French government, very few immigrants returned. During 1975–9 the foreign workforce decreased by only 14 per cent, whilst the total number of non-EEC immigrants actually went up due to family reunion (which was not discouraged by the government).

Another new issue taken up by governmental policy under Giscard d'Estaing was consumerism. The French consumer movement, a couple of decades behind Britain, acquired at last its letters of nobility during Giscard d'Estaing's mandate. Giscard d'Estaing had shown an interest when he was at the Ministry of Finance under de Gaulle and Pompidou. He decided to pinpoint the importance of the issue by appointing a junior minister in 1974. But most of the pressure on manufacturers actually came from the Federal Union of Consumers (UFC), an independent association publishing the monthly *Que Choisir*. The UFC claimed that it was not really backed by the junior minister when it came to implement the legislation and regulations the government itself had initiated. In fact, the official INC acted more as a negotiating body with the manufacturers (not always without results) than as a respected pressure bureaucracy.

But the most worrying new issue was obviously the growth in unemployment. In fact, it is clear that the watershed as far as unemployment is concerned is traceable back to 1965, a key year also in other sectors. But not surprisingly, the situation became visibly worse soon after Giscard d'Estaing took office.

Different factors started working in the same direction: the full influx on to the labour market of the generations of the 1950s; women determined to take up a job and leaving 'reserve' to register on unemployment roles; the slump, cutting job opportunities and increasing the average duration of unemployment between two jobs (10·4 months in 1979). Unions also denounced the growth of 'precarious employment' and the mushrooming of temporary agencies.

Pompidou's last full year in office (1973) coincided with the swansong of the postwar economic boom. In the new circumstances which developed after 1974 social policy during Giscard d'Estaing's first mandate could only be the poor relation of an economic policy that was busy papering the cracks and attempting to regenerate France's industrial muscle.

The easiest and the less expensive reforms, like abortion reform, were swiftly carried out. The fundamental, like the redistribution of power within companies, was never seriously meant by the President nor by his parliamentary coalition. In between, the vast realm of the welfare state was above all marked by actions designed to avoid the disaster of bankrupt welfare services or penniless dole queues. For the rest, there were often delays between the much-publicised announcement of a reform, the passing of the Act through Parliament and the publication by the bureaucracy of the implementation decrees without which nothing can be set into motion. Meanwhile the standard of living of the French continued to rise slightly until 1980 and social protection was maintained for those who knew how to get the proper information. But societal conditions became harder, and worse was probably still to come.

# 5

# Industrial Policy and Policy-Making, 1974–82

*DIANA GREEN*

The Giscardian presidency took place against a backcloth of economic crisis, 'la plus sérieuse, la plus durable, la plus épouvantable, que le monde ait connue depuis les années trente'.[1] Indeed, his accession to power marked a critical economic watershed for the Fifth Republic. The assumption that the 'economic miracle' would continue in an uninterrupted fashion within the framework of a stable international system received a rude awakening in the mid-1970s. Under the combined impact of the collapse of the international monetary system, the emergence of the OPEC cartel and the rapid industrialisation of a number of countries in the Third World, inflation accelerated, growth was halved and unemployment rose alarmingly. Industrial development became a cause of major concern of the government: the competitiveness of French industry would determine the rate of growth and the level of employment, as well as constituting a key weapon in the battle to restore, in the medium term, the foreign balance.

Giscard d'Estaing's accession to the presidency also marked a break with the past to the extent that it signalled the beginning of the end of a decade and a half of Gaullist rule and the possibility of a fresh approach to industrial problems. A key feature of this approach was a belief in the political virtues and economic efficiency of competitive market forces. This new economic liberalism was translated, at least at the level of rhetoric, into a commitment to root out the *dirigisme* which had characterised previous (Gaullist) regimes. 'Rolling back the frontiers of the state' would involve, *inter alia*, the final killing-off of national planning and the abandonment of intervention at the micro-economic level under the rubric of industrial policy. This chapter will draw up a balance-sheet of industrial policy under Giscard d'Estaing. It will also examine the main features of the Socialist government's policies in this area, highlighting where and how these differ from those of the previous regime.

## Economic Policy under the Giscardian Presidency

The Giscardian presidency was framed by two oil-price 'shocks' which brought to an abrupt end the economic miracle of the 1960s. During the seven years of the presidency economic growth was halved (falling from an average of over 5 per cent per annum under the de Gaulle and Pompidou presidencies to 2·6 per cent) (Table 5.1). Inflation doubled and was still rising (prices rose 32·4 per cent from 1976-9 and in 1980 alone rose 13·6 per cent) and the employment situation deteriorated progressively (Figure 5·1). By these indicators, then, economic performance was considerably worse than under previous regimes. The seven years of the presidency must, however, be divided into two distinct phases during which the

Table 5.1  *Economic Growth under Three Presidencies (Average Annual Growth Rates)*

|  | 1959–69 (%) | 1969–74 (%) | 1974–81 (%) |
|---|---|---|---|
| GDP by volume | +5·7 | +5·1 | +2·6 |
| GDP by price | +4·2 | +7·3 | +10·8 |
| Billion franc (1970 prices) | 31·5 | 42·0 | 27·0 |

Figure 5.1  *The worsening employment situation, 1975–80*

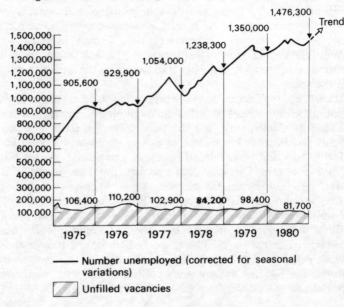

policies pursued were very different, if not contradictory. During the first phase, which corresponded with the premiership of Jacques Chirac, economic and industrial policies manifestly failed to resolve the problems which had to be confronted. This was partly because the Chirac–Fourcade (Minister of Finances) tandem misunderstood the nature and scale of the problem: for some time, it was believed that the crisis was a temporary, if severe, one which required skilful navigation but which, once 'enjambé', would be followed by the return of the high growth rates of the past. At the policy level, the initial response was to treat the major structural changes taking place as if they were simply cyclical ones, that is, short-term measures were adopted rather than attempting to seek any new policy direction. This served only to exacerbate the problem. A freeze, introduced in the summer of 1974, precipitated a recession without having any impact on the rate of inflation. This was followed by a reflationary package in 1975, which sent the economy even further off course, fuelling inflation. The second phase corresponded with the premiership of Raymond Barre. He estimated that it would take at least three years to 'cure' the ills of the French economy, including the effects of the 'medicine' supplied by his predecessor. The Barre Plan, a counter-inflationary stabilisation plan, was designed to put the French economy back on its feet again. Economic health required the establishment of a number of 'basic balances' (the balance of payments, a balanced budget, wage moderation, a stable currency and a moderate growth in the money supply) as a first step to renewed economic stability and inflation-free economic growth. It is against this changing economic background that Giscardian industrial policy has to be examined.

## French Industrial Policy: an Overview

In attempting to draw up a balance-sheet of French industrial policy the analyst has to confront a number of problems. First, it is necessary to distinguish the myths surrounding it from its reality. Thus, since France is generally represented as the home of Western-style national planning, French industrial policy is assumed to be, by definition, rational, coherent and planned. At the same time, in keeping with the right-wing nature of the regime (at least for the first two decades of the Fifth Republic), it was contended that 'industrial policy' was limited to procuring a general framework within which industrial development and change could take place, in response to market forces, that is, that state intervention was essentially marginal. Empirical analysis suggests that 'horizontal' policies have been supplemented by selective intervention on an increasing scale and of an increasingly detailed nature. Moreover, interventions have taken place largely on an *ad hoc* basis. When it became expedient to draw attention to state actions in the industrial area, this was typically achieved by attaching purposeful labels to those actions, for example, the 'industrial imperative' of the 1960s, the 'industrial redeployment strategy' of the 1970s and the 'strategic reinforcement strategy' launched more recently in response to the 'new international economic war' of the 1980s. In other words, even when presented as part of a long-term strategy, industrial policies have frequently tended to conform to the model of crisis management rather than industrial planning. Secondly, the boundaries of 'industrial policy' are almost impossible to draw. Most other economic policies impinge on industrial performance in one way or another: commercial policy, labour market policy and incomes policy, all are critical factors in both the determination and implementation of industrial policies. These boundaries have tended to shift, over time, as the nature of the regime in power and the economic circumstances in which the policies are formulated have changed. Indeed, these changes, in the nature and the scale of intervention, have taken place not only between, but also *within*, the different regimes. It is possible, for example, to detect two distinct phases of industrial policy under Giscard d'Estaing, which correlate with the political complexion of the government and the severity of the economic crisis. Thus, the scale of interventions increased sharply when the impact of the 1973 oil-price rises plunged the economy into a deep recession. The defensive reaction of the government (an instruction to companies to postpone redundancies for as long as possible, the creation of an agency to bail out lame ducks[2] and the launching of a plethora of support 'plans' covering almost all industrial sectors) was only partly a result of its failure to recognise the nature and scale of the problem. It was also in line with the Gaullist approach to industrial problems. Arguably the 'real' Giscardian brand of industrial policy did not emerge until the latter part of the presidential term, after the appointment of Raymond Barre as Prime Minister, in 1976.

Nevertheless, French industrial policy has been characterised by a remarkable degree of continuity, for most of the postwar period. At a general level the main objective which motivated the first three Presidents during the Fifth Republic was to turn France into a major economic and industrial power. If the symbols used to represent this aim changed (that is, 'national grandeur' has been replaced by 'national independence'), this to some extent reflected the more practical nature of the Giscardian regime, faced by the problems posed by the 'changing economic geography of the world'. Whereas under de Gaulle and Pompidou, the economic viability of certain prestige projects was sometimes questionable (for example, *Concorde*), under Giscard d'Estaing this type of project was largely dictated by economic necessity (the nuclear energy programme) or for commercial reasons (the ambitious telecommunications programme).[3] There was similarly continuity in the means adopted in order to realise this objective. Governments continuously intervened in and monitored the pace and direction of industrial change, despite the rhetoric of non-intervention.

Broadly speaking, they pursued a dual strategy, a mixture of protectionism and selective entrepreneurship. If there were also changes, these were primarily changes of scale and emphasis. A key feature of the policy approach under all three presidencies was intervention to prompt, and often underwrite, industrial restructuring in order to create 'national champions', oligopolies capable of competing in foreign markets. This was the cornerstone of the 'industrial imperative' which provided the motivating force for the fifth and sixth national plans. In some cases the aim was political rather than economic, especially in the advanced technology sectors such as computers and nuclear power. The creation of some of the largest conglomerates similarly appeared to be motivated by 'la course au chiffre d'affaires', rather than dictated by any industrial logic. Although restructuring remained a favoured policy approach under Giscard d'Estaing, the emphasis changed. One consequence of the recession was a reassessment of the assumption that bigger companies necessarily meant more efficient and more profitable ones. Since the overriding aim was to increase competitiveness in world markets (that is, there was a shift in emphasis towards *selling*), restructuring focused on rationalisation. At the sectoral level concentration was no longer an end in itself; restructuring was seen as a means of accelerating the specialisation of French industry. At the level of the firm rationalisation meant getting out of unprofitable activities ('couper les branches mortes') or finding a suitable *creneau*, preferably (although not necessarily) in a growth industry. In other words, there was a much more explicit attempt, under Giscard d'Estaing, to distinguish between industrial 'winners' and 'losers'.

In its broadest sense Giscardian industrial policy can be said to have had three main aims. At the macro-economic level the main focus was on removing constraints and providing incentives to the operation of the market. At the micro-economic level the aim was to encourage the traditional industries (especially coalmining, steel, textiles and ship-building) to adapt to the realities of the 1980s and foster the development of the growth industries by promoting technological progress and the spread of innovation. This would enable firms to compete not only with France's main competitors (West Germany, Japan and the USA), but also the newly industrialising countries. At the same time firms should be encouraged to export in order to help pay for France's increasingly expensive imports of oil and raw materials. If these were the policy objectives, what was actually achieved?

## Promoting Industrial Development: Removing the Dead Hand of the State

At the general level Giscardian industrial policy focused after 1976 on removing the constraints (financial and administrative) on the business sector, in order to encourage firms to invest. This was the rationale of the Barre Plan and explains many of the subsequent policy measures. Policy decisions as various as the removal of price controls, fiscal relief to encourage the private investor to buy shares on the stock exchange,[4] a modest reduction in the burden of social charges falling on the corporate sector, as well as increased relief for firms undertaking investment,[5] were taken with this aim in view.

At a different level Giscardian industrial policy focused on changing the habits and attitudes of the entrepreneur. This involved an extensive educational programme, spanning a public-relations exercise designed to underline the costs of too cosy a relationship between government and industry (Barre is reputed to have remarked that, as a first step, industrialists should be prevented from gaining access to ministerial *cabinets!*) and management education in its widest sense (for example, the importance of cash flow, the benefits to be gained from the new technologies and from relocating plant abroad, in low wage-cost countries, and so on).

## The Search for an Industrial Strategy

Giscardian industrial policy was not restricted to removing the constraints on industrial development. Intervention took place at the level of both the sector and the firm, despite the pledge to disengage. Indeed, if intervention was more *selective* than under previous regimes, it took place in industries deemed to be sensitive and/or strategic, with equal disregard for market forces and using broadly the same policy tools (for example, quotas and tariffs to support the ailing textiles and clothing industries, a 'voluntary' import-restraint agreement to protect the car industry from Japanese competition, export subsidies, especially for products in the growth industries, preferential public purchasing to promote the new 'telematics' industry, and so on). Moreover, the government showed no compunction about systematically blocking take-over bids by foreign companies and/or engineering 'French solutions' by prompting (and often underwriting) restructuring operations. It was argued that some encouragement to industry was essential, whilst the constraints on industrial development are being removed. The state was, therefore, prepared to intervene to assist the efforts of efficient firms attempting to pursue an international strategy, (that is, to *support* entrepreneurial initiative, not to supplant market mechanisms). During the first five years of the Giscardian presidency, then, industrial policy offered nothing that was either very new or distinctive. It was not until 1980 that such a policy emerged, when the government published a document outlining its thought on a new strategy for the 1980s and 1990s.

## 'Strategic Reinforcement': a Strategy for the 1980s and 1990s

The first indication that the government was trying to put together a new strategy was a keynote article in *Le Monde* by the Industry Minister, André Giraud, in September 1979. In this he discussed the main problems facing French industry in the medium to longer term and suggested that the way forward lay in an aggressive worldwide strategy based on the 'industries of the future'. Although this did not imply that any sector was 'condemned', the role of the state was not to shore up lost causes. These should be reduced to a defensible segment (*noyau dur*); those resources freed by disinvestment should be moved into new industries, preferably advanced technology industries, where France has a comparative advantage.

The main thrust of the new approach, which was spelt out more fully in a Ministry of Industry document, centred on the promotion of certain key areas (*vedettes*), which were felt to be strategically important to the extent that they are likely to be the source of industrial growth over the next two decades. The failure to develop an effective French presence in these areas would have had serious consequences for French economic and industrial development in the years ahead. Six priority areas were initially chosen (underwater exploration, automation of office procedures, consumer electronics, robotics, bio-industry and energy-saving equipment). It was made clear, however, that this list of strategic areas might be added to. Areas were chosen rather than sectors partly because Giraud, the Industry Minister, believed that sectors 'correspond more to statistical classifications than to the realities or the diversity of French industry'. At the same time it reflected the recognition by the French government that certain of the new technologies are generic to a wide range of industries (for instance, micro-electronics).

The new industrial strategy was based, then, on the rapid development of French technology and particular French products, and underlines the extent to which the government had embraced the Japanese industrial model. It was underpinned by an institutional reform in which some of the previously dispersed industrial policy functions were gathered together and centralised in a new interministerial committee, the Interministerial Committee for the Development of Strategic Industries (CODIS). The creation of this committee is interesting for a number of reasons. First, the composition of the committee, which was chaired by the Prime Minister, gives some indication of its importance in the policy process, as well as underlining the new importance accorded to industrial policy (Figure 5.2). Secondly, it was set up at a time when the importance of the national plan and its relation to (and impact on) industrial policy had become visibly more questionable. It may also be significant that the administrative machinery servicing the CODIS was dominated by Ministry of Industry officials: the interministerial committee preparing its decisions was chaired by the director-general of the key policy division of the Industry Ministry

Figure 5.2 *The Interministerial Committee for the Development of Strategic Industries (CODIS)*

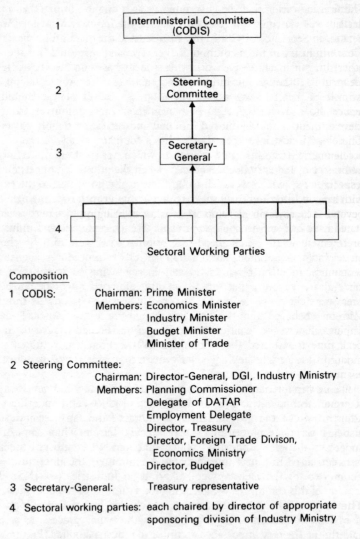

Composition

1 CODIS:          Chairman: Prime Minister
                  Members: Economics Minister
                           Industry Minister
                           Budget Minister
                           Minister of Trade

2 Steering Committee:
                  Chairman: Director-General, DGI, Industry Ministry
                  Members: Planning Commissioner
                           Delegate of DATAR
                           Employment Delegate
                           Director, Treasury
                           Director, Foreign Trade Division,
                             Economics Ministry
                           Director, Budget

3 Secretary-General:   Treasury representative

4 Sectoral working parties: each chaired by director of appropriate
                            sponsoring division of Industry Ministry

and each sectoral working party was chaired by the director of the appropriate sponsoring division.

The strategies devised by the CODIS were 'indicative' (to borrow a phrase from national planning) rather than mandatory. Moreover, the creation of the committee was presented as a means of rationalising the multitude of schemes available to assist private industry and promote industrial development. Arguably it was much more than that. The composition of the CODIS made it possible, for the first time, to co-ordinate interventions and introduce more coherence into industrial policy decisions. The choice of the strategic areas was only the first stage. The next step was to identify the *firms* best suited to spearhead the strategy. In some instances this meant firms already involved in the chosen areas, at other times it meant those which could be persuaded to move into them (despite the insistence that the CODIS was not involved in picking 'winners'). The process was facilitated by the invention of yet another new policy tool: interventions were effected through the medium of 'development contracts' drawn up between the state and the relevant firm. These were a derivative of the 'growth contract' formula, developed to accelerate the growth of selected firms in the electronics sector. Like the latter, these were medium-term contracts in which performance targets (especially export and import substitution targets) are specified, together with sanctions for non-fulfilment. Unlike growth contracts, they extended beyond the provision of financial assistance, bringing different forms of state assistance together in a package (for example, export subsidies, preferential public purchasing and/or temporary import controls, and so on). This regime, then, which had nailed its colours to the mast of economic liberalism, created, *prima facie*, the means of devising and carrying out the most coherent, systematic and detailed industrial policy ever seen in France. It should, however, be pointed out that this new strategy was not comprehensive; it had nothing to say about other important sectors such as aerospace and telecommunications. These were dealt with elsewhere, often in the framework of other plans. The modernisation and development of the telecommunications industry, for example, was covered by both the national plan and the 'informatics plan'.[6] Moreover, whatever the government said about its determination to focus on the industries of the future, those industries facing a major adjustment problem (not only those in structural decline such as steel, but also and perhaps more importantly, the car industry) were not neglected. Indeed, the troubled textiles industry was rapidly added to the list of 'strategic' areas falling within the aegis of the CODIS.

## The Impact of Giscardian Industrial Policy

Did the policies pursued during the Giscardian presidency demonstrably improve the health of French industry and, more generally, that of the economy?

One of the most direct and far-reaching consequences of Giscardian industrial policies is the radical rationalisation which took place. A number of well-known companies disappeared in mergers (often as an alternative to liquidation) (for instance, Boussac and Kléber-Colombes) and many of the big industrial groups moved out of some of their traditional (and often loss-making) activities into new ones.[7]

At the level of the firm investment and divestment are, of course, a natural process. When this is transposed to the wider sectoral level, however, it assumes a much greater importance. The rationalisation of the steel industry, for example, reduced crude-steel production to two main groups (Usinor and Sacilor). Indeed, broadly speaking, the underlying strategy appeared to be a continuation of the one pursued under the two preceding presidencies, that is, building selected companies up into champions for the national, European and international leagues. It was refined, under the Giscardian presidency, however, as was indicated above. The survival of the fittest in each designated 'key' sector generally meant the survival of two firms (Usinor and Sacilor in the steel industry, Renault and Peugeot-Citroën in the motor industry, Thomson and CIT-Alcatel in telecommunications, and so on), presumably on the grounds that this ensured some measure of internal competition.

The process of de-industrialisation which took place under the *septennat*, whether by accident or design, was given an additional impetus by the process of geographical redeployment, encouraged and in some cases underwritten by the government. In a bid to counter the impact of increased competition from overseas a number of firms transferred all or part of their manufacturing process to low wage-cost countries. In the textile and clothing industries, for example, products under the Rodier label are now manufactured in Tunisia, Cacherel opened up plant in Japan, Bidermann transferred part of its production to Colombia and Rhône-Poulenc, which controls 90 per cent of the synthetic-fibre industry, transferred part of its operations to Brazil and Thailand. Similarly, Renault signed agreements with Mack (commercial vehicles) and American Motors (cars) in a first step towards establishing assembly operations in the US market.

The costs of this belated and accelerated rationalisation were high. The number of bankruptcies rose dramatically, increasing 70 per cent over the seven years of the Giscardian presidency. Despite the continued existence of the lame-duck agency the CIASI, the number of bankruptcies per month almost doubled (from 800 a month in 1973 to 1,500 a month in 1979) and in 1980 alone increased by 9·5 per cent (reaching a total of 17,380 compared with 15,860 in 1979). Moreover, companies in the Paris region appear to have suffered more severely than elsewhere in France: the number of companies filing for bankruptcy here increased by 17 per cent during 1980. This reflected the harder-nosed attitude of the Barre government which saw bankruptcies as the inevitable, if regrettable, consequence of France's industrial maturation (exemplified in the decision to tighten up the terms of reference in the CIASI).[8]

The number of redundancies increased substantially, too. As Table 5.2 shows, whereas the industrial labourforce increased under the two

Table 5.2   *Changes in the Pattern of Employment under Three Presidencies (Net Changes, Thousands)*

|  | 1959–69 | 1969–74 | 1974–81 |
|---|---|---|---|
| Agriculture | − 1,700 | − 600 | − 400 |
| Industry* | + 900 | + 380 | − 900 |
| Services | + 2,300 | + 1,180 | + 1,400 |
| Totals | + 1,500 | + 960 | + 100 |

* Includes construction.

Table 5.3   *Industrial Employment as a Proportion of Total Civil Employment in Six Industrialised Nations, 1975–9*

|  | | | (%) | | |
|---|---|---|---|---|---|
|  | 1975 | 1976 | 1978 | 1979 | 1975–9 |
| France | 38·8 | 38·2 | 37·1 | 36·4 | − 2·4 |
| West Germany | 46·0 | 45·6 | 45·1 | 44·8 | − 1·2 |
| UK | 40·7 | 40·0 | 39·7 | 39·1 | − 1·6 |
| Italy | 39·3 | 38·5 | 38·3 | 38·0 | − 1·3 |
| USA | 30·7 | 30·9 | 31·2 | 31·4 | + 0·7 |
| Japan | 35·9 | 35·8 | 35·0 | 34·9 | − 1·0 |

previous presidencies, there was a marked contraction after 1974. The number employed in manufacturing industry overall fell by 8·5 per cent during 1975–9 (from 5,424,600 to 4,800,100). Indeed, all the industrial jobs created in 1970–4 were lost in 1975–8. As Table 5.3 shows, industrial employment declined as a proportion of total employment in most industrialised nations during this period. It declined *more rapidly* in France, however, than in other countries.

Initially, it was the declining industries which were the most severely affected. Manpower levels in the textile and clothing sector, for example, fell by 135,000 in 1974–8. During the latter part of the Giscardian presidency, however, the increasing severity of the problem can be gauged from the fact that the number of redundancies increased sharply both within these industries (for instance, 27,000 jobs were lost in the textile industry in 1980 alone), and also spread to a much wider range of industries, including the car industry. This industry, which during the 1970s was regarded as the most successful of French industries (measured in terms of its growth, employment and exports),[9] had recently been affected by the crisis affecting that industry in other industrialised nations (for example, Chrysler in the USA and British Leyland in Britain). Thus, whereas the French motor companies were able to ride the 1974–5 crisis (indeed, employment increased by 20 per cent during 1970–9, whilst in the steel and textiles industries it fell by the same amount), they had by 1981 been forced to resort to lay-offs, early-retirement schemes and short-time working. In all, 28,000 jobs were lost in 1980 and Renault, the most successful of the two groups, decided to cut its workforce by a further 3,600 during 1981. The Giscardian presidency was marked, then, by a massive shake-out of labour which helped swell the ranks of the unemployed.

If French industry was slimmer, was it any healthier than it was in 1974? The various measures introduced to improve company profitability appear to have had some success. Those firms which weathered the first crisis clearly benefited from the abolition of price controls. Company profits increased after 1978 as firms used their new-found freedom to put up prices and liquidate their debts. The government's strategy here was quite clear: profitability was a prerequisite of increased output and employment, that is, to increase profits was the only way to create 'genuine' jobs. Indeed, perhaps the most important difference between Giscard d'Estaing's policy and that of his predecessors was not so much the priority

Figure 5.3   *Volume of private productive investment in France, 1978–80 (see INSEE, 1981)*

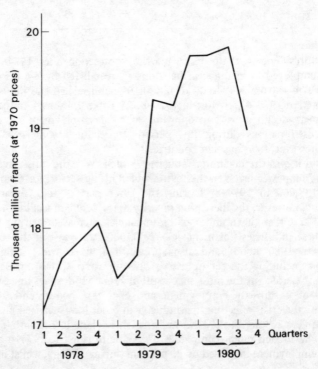

accorded to restoring profitability as the way this was carried out. In other words, in a clear bid to redress the balance between the personal and business sectors the burden of paying for the growing oil-bill was shifted from industry to the higher-paid wage-earner and consumer. Unfortunately, although profits increased, after that initial increase, the volume of private investment slumped dramatically during 1980 (Figure 5.3).

It also proved more difficult than expected to reduce the administrative burden on companies. Despite the constant references to the need to decentralise industrial decisions (that is, reduce interference by central government), little real progress was made on this front. Indeed, the fate of the Mayoux Report (on the de-centralisation of finance to the regional and local levels) provides a pointed illustration of the power of vested interests and administrative inertia. It similarly proved difficult to arrest the growth of public expenditure, seen as both a symbol of state intervention and a constraint on the entrepreneurial spirit, 'crowding out' private initiative. Whilst public expenditure grew relatively slowly in France before 1973, it accelerated after that, rising from 38·1 per cent of GDP in 1973 to 44·5 per cent in 1977 (compared with an increase from 41·9 to 43·4 per cent in Britain over the same period).

## An Experiment in Economic Liberalism which Failed?

One of the most critical problems facing France and other industrialised nations in the 1980s is how to reverse the industrial stagnation which took place in the last decade. It is a problem which highlights the issue of the state's role in economic life and, more generally, government–industry relations, an issue which is particularly contentious in liberal, free-market economies. Those who had hopes of an era of full-blooded liberalism when Giscard d'Estaing acceded to the presidency in 1974 were disappointed. Despite the pledge to disengage, the state took an active role in French industrial life, orchestrating the rationalisation of the activities of the main industrial groups ('la redistribution des cartes') and extending even further the battery of mechanisms used to direct structural change.

State intervention is, of course, traditional in France. Under the first three presidencies of the Fifth Republic, government-inspired programmes, designed to modernise French industry, constituted the backbone of French industrial development. During the 1960s priority was given to the development of the nuclear and aerospace industries primarily for strategic reasons (for instance, de Gaulle's nuclear policies were designed to secure military independence). Although these programmes were continued under the Giscardian presidency, they became part of a *broader commercial* strategy, partly dictated by the need to come to grips with France's growing oil-bill.[10]

Giscard d'Estaing pursued his main and unambiguous aim – to secure a

French presence in international markets in certain key sectors – and with an extraordinary single-mindedness. Indeed, French foreign policy seemed to become simply an extension of economic and industrial policy. The intention was clearly to break with the past, first, by separating industrial policy from social policy – the state should not be involved in propping up declining industries and inefficient firms in order to save jobs. In line with the determination to instil competitive free-market habits into the business community, there was an attempt to use public funds in the most *efficient* way possible, assisting only *efficient* firms, especially in those growth industries where France has a comparative advantage. Secondly, there was an attempt to break with the past by intervening in a more 'methodical' way. Neither of these aims appears to have been fully realised.

In the 1981 presidential elections Giscard d'Estaing was judged by, and found wanting in respect of, his economic and industrial policies. But did the policies really fail? As far as more general macro-economic policies are concerned, and judged by its own performance targets, this appears to be the case. For example, the attempt to bring down the rate of inflation clearly did not succeed. To what extent this failure is attributable to the inadequacy or inappropriateness of the policies pursued[11] or to factors over which the government had no control (for instance, the oil price rises), is debatable. It is also true that the failure of its macro-economic policies made it more difficult for the government to achieve its aims in the industrial policy area. Firms claimed, for example, that the high rate of inflation, the strength of the franc and high interest rates were making it difficult to compete in overseas markets. Yet it could be argued that rather than constituting a failure, the attempt to encourage industrial adjustment (by encouraging specialisation and by promoting industrial 'winners') was too successful. More specifically, the consequences of Giscardian industrial policy (in the shape of the disappearance, at too rapid a rate, of sectors, firms and jobs), proved to be electorally unacceptable. In other words, what mattered to the French electorate was not so much inflation (which they have learned to live with) as unemployment. This suggests that Giscard d'Estaing's main error was in giving the control of inflation priority over all other policy objectives.

## The Socialist Alternative

Several months after taking office, the precise nature of the Socialist government's industrial policy was still unclear, if indeed it has such a policy. Arguably it is easier to define their approach to industrial problems *negatively* rather than positively, to the extent that this constitutes a reaction to the policies of the old regime. Thus, the Socialists reject the specialisation strategy pursued under Giscard d'Estaing. Their basic premiss is that neo-liberalism was demonstrably incapable of responding to the country's needs in the 1980s. It was producing a dual economy, characterised by the privatisation of profits and the socialisation of losses (a trend accentuated by Giscard d'Estaing's policy of 'helping the strong'). They argue that a wider and more diversified industrial base should be retained, including the 'mature' and growth industries. Secondly, they reject the 'fatality' of the thesis of international division of labour. Some degree of protectionism may be necessary as a temporary measure (for instance, import controls may be used to assist the development of new technologies as well as preserving those in structural decline). More importantly, import substitution (*le reconquête du marché intérieur*) is essential to recapture 'lost' industries. In itself this is not new: protectionism is a traditional response to the problem of industrial adjustment, used by governments of the Right and the Left, in line with the general scepticism about the market mechanism. The change is likely to be one of *scale*. Putting it another way the Socialists are likely to reinforce the traditional nationalism of French governments in this policy area. One indicator of this is the concern which has been expressed, at the political level, about the relative backwardness of French technology and the extent to which 'French' technology is actually imported.[12] This has resulted in a massive increase in the budget of the powerful Ministry of Research and Technology. Again this is not so much a change of policy direction (the CODIS procedure had identified the importance of the new technologies) as of emphasis. In other words, the Socialists are building on the foundations of the earlier strategy and underwriting it with an increase in public funding.

Thirdly, the growing unemployment problem, exacerbated by demographic and technological changes,[13] means a softer line on 'lame ducks'. Indeed, the Giscardian thesis (that profits lead to investment which produces jobs) has been stood on its head. The Socialists' main policy objective is to *create and maintain jobs* (summed up in the government's battle-cry, the 'war against unemployment'). This is to be achieved by 'offensive' measures, in the shape of a neo-Keynesian approach focusing on the stimulation of demand (through a modest reflation and the increase in the number of civil servants) and 'defensive' measures (such as the introduction of various work-sharing schemes).[14]

The most positive feature of the Socialist government's industrial policy – and certainly the most contentious aspect – is its nationalisation programme. There seems to be some confusion as to the precise purpose of this programme (under which the state has taken over a number of industrial interests and a large part of the private sector financial institutions). Apart from its symbolic value, there appears to be some doubt as to whether nationalisation is an end in itself, or a means to some other (unspecified) end. In the case of the industrial interests, for example, the government has been at great pains to emphasise the non-ideological nature of its actions. Nationalisation is presented as both a means of rationalising the state's holdings and, more generally, as a tool of industrial policy. Thus, the nationalisation of the steel industry is presented as the juridical ratification of the *de facto* transfer of ownership from the private to the public sector which took place under the 1978 steel plan. The public ownership of Dassault (in which the state already had a minority holding) and the missiles and space division of Matra is justified in a similar fashion, given that these companies are virtually dependent for their existence on government contracts. At the same time, and to avoid being accused of 'nationalisations rampantes', the government has confirmed its intention of 'privatising' (that is, selling back to the private sector) the industrial assets of two private sector investment companies, Paribas and Suez, which were nationalised. More positively, the nationalisation of the five industrial groups (CGE, Saint-Gobain, PUK, Rhône-Poulenc and Thomson Brandt), is presented as a means of securing a French presence in key technological areas to maintain and consolidate France's position as a leader in the league table of industrial power. Nationalisation in this respect is seen as the basis of 'une force de frappe pour l'avenir'.

After nationalisation, what then? Does the nationalisation programme correspond to any coherent strategy? This is not really clear. The first Industry Minister, Pierre Dreyfus, appeared to have a fairly precise master plan, according to which, after a further reshuffling of the industrial pack, the five *nationalisables* would emerge as the 'poles' in their designated sectors. Thus, Rhône-Poulenc would become a leader in the chemicals and agrochemicals branches as well as becoming the main French pharmaceuticals producer (a sort of 'French Pharmaceuticals Inc.'). Similarly, PUK would improve its share of the aluminium and non-ferrous metals markets and seek 'synergie' (that is, merge its interests with other companies) in pharmaceuticals and special steels; CGE would become a champion in electronics and telecommunications (via Cit-Alcatel), in shipbuilding (via Alsthom-Atlantique) and in construction (through the Société Générale d'Enterprise); Saint-Gobain would become the market leader in informatics and automated office equipment (via its interests in CII-HB and Olivetti); whilst Thomson is being encouraged to expand its interests in consumer electronics. To what extent this is government policy or simply Dreyfus's personal vision was unclear. It may be significant that there was some disagreement, even between the minister and his advisers as to the 'right' strategy for France.[15]

Whether or not the list of nationalisations corresponds to any specific industrial strategy, it will nevertheless radically alter the shape of French production. As Table 5.4(*a*) shows, after nationalisation, over 30 per cent of French industry is now state-owned/controlled, compared with just over 16 per cent at present. The change is even more dramatic at the level of the individual branch. Thus, after nationalisation, state-owned companies account for 79 per cent of turnover in the steel industry (compared with 1 per cent today); 75 per cent of turnover in the synthetic-fibre industry (compared with 0 per cent); 74 per cent of turnover in the arms industry (compared with 58 per cent) and 52 per cent of basic chemicals (compared with 16 per cent) (Table 5.4(*b*)).

The nationalisation of a large proportion of the private banking sector (in all, some eighty-eight banks representing 26·3 per cent of total banking deposits and 30·1 per cent of total credits) is justified in the same non-ideological fashion. The aim here is to underwrite industrial policy. It is argued that the state does not have adequate control over the provision of credit. Private banks tend to lend short, or give priority to housing, showing little interest in riskier industrial ventures. Nationalisation will allow the state to direct funds into longer-term industrial investment projects, as well as providing a means of assisting small firms (by reducing the cost of credit and providing equity in the shape of 'participatory loans').[16] Here, too, the government has adopted a minimalist position, avoiding the creation of a National Investment Bank to direct funds into industry in line with the objectives of the national plan (a sort of 'Gosplan

Table 5.4   *The Nationalisation Programme of 1981–2*
(a)   *Share of Public Sector in French Production,
before and after Nationalisation*

| | (%) | |
| --- | --- | --- |
| *Sector* | *Before* | *After* |
| Production and distribution of energy | 61·3 | 61·8 |
| Intermediate capital goods | 6·8 | 29·8 |
| Capital goods | 15·1 | 29·8 |
| Consumer goods | 1·6 | 6·0 |
| Miscellaneous industries | 0·0 | 0·1 |
| Total of industrial production | 16·8 | 30·8 |

(b)   *Percentage of Turnover Accounted for by
State-owned Firms, by Branch*

| | (%) | |
| --- | --- | --- |
| *Branch* | *Before* | *After* |
| Steel | 1 | 79 |
| Synthetic fibres | 0 | 75 |
| Arms | 58 | 74 |
| Extraction and processing of iron | 0 | 71 |
| Metallurgy | 16 | 66 |
| Basic chemicals | 16 | 52 |
| Consumer electronics | 0.3 | 42 |
| Glass | 0 | 37 |
| Office machines and treatment of information | 0 | 34 |

français'). Instead, nationalisation of finance is presented as another tool of industrial policy.

In adopting this line the Socialists appear to be arguing that they are simply pushing the concept of state intervention (to create jobs, to win new markets and fund growth by channelling investment into industry) a step further than their liberal and Gaullist predecessors. They justify their actions by the use of the same argument – that the market is sometimes 'blind' – and with the same arrogance assume that the state has the sole competence, and the sole right to interpret the national interest. The difference is mainly one of degree. For example, the state already had considerable control over banking and credit (it controlled the three main groups which accounted for 58·6 per cent of deposits and 49 per cent of credit). Nationalisation therefore merely *extends* their ability to direct credit.

Finally, are changes likely at the policy-making level? The Socialists have said they wish to 'restore the plan' but its precise relationship to industrial policy (in respect of both the determination of industrial priorities and policy implementation) and, at the institutional level, the relationship of the Planning Ministry to the proposed 'Superior Council of Industrial Development'[17] is as yet unclear.

The Socialist alternative, in the industrial policy area, does not therefore appear to constitute a really radical departure from past practice: the changes appear to be primarily changes of scale and emphasis (more intervention, a greater emphasis on employment maintenance, and so on). Nor, if the government is to be believed, will more intervention mean more control: they have pledged their belief in the mixed economy and the autonomy of the firm (to be preserved by 'de-centralising' decisions). To some extent this reflects the constraints – both economic and political – within which it is operating. The economic crisis shows no sign of abating and the extent to which radical economic and social change is feasible and desirable is unclear; *prima facie*, then, the accession to office of the Socialist regime is unlikely to mark a revolution in French economic and industrial policy. Whether or not the 'Socialist alternative' will turn out to be a real alternative – in the sense of constituting a more coherent and rational approach to the problem of industrial development – or be simply another method of managing industrial crisis must, for the moment, remain an open question.

## Notes: Chapter 5

1 Giscard d'Estaing, speech delivered on the occasion of twentieth anniversary of the OECD, December 1980.
2 The CIASI (Inter-ministerial Committee for Managing Industrial Structures) was set

up in 1974 to recommend intervention in firms (mainly in the small business sector) which were experiencing temporary financial difficulties ('lame ducks'). Rescue operations are a joint venture, involving both public and private capital.

3 The modernisation of the telecommunications network which started in 1976 was partly undertaken in response to the somewhat belated recognition that France had one of the most antiquated networks in Western Europe. The modernisation programme, based on the new digital technology, and funded within the framework of the seventh national plan, has provided the French with a highly sophisticated system which has enabled them to win a number of impressive export contracts.

4 Introduced under the Law of 13 July 1978, 'Loi Monory', named after the Economics Minister.

5 The most recent package was introduced in the 1981 budget, providing 25,000 million franc over the next five years.

6 The name given to the government's programme to computerise French society, launched in response to the report by Simon Nora and Alain Minc on this theme ('L'Informatisation de la Société', 1978). Like other plans, it is a label attached to a number of policy initiatives relating to information technology, some of which fall within other programmes (for example, the peri-informatics plan, the plan for components, the micro-electronics plan, and so on).

7 For example, BSN-Gervais-Danone sold its glass-making activities to Pilkingtons of the UK, in order to concentrate on food; Saint Gobain Pont à Mousson (now renamed Saint Gobain) moved, via the purchase of minority holdings in CII-HB and Olivetti, into electronics; and Matra, the successful missiles and electronics combine, extended its activities, amid much controversy, into publishing.

8 The terms of reference were changed to allow CIASI to take a catalytic role, intervening in and accelerating the expansion of efficient firms.

9 For example, Renault increased its sales by 17 per cent in 1980 and produced a record 2 million vehicles. Over 50 per cent of the total output of the industry is exported.

10 The increase in expenditure on imported energy was the main element in a big increase in France's trade deficit in 1980 which rose to 60·4 thousand million franc (compared with 13·6 thousand million franc in 1979).

11 According to the Bloch-Laîné Report (Commission du Bilan, Lettre au Premier Ministre, 15 September 1981), the economic policies pursued by the Barre government were both inappropriate and inadequate, given the problems faced by the French economy. Instead of relying on traditional macro-economic tools to check inflation (for example, control of the money supply and curbing the budgetary deficit), the government should have deployed more sophisticated weapons, attacking the structural characteristics of French inflation (for example, incomes policy).

12 The Industry Minister, Pierre Dreyfus, said in an interview that the government has no intention of allowing firms to continue the practice of putting French labels on imported technology as a means of bypassing research and development (interview in *L'Expansion*, 6-19 November 1981).

13 The active population grew by 254,000 in 1980. More than 200,000 additional people are expected to enter the job market each year until 1984, declining slowly after that date.

14 For example, the reduction of the working week, initially to thirty-eight hours, to thirty-five hours by 1985.

15 Where Dreyfus favoured a policy based on *national* (and more specifically, state-owned) champions, Ministry of Industry officials appeared to support a strategy based on restructuring at the *European* level.

16 Long-term loans (up to seventeen years), equivalent to equity capital.

17 In a speech to the National Assembly on 15 September 1981 the Prime Minister pledged that this latter (bringing together the Prime Minister, the Minister of Industry and industrialists in the public and private sector) would be set up by the end of the year.

## Select Bibliography

Bonnaud, J.-J. (1975), 'Planning and industry in France', in J. Hayward and M. Watson (eds), *Planning, Politics and Public Policy* (Cambridge: Cambridge University Press), pp. 93–110.

CNPF, (1979) *De l'Exportation à la Croissance Internationale? Propositions du CNPF pour une politique active d'investissement à l'étranger* (Paris: ETP).

Commissariat Général au Plan (1980a), *8è Plan: Rapport de la Commission Développement* (Paris: La Documentation française).

Commissariat Général au Plan (1980b), *8è Plan: Rapport de la Commission Industrie* (Paris: La Documentation française).

Commissariat Général au Plan (1980c), *8è Plan: Projet* (Paris: La Documentation Française).

De Bandt, J. (1978), *Politiques industrielles et objectifs d'industrialisation* (Paris: Cujas).

Green, Diana, (1979), 'Individualism versus collectivism: economic choices in France', in V. Wright (ed.), *Conflict and Consensus in France* (London: Frank Cass), pp. 81–96.

Green, Diana (1980), 'The Budget and the Plan' and 'Economic policy and the governing coalition', in P. G. Cerny and M. A. Schain (eds), *French Politics and Public Policy* (London: Frances Pinter), pp. 101–24 and 159–76 respectively.

Green, Diana (1981), *Making Industrial Change?* (London: HMSO).

Ministère de l'Industrie (1980), *Pour une Industrie de Performance: éléments de politique industrielle* (Paris: La Documentation Française).

Pisani, Edgard (1979), *La France dans le conflit économique mondial* (Paris: Hachette).

Stoffaes, Christian (1978), *La Grande Menace Industrielle* (Paris: Calmann-Levy).

Stoleru, Lionel (1969), *L'Impératif industriel* (Paris: Seuil).

Zysman, J. (1977), *Political Strategies for Industrial Order: State, Market and Industry in France* (London: University of California Press).

# 6

# From Planning the French Economy to Planning the French State: The Theory and Practice of the Priority Action Programmes

*J. HAYWARD*

Twenty years ago the importance of planning as an institution and as an activity was probably overestimated. Though not quite at the summit of its prestige among decision-makers and pervasive influence upon leaders of opinion, the national plan fitted well into a period of economic revival and reinvigorated political ambition, within a context of international economic expansion and political détente. Whilst allowance must be made for the gap between a somewhat pretentious rhetoric (intended to impress and undoubtedly successful in this objective, partly because it coincided with a generally impressive economic performance) and a reality that was patchy, the claims that were made for the plan as an institution had an undoubted plausibility. The French plan won many unlikely friends at home and abroad because it appeared to combine the virtues of a heroic style of policy-making with a rationalistic analysis of the problems to be resolved. It sought to modernise a backward economy and conflict-ridden society without using coercion, by a process of consensus-building and self-confident public leadership that was breathtaking in its boldness yet prudent in measuring what it was possible to achieve in the medium term. In 1963 the government's counter-inflationary stabilisation plan (which de Gaulle boasted had been 'imposé à Giscard et outre Pompidou') marked the start of a series of reverses that undermined the credibility of the French plan both inside and outside the public decision-making process; with the May–June 1968 'events', the oil crisis of 1973 and the election to the presidency in 1974 of Giscard d'Estaing – whose personal disbelief in planning and frequent interventions in decision-making were unmistakable signals that henceforth it was enough to 'manage the unforeseeable' – representing some of the decisive steps in the degeneration of the plan's image as the prime instrument of the national strategy and the programme of action to be implemented in the public and private sectors.

Until the Mitterrand victory of 1981 the plan was widely regarded as discredited but it did not merit the depths of its recent abasement any more than, in retrospect, it merited the heights of its earlier apotheosis. Much of the difference was the result of the previous 'myth' of the plan having been dissipated, even though the reality – if only for reasons of political and administrative inertia – had not changed to anything like the same extent. The phrase that caught the imagination in the 1960s was spoken by General de Gaulle but prepared in the Planning Commissariat and amended by the then Prime Minister, Michel Debré, to be somewhat less misleading than in its original formulation. As the former Planning Commissioner, Michel Albert, has recalled, the original formula – *obligation ardente* – was reversed by the punctilious Michel Debré 'to make clear that the Plan has a political rather than a legal character'.[1] It was still widely misinterpreted and as the ardour of the successive Presidents of the Republic ebbed the planners found it increasingly difficult to secure the high-level support that is essential to impart the necessary impetus to securing the implementation of their plans. Even the sceptical Georges Pompidou and his *cabinet* kept in close touch with the Planning Commissioner and ensured that he was a former close collaborator of his – so that there was a sense that the necessary political backing could be secured for policies connected with the plan's objectives.

However, as economic policy-making was concentrated increasingly in the hands of the President and his staff, it was harder to disguise the fact that the plan was that of the government rather than of the nation, and as circumstances or the government's priorities changed, the commitments ceased to be much more than expressions of provisional intentions. So, paradoxically, increased political control was combined with decreased political commitment. The Planning Commissioner's membership of the Central Planning Council, instituted by President Giscard d'Estaing in 1974, provided regular monthly occasions for the concerns of the Planning Commissariat to be ventilated at the highest level but the Planning Commissioner tended to be informed rather than fully to share in decision-making. The *ad hoc* and short-term preoccupation of the President, his ministers and their *cabinets* meant that the planners increasingly had to concern themselves at best with piecemeal programming rather than achieving an *overall* strategy. While the day-to-day influence of members of the Planning Commissariat had not necessarily been reduced substantially in the inter-ministerial committees, the decline in the significance of the medium-term, macro-economic framework within which particular decisions had their place, meant that the plan had to adapt itself to fit the immediate requirements that it was unable to anticipate or bend to its purpose. As a result, the plan lost something of its distinctive character; like most innovations, it had adapted itself to its environment. Michel Albert claimed that the commissariat's 'mission is to organise the conditions of its own redundancy; the Plan invents and then it leaves it to others to carry out'.[2] This capacity to engage in permanent intellectual revelation and to get one's ideas accepted and acted upon by those concerned is compatible with non-vegetative survival only if the planners are able to discover new functions replacing those that have become redundant. Did the priority action programmes (PAPs) of the seventh plan (described below), the major positive innovation of the 1970s in terms of French planning methods, allow the Planning Commissariat to overcome the danger that it had all too successfully organised its own dispensability in the context of an economy at the mercy of the international market, whose rigours it had prepared French firms to face? Far from planners in France having sought to impose administrative criteria upon the market, an examination of the PAPs will show that they tried to import market criteria into the administration which is as allergic to planning and programming as the business world was to competitiveness.

The plan's enduring prestige is due to its share in the twin achievements of making the internationally competitive industrial firm the reference-point of national economic policy and taking the edge off the conflicts that this shift in public priorities was bound to provoke. The much-vaunted *concertation* practices, notably through the modernisation commissions but also in the Economic and Social Council, made it possible to test the intensity of opposition to a policy dictated not by the time-honoured preservation of a socio-political equilibrium, but by a deliberate intention to redeploy state support towards the big industrial firms.[3] The planners were not only able to warn political decision-makers of the domestic and international constraints upon their choices; they performed an invaluable role of *réducteurs d'intransigeance*, as Léo Hamon put it, helped notably by the leaders of the CFDT trade union, which in the late 1950s and early 1960s believed that planning could be made democratic both in its procedures and in its objectives. Yet, by the mid- and late 1960s, policy priorities such as full employment were being abandoned in favour of what a planner and future minister popularised as an 'industrial imperative' based above all upon competitiveness, the economic policy of the government becoming an extension of this industrial policy.[4]

The commitment to this strategy was to culminate in the late 1970s under the premiership of Raymond Barre when, with an additional stimulant of the world economic crisis, everything was done to promote the profitability of firms to whom the fate of the nation and the state was entrusted. This meant abandoning instruments of state intervention such as price control and also tolerating rates of unemployment that were previously unacceptable, temporarily cushioning the firms, the regions and the families that felt the full brunt of the shock. This would allow the country's industrial champions to take up the cudgels on a solid, self-financed foundation, albeit with financial assistance from state banks and public funds. Such a policy was not to be confused with the doctrinaire *anti-dirigisme* preached across the Channel in Britain; rather than a withdrawal of government, it involved a new approach, in which planning and the state machine generally had to be adapted to fulfil its subsidiary role in the service of industrial competitiveness. The attempt to combine an increasingly selective policy with one that sought to retain an overall consistency of public action had, furthermore, to be introduced in a situation in which it was desired to reduce the share of public expenditure within GNP, whilst expanding the share of military relative to civil expenditure. (The increase in military expenditure, for 1976–80, was three times that over the period of 1970–5, and 60 per cent greater than the increase in civil expenditure, the military share of the budget being due to rise to 19 per cent in 1980 and 20 per cent in 1982.) To overcome the inertia of institutions well experienced in the arts of self-preservation, redeployment of public expenditure provided an attractive instrument for bringing about the desired changes, particularly when the idea of extending to the state sector a theory of investment decisions inspired by the most advanced American firms seems to offer the appropriate management technique: the *rationalisation des choix budgétaires* (RCB).

## Rethinking French Planning in the Early 1970s

The medium-term programming of public expenditure became an active issue in the late 1960s and early 1970s when the desire to resist the further increases in taxation which had inspired the pioneer American PPBS ventures encountered the planners' desire to combine programming capital investment with that of current expenditure. Even before they became conscious that the era of big public investment projects was on the wane, the period between plans (which has always been the occasion for reconsideration of the methods and objectives of the plan) was put by the planners to especially intensive use in the years 1971–3. Why did this period, between the start of the sixth plan's implementation and the preparation of the seventh plan, give rise to a particularly searching rethink of the function of planning in France, including consideration of whether it should be abandoned altogether? The plan's dependence on the personal role of the Planning Commissioner had meant that the extended illness of René Montjoie, who was to be followed by a conscript, Jean Ripert, seriously weakened its standing. Many of the old ailments had become worse. Forecasting was increasingly difficult, with an increasingly unpredictable international and domestic situation. It was possible to mobilise a divided French society only to a limited extent, particularly when the planners were so closely identified with the government. The pursuit of overall consistency made innovation difficult, while the attempt simultaneously to make a large number of choices meant that they were not made in the best conditions. The credibility of the sixth plan was in question: the two major trade unions had dissociated themselves from it, the senior civil servants seemed to have less commitment to it and the government was reluctant to face the criticism that would result from openly disclosing its policy. To avoid the seventh plan being reduced to general rhetoric that would be received with increasing scepticism, it was regarded as essential for there to be a 'hard core' of precise programmes, to be fitted into a precisely specified financial framework. In the event, with the election of Giscard d'Estaing to the presidency in 1974, the planners had to consider themselves lucky to have survived the new dispensation. They were compelled to prepare their priority action programmes without benefit of the detailed overall allocation of resources between ministries and between regions, the former to be based upon medium-term plans which never saw the light of day.

However, the ministry programme budgets that formed the core of the exercise in rationalising budgetary decisions, launched by Michel Debré as Finance Minister in 1968, offered the prospect that programming might not only be linked forward to budgeting but backward to planning. Not only would it be possible to relate the programming of means to the objectives planned, but through a decentralised management by objectives and indicators of the results to be achieved, it would be possible to check intentions against performance. The fact was that this would require not merely a revolution in planning methods, but a revolution in budgetary processes and in administrative practice. In 1973 a former Budget Division official who moved to the Planning Commissariat to realise this extraordinary ambitious series of innovations declared:

all programming implies prior planning. When the Seventh Plan is prepared, which it would be judicious to base, as far as possible, upon the programming ideas advanced by the ministries that have experimented with programme budgets, it seems timely to move towards the integration of a general planning, with a five year fixed timescale in terms of objectives and impact and a set of rolling partial programmes in terms of achievements and costs. The new system will be characterised by a greater reciprocal flexibility of the present annual structure of budgetary expenditure and the structure of state objectives,[5]

the plan and the budget each influencing the other.

The head of the Finance Ministry's RCB *mission* recognised that if these ambitious objectives were to be attained, it would be necessary to overcome the semi-feudal compartmentalisation within and between ministries and that existing methods of co-ordination were inadequate. Reliance upon inter-ministerial committees and working parties meant that 'the communication of data is conceded only late, incompletely and with reticence, the discussion becomes conflict even before it has been fully informed and an arbitrated compromise based upon pleadings replaces the desirable synthesis, whose constituent elements have not been brought together by a common search for alternative solutions'.[6] Furthermore, another prerequisite of successful programme budgeting was de-concentrated decision-making:

> Attempts at deconcentration have not hitherto succeeded owing from the start to the lack of an adequate system of information of those to whom powers are delegated. They are ill-informed about the objectives pursued; they do not receive the information that is indispensable if they are to carry out public action; lastly, they have no latitude to adapt the means and their use to the specific requirements of their field of responsibility.[7]

The rigidity of public expenditure was due to the related fact that:

> little is known, if anything at all, about the use made of administrative resources; the product of administrative activity remains undefined, *a fortiori* not measured, and the relationship between this product and the objective to which it corresponds is all the less clear because the objective itself, the practical result to be achieved, has often never been clearly settled or communicated to an administrative authority, which would be accountable for it.[8]

Now although most ministries produce three-year programme budgets, they are usually mere projections that have contributed to the ministry's internal budgetary discussion but are used neither for its discussions with the Budget Ministry nor for measuring the efficiency of management within the ministry.

While the development of programme budgeting seems to have led to some improvement in intra-ministry collaboration, the attempt to substitute rational allocation for political bargaining quickly ran into difficulties, especially because 'it is not so much the objectives of ministerial programmes which tend to be contentious, as the *priorities* attached to the respective programmes ... in terms of funding'.[9] The seventh plan priority action programmes which sought to grasp this nettle had been preceded by sixth plan innovations that did not attract much attention. First, 20 per cent of the public-investment projects were declared to have priority over the others in that the funds allocated to them would be guaranteed unless the plan was formally revised. Secondly, six 'finalised programmes' were selected, involving only 3 per cent of public-investment funds, to undertake a more ambitious RCB-like operation. Precise objectives were to be fixed, with indicators so that results could be accurately monitored. Not only would the funding cover both capital and current costs, but these programmes would be necessary to attain their targets. Two of these six experimental programmes – those concerning helping old people to remain in their own homes and road safety – were to reappear among the seventh plan PAPs.

The problems of implementation encountered in the sixth plan and the consequent loss of credibility in medium-term public investment planning, led the team which was rethinking the strategy for the seventh plan to the conclusion that it was vital to secure stronger links both with the budget and the spending ministries, backed up by the top-level political support necessary to overcome the traditional administrative reluctance to engage in medium-term planning. The political commitment accorded to anti-inflationary balanced budgets and the avoidance of increases in taxation and social security contributions, coupled with the increasing cost of social and economic transfer payments and of the civil service which (along with military expenditure) were not programmed by the plan, 'led almost inevitably to the abandonment of the other objectives' notably the planned public investment programmes. As the former Head of the Commissariat's Economic Service put it:

experience has shown that the plan's participation in the annual budgetary discussions is not sufficient to change the direction of the decisions made year by year ... The lack of a real medium-term programming in more spending ministries, the inadequate integration of the plan's programmes with the plans prepared by the ministries, can lead in the course of the plan's implementation to budgetary decisions that are contrary to the plan's guidelines or priorities. In the annual budgetary negotiations with the Ministry of Finance, the ministries may propose, often rightly, an allocation of funds favouring current as against capital expenditure, leading to the non-implementation of the plan's programmes which are confined to investment projects. Similarly, the low rate of implementation of some of the plan's priorities shows that even within capital expenditure, the *de facto* choices of the ministries at the centre or in the regions do not conform to the plan's guidelines.[10]

As we shall see, the PAPs were – following the sixth plan *programmes finalisés* – to try to ensure that current and capital expenditures were treated as complementary parts of a single project.

However, the other main weakness was that despite the finance–plan collaboration developed in connection with the preparatory stage of the sixth plan, the budget officials (in the pre-Barre era) could not rely upon the ministers to hold the anti-inflationary line and as a result regarded 'commitments entered into in the planning context as being excessively ambitious. It is as though, when the Plan is prepared, the planners, relying upon the spending ministries and the concertation bodies, forced the hand of the Finance Ministry so that subsequently, when the Plan is implemented, the budgetary authorities reduce the effective commitments to the level that they consider ... to be more realistic'.[11] Such realism implied that medium-term planning of public finance should include programmed decreases as well as increases in public expenditure, an attitude that – whatever its logic – was bound not to commend itself to the spending ministries. Yet in hard financial times an insistence upon redeployment rather than simply increasing public expenditure was inevitable and became the price of protecting medium-term priority projects from being abandoned *en cours de route*, under short-term pressures.

Whilst an emphasis on the consensus-building role of the modernisation commissions had always been accorded a disproportionately large place relative to their importance in decision-making, in the new arrangements envisaged for the seventh plan their role was to be scaled down dramatically, especially in the second, programming phase of the process. The commissions would continue to be consulted during the first, guidelines phase of the planning process, when the secretive ministries could be induced to disgorge some information; but once the government had made its major policy choices, the detailed programming would be left to the ministries and agreed with the budget. The major shift in the subject-matter of the planning process away from planning the whole economy towards programming part of public expenditure was thus accompanied by a shift away from the emphasis upon the 'social partners' – always prone to make excessive demands – towards an increased stress on the public administrators with no mean appetites of their own. In turn, this presupposed that the ministries would be willing to engage in an exhaustive medium-term programming of their activities of an entirely novel kind and the PAPs were to be the instrument of bringing this major change about.

## The PAPs: Vicissitudes of Conception and Application

In the anti-planning climate of 1974–5 it was possible only to put into operation part of the strategy worked out within the Planning Commissariat in 1973. It was not possible either to get the ministries to engage seriously in detailed medium-term planning or to fit their plans into an overall rolling public expenditure plan. However, on 30 June 1975, Prime Minister Chirac asked each minister, working on the assumption of a standstill total budget, to send to the Planning Commissioner by 1 October 1975 a ten-page document setting out the 'main guidelines of the action of your ministry for the period of the Seventh Plan ... indicating the strategic direction of your action and what modifications you propose to make to it in the light of the priority objectives and the preliminary guidelines of the Plan'. Given the fact that this exercise had to be performed in the 'deadest' three months of the year, it is even less surprising that the results were more a testimony to the rhetorical skills of the authors than anything like the serious medium-term planning effort which it had been hoped to promote. However, doubtless in the belief that precise proposals would yield increased allocations, the ministries came up with numerous schemes. In addition, because it was hoped to overcome the irrational effects of compartmentalised administrative responsibilities, twenty-eight inter-ministerial study groups were established to report by the beginning of October 1975 on themes inspired by the seventh plan guidelines that the Planning Commissariat believed might suggest appropriate PAPs. In the event, these groups came up with relatively few practical suggestions. Most of the PAPs were inspired by proposals from the ministries, a fact that was to make it subsequently even more difficult to promote the inter-ministerial collaboration that was an important objective of the whole exercise. Lastly, the regional dimension – which was to be covered by the PAPIRs, the PAPs that were to be based upon *initiative régionale* (*et locale*) but which for reasons of space are not discussed here – was included in the form of information from the regional prefects about the policy preferences of their areas. These naturally varied but indicated a general priority for health and transport, with environment somewhat behind and education bringing up the rear.

The criteria which the planners had in mind, with a view to selecting from among the 132 programmes proposed, involving a cost of 432 billion francs (of which 262 billion francs would not involve either new or redeployed funds) were subject to two overriding considerations. It was, first, felt desirable to have rather more than the six 'finalised programmes' of the sixth plan to ensure a sufficient coverage and impact, yet not so many that the whole exercise would become fragmented into a multitude of mini-programmes. Furthermore, the amount of money that could be devoted to the PAPs – after prolonged and heated bargaining with the budget – was agreed to be about 200 billion francs (of which nearly half would go to one super-priority directly attributable to the presidential decision, the development of the telephone system). Within these constraints, it was felt that politically, the PAPs needed to be related to both the government's objectives and the plan's options, as well as being capable of mobilising public support. (Apparently the reinforcement of the 'struggle against tax fraud' proposal was ruled out on this latter ground.) Administratively it was hoped that the PAPs chosen would promote inter-ministerial co-ordination. Procedurally a RCB-style linkage between clearly specified objectives, the means to achieve them and the capacity to monitor the physical as well as the financial results of the actions undertaken was rather optimistically required, necessitating formulating operational indicators for each action contemplated. Financially the programmes were not normally intended to last beyond the life of the plan, thereby overcoming the built-in tendency of public expenditure to accretion by inertia, and were to fulfil a pump-priming role for innovative programmes. Lastly, the hope was that despite the exclusively administrative character of the PAPs' preparation, the programmes would be accepted by the non-administrative 'partners' in public action, notably the local authorities and social security organisations, with whom it might be possible to enter into contracts.

Some ministries, instead of selecting priorities from among their activities, tried to cover all aspects of their work. This was often due to the fact that in terms of intra-administrative politics it was 'not possible' for the minister or his *cabinet* to choose between the proposals of the various *directions*. This meant, in addition to their inadequacy as a basis for medium-term planning of public expenditure, that there were too many proposals most of which were only remotely related to the seventh plan's preliminary guidelines. For these reasons, and because the financial implications exceeded by far the amount of money set aside to cover the PAPs, the Planning Commissariat excluded or conflated many of these proposals to about a quarter of the initial number. Small working parties of from three to seven officials from the various ministries concerned (but always including representatives of the plan and the budget) then worked out the details. The selection was hammered out by inter-ministerial meetings at the Hôtel Matignon chaired by a member of the *cabinet* of the Prime Minister, composed of other members of the Prime Minister's *cabinet*, the Director of the Budget and his staff, the Planning Commissioner and his staff and a member of the *cabinet* of the President of the Republic and of the Finance Minister.

The budget representatives made no secret of their scepticism about the whole exercise. They were prepared to take on board questionable proposals such as the Rhine–Rhône waterway (which was inserted at the express request of the President of the Republic, following a personal commitment he had given to the Conférence Inter-régionale pour la Liaison Rhin–Rhône at Dijon on 24 November 1975) despite the fact that it was not supported as a priority either by the ministries of Infrastructure or of Transport and that the plan was unenthusiastic to put it mildly.[12] They argued that most of the proposed PAPs should simply be abandoned as threatening insoluble financial problems and that as a matter of 'realism' they should concentrate on a very few genuine priorities, such as the EDF electro-nuclear programme. However, this onslaught was beaten back by the Planning Commissioner, who argued that the number, content and cost of the PAPs was for the government rather than the Finance Ministry to decide. As for the electro-nuclear programme, the Minister of Industry did not want it included among the PAPs as this would involve entering into public commitments farther ahead than the government was politically prepared to go on this sensitive issue at the time. Having failed to avoid what was seen as an attempt to allow the spending ministries to have guarantees for their non-priority projects – their real priorities being financed anyway – the budget officials refused to regard the PAPs as anything more than empty financial *enveloppes* that could be filled from year to year as circumstances permitted. This was why the budget (successfully) resisted the idea that there should be a commitment to a precise timetable of the sums to be spent in each of the five years. The prime concern was to avoid building medium-term constraints into the budget procedure that would hamper the flexibility needed to deal with short-term problems and changing priorities.

The initial enthusiasm of the spending ministries for the PAPs waned once they realised that if the new procedures worked as was intended, they would have to redeploy their existing funds – admittedly easier over five years than annually – rather than obtain additional resources and would be more rigorously accountable than they had been previously. Unlike the blank cheques for public investment of the past, the PAPs might allow the plan and budget to check for the first time on the efficiency with which the ministries utilised their existing resources. It was particularly the ministries such as Health, that had weak bargaining power in the traditional budgetary process, which threw themselves most wholeheartedly into the PAP innovation. When it became clear that the Ministry of Health would receive little extra money (for instance, by redeployment from other ministries) and was expected to redeploy within its own exiguous existing funds, it felt that it had been misled. The process of redeployment became especially difficult for a ministry when a large part of its estimates were covered by PAPs, as was the case with Health and another small ministry, that of Trade and Craft Industries.

Even in large ministries the same problem could occur in particular divisions when most of the money went to those activities concerned by a PAP. In the Roads Division of the Ministry of Infrastructure, this led to a massive *de facto* redeployment away from the Paris region. However, whilst most ministries managed to take the RCB sting out of the PAPs and submerge their operation in the bureaucratic inertia of routine administration, departments such as the Ministry of Justice, which had hitherto escaped the potentially revivifying effects of involvement in planning, were affected for the first time.

A major failure of the partial programming innovation was in the practical arrangements for ensuring a proper implementation of the PAPs. This was to be done first by preparing confidential *dossiers administratifs*, only extracts of which were published in the second part of the text of the seventh plan, where the objectives, content, organisation and finance of each PAP were succinctly set out. Partly because of the speed at which the work was done – even though many of them were not completed until well into July 1977 – but mainly because they had no official status, they failed to provide the intended basis for interministerial collaboration and joint action. The programme indicators[13] were usually inadequate or over-ambitious, with the result that it became impossible to check up on their implementation when annual reports were prepared for publication each year in the *Rapport d'Exécution* appended to the Finance Act. The lack of a formally signed agreement, which meant that it was not always possible to know which document was the final version, enabled the Budget Division to refuse to be bound by it, though it was unofficially used. Somewhat more surprising is that the other ministries did not consider themselves bound either, so that little procedural pressure was exerted to break down the barriers of mutual suspicion between them.

Predictably, in the absence of pressure to co-ordinate, customary departmentalism quickly reasserted itself. Each PAP had a designated ministry as programme leader (*chef de file*), the minister selecting – after consulting the other ministries concerned – a project leader (*chef de projet*) who was responsible for supervising the programme's implementation and calling regular meetings of a co-ordination group. Because of the heterogeneous character of some of the PAPs and the reluctance of ministries to concede the leadership in any matter in which they were involved to another ministry, what happened in practice was that each ministry managed its own piece of the PAP, thereby circumventing entirely a major purpose of the whole venture: co-ordinated implementation. The ministry formally in charge naturally tended to favour those actions that were its own primary responsibility. More serious, ministries appear often to have had only a single copy of the *dossier administratif* and to have taken no steps to ensure that its contents were communicated at all relevant administrative levels through a circular or by meetings of the officials concerned. Implementation went best when for all practical purposes one bureau in a single ministry was responsible. The hope that it would be possible to start by rationalising a small part of a ministry's activities and that its effects would spread – part of the logic of partial planning – turned out in practice to be much too optimistic. Frequent changes of minister (four at the Ministry of Labour during the seventh plan) or of project leader did not help. Co-ordination groups often either did not meet at all or were attended by junior officials without the authority to give joint action the necessary impetus. Ministries sometimes would have been prepared for Planning Commissariat officials to play the co-ordinating role but they were reluctant to take on this task, which would have probably been beyond the capacity of a very small staff that was not intended to involve itself in detailed management and lacked the authority to impose co-ordination on unwilling partners. Ministries were also reluctant to enter into formal contracts with non-administrative bodies and even when arrangements existed for an annual conference of all those concerned with carrying out a PAP, as was the case with the one concerning 'helping old people to remain in their own homes', it never met.

If the attempt to use the PAPs to teach the ministries new administrative tricks and to modify their traditional behaviour would seem to have made little headway, did they work better in terms of guaranteeing the priority in budgetary terms of certain programmes as reflected in the extent to which they were financially and physically implemented? The bare figures suggest quite a good overall performance, reflected in an implementation rate of 93·5 per cent, with the telephone maxi-PAP's 92 per cent concealing the welcome fact that it proved possible to meet the physical targets at lower cost.[14] However the 95·1 per cent implementation rate for the other twenty-four PAPs covered very variable results, with the general rule being that those of an economic character were better implemented than those that did not directly serve the dominant industrial strategy. Some of the figures were also very misleading. The 78 per cent implementation rate for the Rhine–Rhône PAP did not take into account the fact that the target had been halved by the mid-term adaptation of the seventh plan, so that the real implementation rate was more like 39 per cent! The 88·5 per cent implementation rate for the Manpower Agency (Agence Nationale pour l'Emploi) PAP looked good in quantitative terms but, in fact, many of the new posts were given to unemployed managerial staff under the government's *pactes pour l'Emploi*. This recruitment was not calculated to improve the quality of the staff, which was one of the PAPs' objectives in an attempt to make the agency a more attractive and effective unemployment service at a time of increasing unemployment. After two years, in which the PAPs explicitly received priority in the Finance Acts of 1977 and 1978, they had to take their chance in the annual budgetary meetings. The planners had envisaged that the PAPs would be dealt with preferentially at the start of the budgetary process, following a go-ahead from the Central Planning Council ensuring that they would not compete directly with other expenditures, but this guarantee did not survive the harsher situation once Prime Minister Barre's more stringent policy prevailed.

## Planning and Political Decision-making

What captured the imagination of so many people, beyond as well as within her borders, about French planning was not so much the rationality of its techniques as the sweep and boldness of its ambitions and achievements. So that when, during the Giscard d'Estaing presidency, there was a retreat from this 'heroic' conception of national economic and social planning, the somewhat mythical primacy of the plan was questioned. Perhaps, after all, the emperor had no clothes! Although it might be demonstrated that 'The vast exercise of putting more than a hundred of the most promising *variantes* through the (Dynamic Multisectoral) DMS model [involved] one of the most ambitious exercises in measuring the trade-off between vastly complicated policy options which has ever been undertaken',[15] still there was a disheartening disproportion between technical skills and the political will to use them. It was all too evident in the eighth plan that these increasingly refined techniques were used too little and too late, being at the service of what appeared to be an accommodating defeatism that deferred to external market constraints in the name of classical economic orthodoxy. Gone was the indomitable and tenacious political will that united Jean Monnet (the first planning commissioner) and de Gaulle in their view that rebuilding national power and influence were the prime objective; a view that Pierre Massé (an influential ex-planning commissioner) still shares, when he argues that a strong and *solidaire* France is essential, even if isolated salvation is no longer possible.[16] The protagonists of a plan based upon a calculated assertion of political will, whether from the political Right such as Michel Debré or Jacques Chirac or from the left-wing as embodied in the varied views of the leaders of the Socialist and Communist parties, were out of power and appeared destined to stay there indefinitely.

Jacques Delors, former head of Social Affairs at the Planning Commissariat (CGP) who in 1981 became Minister of Finance in the Mauroy government, has argued that from the start 'The Plan existed alongside but parallel to the state' and had problems in achieving consistency with day-to-day government decision-making, notably budgetary decisions.[17] Whilst decisions had always largely been taken outside the planning process, the more recent tendency had been for ministers, senior civil servants and the heads of major economic firms to free themselves from such constraints upon their freedom of action as planning might impose. In the case of the preparation of the eighth plan, the proximity in time of the launching of the plan and the start of the presidential election campaign, made all concerned especially sensitive to the fact that controversial issues like increasing unemployment and remedies such as increasing public investment or reducing working hours, might be embarrassingly spotlighted. Yet, at the same time, the President and Prime Minister wished to utilise the fund of public goodwill still attaching to the Planning Commissariat as an institution, owing to its past reputation for relative autonomy from the government, to provide a spurious appearance of consensus about its policies. This kind of 'virtue by association' meant that although 'the work undertaken by the *Commissariat au Plan* has been relegated to secondary status by decisions taken in the Central Planning Council . . . by talking of the plan without actually planning, one can attach the reputation and authority of the plan to whatever particular initiative has been decided on by the government'.[18]

The extent to which the politicisation of planning involved the direct intervention of the Prime Minister and his personal staff in the text of the plan became clear in the final report of the eighth plan, while the refusal to debate it before the 1981 presidential election underlined the explosiveness of the issues that were to be postponed until after the decisive moment of political choice. It transpired in extracts from a confidential letter on 14

August 1980 from the Planning Commissioner to the Prime Minister, that he considered it unusual and undesirable that the 'text of the plan should be used by the Government to award itself congratulations on its performance and that this innovation is in danger of being criticised because of the political timetable'.[19] This letter also frankly admitted that the draft plan 'attempted to elude' the problem of increasing unemployment and 'presented as a risk what is a certainty', as well as declaring that the increased public investment proposed in the plan was not consistent with the 1981 budget decisions.

Such an open disclosure of the extent to which national planning strategy was being subordinated to the government and the President of the Republic's tactical convenience was crowned by the postponement of the parliamentary debate on the eighth plan until after the presidential election. This was because Chirac's Gaullist party was highly critical of the eighth plan's priorities and threatened to vote against them if they came to a vote. Also it would not have been helpful to a Giscard d'Estaing candidacy to focus attention upon the medium-term sacrifice of unemployment to the defence of the currency and the balance of payments. An occasion on which the plan might, owing to the coincidence of timing, have become the centrepiece of a presidential election campaign, in the way envisaged by Pierre Mendès-France in *A Modern French Republic*, was deliberately evaded, incidentally stressing Giscard d'Estaing's unwillingness to subordinate political improvisation to the constraints of planning. So the eighth plan, whilst including twelve PAPs[20] – without any precise financial commitments and shorn of the ambitious objectives that had marked their seventh plan predecessors – in practice concentrated upon the development of France's much-envied electro-nuclear programme and the need to increase the country's birth rate. After all, Giscard d'Estaing having been criticised for stating that France would soon account for only 1 per cent of the world population, it became a great national priority to exhort the people to procreate and stem if not reverse the demographic tide that threatened to submerge France.

## The Implications of the 1981 Socialist Victory

Whilst the defeat of Giscard d'Estaing at the presidential election was to have as one of its byproducts the advance of economic planning, if not to the centre at least to the spotlighted forefront of the stage, its immediate effect was to paralyse the eighth plan: 1981 became a hiatus in the planning process because it took Michel Rocard, the new Minister for National and Regional Planning, several months to prepare a two-year interim plan to cover 1982–3. This transitional arrangement was intended to serve the twofold function of getting France back on to the path of pre-recession economic growth and fuller employment, as well as to enable a drastic change in planning methods to be adopted for the return to medium-term planning covering 1984-8, the last five years of President Mitterrand's term of office. The spirit in which planning was to be operated under a Socialist government was reflected in the appointment as Planning Commissioner of Hubert Prevot, initially *chargé de mission* to Rocard, who - after serving in 1961-74 in the Finance Ministry's Forecasting Division - had been seconded to the trade union CFDT as a confederal secretary during 1974-81. Furthermore, this appointment was quickly followed by the return of a distinguished planner from the 1963-73 era, Yves Ullmo, as deputy planning commissioner. However, this should not be taken to mean that the intention was to recapture the glamour of early 1960s planning because, as part of the strong commitment to de-centralisation reflected in the Defferre local and regional reforms, it is proposed to give priority to regional planning from below. Although it is too early to say how this ambitious objective will be implemented, it is worth examining the only experience we have to go on, the seventh plan's instructive PAPIR experiment to which we have alluded already.[21]

As the national PAPs did not necessarily correspond to subnational priorities, it was suggested that towns, *départements*, or regions should initiate PAPIRs, for which they might receive state financial support provided they were prepared to contribute towards the cost themselves. In this way it would be more likely that the real needs of local communities would be met and the programmes rationally administered in a de-concentrated or even de-centralised way. The sixth plan experience had all too often taken the following form:

the mayors and other elected representatives found themselves bound hand and foot in the so-called debate on the plan which was often reduced for them to this: they are summoned (by the Prefect) to a meeting (chaired by the Prefect) where a *dossier* is distributed (prepared by state officials) whose content is known to them (because the Prefect has spoken to them about it) and the Prefect requests their agreement.[22]

Local authorities should be persuaded to prepare their own medium-term 'action programmes' which should be the basis for pluriannual contracts between the government and towns, *départements*, or regions. This was the view of the plan's *Service Régional et Urbain*, and the Ministry of Infrastructure's Service des Affaires Economiques et Internationales, the latter hoping that this de-centralist approach would give a new impetus to urban planning.

Like the inspiration behind the PAPs, it was hoped to introduce by procedural reform local action programmes that would have three defining characteristics. They would be problems selected as crucial by a political authority (a local or regional council) committed to carrying out the programme through successive budgets. They would cover both capital and current expenditure and have a precise timetable. They should include agreements with both state and non-state actors (for instance, chambers of commerce, voluntary associations, and so on) in the spirit of the 'plan contracts' launched by the 23 December 1970 decree on urban communities.[23] This project – wryly described by its authors as the 'histoire d'une circulaire non signée' – nevertheless influenced the PAPIR venture, although there was a political fear that a general invitation to local authorities to make programme proposals would arouse unsatiable expectations and unleash a rash of embarrassing *cahiers de doléances*. It was felt to be safer to entrust the operation to the regional prefects, who chose their own ways of consulting local and regional *notables* and selecting programmes to propose, characteristically tending to ensure that there was something for everyone. The plan's Regional and Urban Service then discussed the proposals with each ministry in turn. This approach favoured mono-ministerial and sectoral rather than spatial projects. The Ministry of Agriculture was the most popular and so were other territorial ministries such as Infrastructure and Education, but not Industry which lacked their well-developed field services. However, these ministries were facing a financial squeeze and were unwilling to devote money from redeployed budgets to PAPIRs in addition to the PAPs.[24] The PAPIRs were able to play a part in the region's economic strategy where it existed (notably in Nord, Alsace, Aquitaine and Pays de la Loire). They sometimes took the form of co-ordinated operations, associating *départements* within a region or collaboration between regions. Lastly, they promoted planning and a willingness to enter into contracts for the joint financing of medium-term programmes with the central government.

Clearly, the replanning of the French state which is being undertaken by the Mauroy government, with its promotion of the role of the representative President of the elected regional council and the demotion of the regional prefect, will potentially produce a very much more drastic redeployment of resources than the techno-bureaucratic experiments of the Giscardian era. However, despite his 1960s reputation for seeking to 'decolonise the provinces', Rocard is committed to using the planning process to integrate rather than disintegrate France, a point repeatedly stressed by Defferre when explaining that greater de-centralisation would be within the limits fixed by the plan. Clearly, it is intended to reverse the long retreat from national and regional planning. The relentless pressure of economic circumstances, that played so large a part in the defeat of Giscard d'Estaing, will nevertheless have to be successfully resisted if this change is actually to materialise. Given that a traditional problem has been to secure collaboration between budgeting and planning, it might be considered an astute move by President Mitterrand to have appointed a former planner as Minister of Finance (Delors) and a former Finance official as Minister of Planning (Rocard).

## Notes: Chapter 6

An earlier version of this paper was presented to the Fiftieth Congress of the International Institute of Administrative Sciences, Madrid, July 1980.

1  Unpublished lecture by Michael Albert on 'La Planification française', delivered at the Institut d'Etudes Politiques de Paris, 8 November 1979.
2  ibid.
3  See the extended extract from the May 1975 speech by the Minister of Industry, Michel d'Ornano, opening the colloquium on 'Le Redéploiment industriel', in *Les Cahiers français*, special issue on the seventh plan, no. 182, supplement, July–September 1977, p. 19; and cf. *Etudes de politique industrielle*, no. 6, 1975 (La Documentation Française).
4  Lionel Stoleru, *L'Impératif industriel* (Paris: Editions du Seuil, 1969). The key document is the Montjoie Report on *Le Développement industriel*, April 1968 (La Documentation française). More generally, see Liliane Sardais, 'La Planification industrielle', in *Les Cahiers français*, op. cit., supplement 4–5, and especially by the same author, 'L'Etat et l'internationalisation du capital. Un essai sur la politique industrielle en France', doctoral thesis, Université de Paris X (Nanterre), 1977. See also the discussion of French industrial policy by Jean-Jacques Bonnaud in Jack Hayward and Michel Watson (eds), *Planning, Politics and Public Policy* (Cambridge: Cambridge University Press, 1975), ch. 4. The quotation from Hamon is in 'Le Plan et sa signification politique', Jean-Daniel Reynaud (ed.), *Tendances et volontés de la société française* (Paris: Futuribles, 1965), pp. 210, 212.
5  Jacques Bravo in Philippe Huet and J. Bravo, *L'Expérience française de rationalisation des choix budgétaires* (Paris: PUF, 1973), p. 151. On RCB and the seventh plan, see Jean Carassus, 'The Budget and the Plan in France', in Jack Hayward and Olga Narkiewicz (eds), *Planning in Europe* (London: Croom Helm, 1978), ch. 2.
6  Philippe Huet, in Huet and Bravo, op. cit., p. 16; cf. 12–14.
7  ibid., p. 10.
8  ibid., p. 22
9  Diana Green, 'The Budget and the Plan', in Philip G. Cerny and Martin A. Schain (eds), *French Politics and Public Policy* (London: Francis Pinter, 1980), p. 110; cf. 105 ff. On the unsuccessful application of programme budgeting to achieve improved planning and co-ordinating within the Ministry of Education, see M. Praderie, in Huet and Bravo, op. cit., ch. 2; and Jack Hayward, *The One and Indivisible French Republic* (London: Weidenfeld & Nicolson, 1973), pp. 201–3.
10  Gabriel Mignot, Lectures at the Institut d'Etudes Politiques de Paris on 'La Planification française', 1976–7, mimeo., p. 180.
11  ibid., p. 182.
12  On this whole complex issue, see *Un Dossier: la liaison Rhin-Rhône*, Notes et Etudes Documentaires, No. 4547–8, Paris, 28 December 1979.
13  On this rather technical subject, see the very clear exposition by Jacques Bravo and Bernard Walliser, 'Les systèmes d'indicateurs de programmes', *Statistiques et etudes financières*, 1975–9, esp. pp. 12–17.
14  *Rapport d'exécution du VIIè Plan*, Annexe au Projet de Loi de Finances pour 1980 (Paris: Imprimerie Nationale, 1979), pp. 33–5.
15  Sir Andrew Shonfield, 'The VIIIth Plan: assumptions and constraints', *Revue economique*, no. 5, September 1980, p. 830. On the DMS model and its use for exploring alternatives, see two other articles in this special issue on the eighth plan, p. 894 ff. On the context in which the eighth plan was prepared, see Jack Hayward, 'France: the strategic management of impending collective impoverishment', in Andrew Cox (ed.), *Politics, Policy and the European Recession* (London: Macmillan, 1982).
16  Pierre Massé, 'Repenser le Plan', in ibid., p. 818; and cf. Jean Monnet, *Mémoires* (Paris: Fayard, 1976), p. 270.

17  Jacques Delors, 'The decline of French planning', in Stuart Holland (ed.), *Beyond Capitalist Planning* (Oxford: Basil Blackwell, 1978), p. 10. See also Jean Boissonnat, 'Le Budget contre le Plan', *L'Expansion*, 5 September 1980, pp. 60–6.
18  Delors, op. cit., p. 26.
19  This letter was leaked to *Le Canard enchaîné* and partially published in its issue of 10 September 1980, p. 3; cf. ibid., 17 September 1980, p. 2.
20  *8è Plan de développement économique et social, 1981–1985* (Paris: La Documentation française, 1980), pt III, pp. 217–49.
21  For a fuller discussion, see Jack Hayward, 'Incorporer la périphérie: l'essor et la chute de la régionalisation fonctionelle en France', *Pouvoirs*, November 1981, pp. 103–18.
22  Quoted in Jacques Chobaux and Jean Grammont, *Réflexions sur les conditions d'une programmation locale*, Ministry of Equipment, SAEI, August 1974, p. 19.
23  ibid., p. 61, and cf. p. 51.
24  For the rate of implementation of the PAPIRs by ministry, see *Rapport d'Exécution du VIIIè Plan*, 1979, op. cit., p. 128. See also Charles Vigouroux, 'Quelques éléments pour un bilan des établissements publics régionaux', Commissariat Général du Plan, Service Régional et Urbain, November 1979, mimeo., pp. 39–42.

## Bibliographical Note

On the situation of French planning at the start of the Giscardian presidency, see Jack Hayward and Michael Watson (eds), *Planning, Politics and Public Policy. The British, French and Italian Experience* (Cambridge: Cambridge University Press, 1975). More recent discussions are available in Bernard Brunhes, 'Preparing a national plan. Thirty years of French experience', *Futures*, June 1977, pp. 175–81, and the special issue of *Revue Economique*, 'Le VIIIè Plan', no. 5, September 1980. For critical reviews of French experience, see Diana Green on 'The Budget and the Plan' and 'Economic policy and the governing coalition', in Philip G. Cerny and Martin A. Schain (eds), *French Politics and Public Policy* (London: Methuen, 1980), chs 5 and 8; as well as Jack Hayward, 'France: the strategic management of impending collective impoverishment', in Andrew Cox (ed.), *Politics, Policy and the European Recession* (London: Macmillan, 1982). For a revealing case study, see N. J. D. Lucax, *Energy in France. Planning, Politics and Policy* (London: Europa Publications, 1979), esp. ch. 5.

# 7

# The Presidency and the Media, 1974-82

*R. KUHN*

## Introduction

Virtually the final political act of Valéry Giscard d'Estaing as President of the Republic in 1981 was a television broadcast in which the defeated President gave the nation his valedictory address. At the end of this broadcast, in a Gaullian attempt to highlight the political vacuum which France was now supposedly entering, the television camera zoomed in on the empty chair vacated by the outgoing Head of State. The king was indeed dead and his political demise was played out as a media event for all to see.

It was appropriate that the broadcasting media, which Giscard d'Estaing had used so skilfully in his successful 1974 election campaign, should provide the stage for his departure from office in 1981. During the period of his presidency Giscard d'Estaing had frequently appeared on radio and television to explain his policies, defend his government, sketch out his vision of France in the third millenium and publicise his own literary contribution to political debate, *Démocratie française*.[1] Changes in the content of presidential decision-making in a variety of policy areas were reflected in a marked alteration in broadcasting style, with the casual fireside chats of the early reformist months giving way to a more regal posture towards the end of the *septennat*. Moreover, the structural relationship between the Giscardian regime and the broadcasting media had itself been an important feature of Giscard d'Estaing's presidency. Alleged governmental control of the broadcasting services was a constant source of political controversy throughout Giscard d'Estaing's term of office, not least during the 1981 presidential election campaign.

Yet at the start of his presidency Giscard d'Estaing had pledged to remove broadcasting as an issue of contention in French politics. One of his first acts had been a reform of the state broadcasting services, which under his Gaullist predecessors had been the object of close governmental control. Thus, Giscard d'Estaing's avowed aim to make radio and television independent of the government emphasised broadcasting as a key area in which the new President's espousal of gradualist change and his aspirations to create an advanced, liberal society in France could be usefully evaluated. Seven years later it was the turn of the successful Socialist challenger for the presidency, François Mitterrand, to condemn the control of the Giscardian authorities over the state broadcasting media and the resultant inequalities in political coverage. Ironically, one of the first pledges of the new Socialist President was a reform of state broadcasting. The wheel had apparently come full circle.

This chapter is concerned with an examination of the relationship between the government and the broadcasting media during Giscard d'Estaing's presidency. In particular, it will concentrate on the extent to which the public service norms laid down in the 1974 reform statute were respected in practice. More generally, broadcasting will be used as a case study to exemplify certain institutional and political developments which took place during Giscard d'Estaing's presidential term. In the concluding section the changes already made by Giscard d'Estaing's successor in this controversial field and the reforms the new Socialist administration has proposed to introduce will be briefly analysed.

## The 1974 Reform

The reorganisation of state broadcasting was the first major substantive reform to be introduced by Giscard d'Estaing after his success in the 1974 presidential elections. The recent history of scandals at the Office de Radiodiffusion Télévision Française (ORTF), a succession of critical parliamentary reports, the Office's reputation for mismanagement, its allegedly strike-prone trade unions and a financial loss in 1973, all made the ORTF a suitable case for treatment at the start of the new presidency.[2] More importantly, a reform of broadcasting neatly fitted in with Giscard d'Estaing's electoral campaign in favour of change. In fulfilment of his electoral pledge the President wanted to settle the broadcasting problem with an impressive flourish so that the new companies could be in operation by the start of 1975.

The break-up of the ORTF, an institution which represented one of the more unattractive faces of Gaullism, was one of a series of measures designed to aid the consolidation of the new Giscardian regime and distinguish it from its predecessor. Whilst some of these innovations, including changes in protocol at the official inauguration ceremony, were superficial gimmicks, others were of more substance. Giscard d'Estaing's early reforms included such diverse measures as the suppression of telephone-tappings 'if they existed', the lowering of the age of majority from 21 to 18, liberalisation of the laws on contraception, and promised changes in abortion and divorce legislation. It was in the context of these 'liberal reforms' that the reorganisation of state broadcasting was placed by government spokesmen.

At the time of Giscard d'Estaing's election to the presidency there was no shortage of proposals for a reform of broadcasting. The director-general of the ORTF, Marceau Long, had already drawn up his own proposals for a functional de-centralisation of decision-making within the huge organisation. Private interests were actively campaigning for the establishment of a commercial television channel. Yet during the 1974 election campaign the broadcasting issue did not assume nearly the same degree of importance as it had done during the 1969 contest between Georges Pompidou and Alain Poher. Thus, while it was well known that the majority of the Independent Republican Party, including Giscard d'Estaing's close personal adviser, Michel Poniatowski, had previously declared its support for commercial television, Giscard d'Estaing's own views on broadcasting were by no means clear. This gave the new President wide freedom of manoeuvre, which was curtailed only by his dependence on the Gaullist party in Parliament to support his legislative proposals. With the Prime Minister, Jacques Chirac, acting as the linkman between a demoralised Gaullist party and Giscard d'Estaing, the necessary parliamentary support was soon forthcoming.

By the statute of 7 August 1974, the ORTF – a pillar of the Gaullist state – was abolished.[3] It was replaced by a new broadcasting structure made up of seven companies organisationally independent of one another: a transmission company, Télédiffusion de France (TDF), a production company, Société Française de Production (SFP), an archive and research institute, Institut National de l'Audiovisuel (INA), a national radio company (Radio France) and three television companies (TF1, Antenne 2 and FR3). FR3 was made responsible for both regional radio and television. The ORTF was thus broken up into its constituent parts with no central body to co-ordinate the running of the different companies. The monopoly was retained, but the two main national television companies, TF1 and Antenne 2, both heavily dependent on revenue from commercial advertising, were to compete with each other for viewers.[4]

Apart from the aim of making the new, slimmer companies more efficient than the highly centralised ORTF, the 1974 reorganisation was explicitly intended to sever the umbilical cord which had linked the government and the state broadcasting services during the de Gaulle and Pompidou presidencies. Thus, in a letter to the heads of the new companies in January 1975, Giscard d'Estaing declared that the government would not seek to interfere in the internal running of the companies and asked that any infringement of this principle be reported to him personally.[5] Moreover, in his best-selling, pretentious work on French democracy, published in 1976, the President defended the break-up of the ORTF as a necessary prerequisite for the establishment of pluralism in the broadcasting media.[6] Thus, the public service norms of independence and pluralism lay at the very heart of the 1974 reform. Not for the first time in the Fifth Republic a French government was apparently seeking to give the state broadcasting services a similar status to that enjoyed by the BBC in the UK.

## Broadcasting in the Giscard d'Estaing Presidency

The causes of the break-up of the ORTF and the principles underpinning the 1974 reform are clear enough. If one strips away the liberal rhetoric, however, to what extent did the relationship between the government and broadcasting during the Giscard d'Estaing presidency differ in practice from what it had been under his Gaullist predecessors? This section concentrates on three areas in particular which highlight certain similarities and differences: appointments, political coverage and the state monopoly.

### Appointments

Whilst all French governments since the Second World War have made partisan political appointments to key decision-making posts within state broadcasting, the practice has become more systematic during the Fifth Republic. For example, the longest-serving Minister of Information during de Gaulle's presidency, Alain Peyrefitte, who was responsible for drawing up the 1964 broadcasting statute, placed several members of his ministerial *cabinet* in top posts at the newly created ORTF. Several members of 'the Peyrefitte clan' held important posts in the new broadcasting companies after 1974.

By the provisions of the 1974 legislation the government's right of appointment in the broadcasting companies was quite limited. For example, with regard to the four programme companies (TF1, Antenne 2, FR3 and Radio France) the government was to appoint only the head of the company, who normally combined the functions of managing director and chairman of the board of governors. The heads of the new companies were guaranteed a minimum statutory three-year term of office. It was perhaps not surprising, though none the less disappointing given Giscard d'Estaing's electoral commitment to change, that when the first appointments were announced at the end of 1974 there was nobody who had any connections, however tenuous, with the ranks of the left-wing opposition. Moreover, three of the four heads of the new programme companies had worked in some capacity at the defunct ORTF: Jean Cazeneuve (TF1), Claude Contamine (FR3) and Jacqueline Baudrier (Radio France).

The only newcomer to broadcasting management placed at the head of a programme company was Marcel Jullian (Antenne 2). Jullian's appointment, as he himself recognised, exemplified the new President's desire for change.[7] However, after a series of disputes within the company, and in particular a succession of directors of news and news editors, confidence in Jullian's ability to manage Antenne 2 quickly evaporated. It was no surprise, therefore, when Jullian's contract was not renewed at the end of 1977. Jullian's replacement by a former civil servant, Maurice Ulrich, marked the return to prominence of high-ranking civil servants in the top broadcasting posts. Thus, whilst in 1975 only two of the seven broadcasting companies were headed by former civil servants, by the end of 1979 this total had climbed to five.

The 1974 reform, therefore, did not constitute a radical break with past experience in terms of either the professional background or political sympathies of those appointed to manage the new companies. Moreover, whilst none of the heads of the four programme companies was removed from his post in mid-term, in marked contrast with their predecessors at the ORTF, the government's power to terminate or renew their appointments represented a useful potential sanction. The example of Jullian amply demonstrated that if for some reason the performance of a company head was deemed to be unsatisfactory, he could be dismissed with a minimum of fuss *pour encourager les autres*.

Once appointed, the heads of the programme companies had in theory complete autonomy in the choice of their immediate subordinates. However, this did not prevent the government from exerting pressure where necessary to ensure the appointment of certain candidates. Once again the main target of this pressure was Jullian, who was instructed to accept Xavier Larère and Armand Jammot as his directors.[8] The managerial posts in all the new companies were overwhelmingly filled by people who had previously worked at the ORTF.

Governmental intervention to ensure the appointment of politically suitable candidates was, of course, particularly important in the field of news programming. In late 1974 the Minister of the Interior, Poniatowski, and his staff exercised a power of veto over appointments to the top news posts.[9] The use of this veto was most in evidence at Antenne 2 where various candidates for the post of news editor were rejected on what could only have been political grounds. The longest-serving director of news at Antenne 2, Jean-Pierre Elkabbach, was appointed in January 1977, just over a year before the crucial parliamentary elections of March 1978. Jullian admitted that Elkabbach had been imposed on the company from outside and, after leaving Antenne 2, was particularly scathing about the pro-Giscardian sympathies of Elkabbach.[10]

Usually, however, the company heads were more willing than Jullian either to accept ministerial suggestions regarding acceptable candidates, or, more normally, to make the appointments themselves with full knowledge gained from long professional experience of who were *persona non grata* in the eyes of the government. Generally the heads of the companies knew the rules of the game and did not attempt to infringe them.

Prior to 1976, a certain balance in the appointments process was maintained between Gaullist and Giscardian sympathisers. After the resignation of Chirac from the premiership, however, this balance tilted quite sharply in favour of those either faithful to the President or, for career reasons, at least generally uncritical of his regime, to the point where one could speak of a pattern of control via presidential appointments. Apart from the heads of the companies, persons with Giscardian or pro-regime sympathies employed in important decision-making posts in the broadcasting media or related organisations included *inter alias*: Patrice Duhamel, head of the politics desk at TF1 after autumn 1976 and promoted to the post of news editor in December 1980; Elkabbach, director of news at Antenne 2 from January 1977; Roland Faure, former head of the right-wing newspaper *l'Aurore*, director of news at Radio France from September 1979; Xavier Gouyou-Beauchamps, former head of Giscard d'Estaing's press service at the Elysée, as head of Sofirad, which controls most of the peripheral radio stations, from April 1977; Yves Cannac, formerly Giscard d'Estaing's deputy secretary-general at the Elysée, as head of the Havas advertising agency, which has a controlling interest in Radio Télévision Luxembourg (RTL) from June 1978; Michel Bassi, former head of the Giscardian propaganda organisation Association pour la démocratie, as head of Radio Monte Carlo (RMC) from November 1978; Antoine Schwartz, a former member of Raymond Barre's *cabinet*, as Bassi's deputy at RMC also from November 1978; Jean-Luc Lagardère, chairman of Matra since 1977, as director-general of Radio Europe 1 from October 1974; Etienne Mougeotte as Director of News at Radio Europe 1 from October 1974; Gérard Montassier, Giscard d'Estaing's son-in-law and unsuccessful Giscardian candidate in the 1979 cantonal elections, as head of the government's think-tank on broadcasting, the Haut Conseil de l'Audiovisuel, from October 1976; and Henri Pigeat, head of the French news agency, Agence France Presse, from October 1979.[11]

Giscard d'Estaing denied that these appointments represented a conscious political strategy on his part, arguing that they were made on the professional ground of merit alone.[12] However, his parliamentary supporters were less equivocal. Replying to criticisms made by the Gaullist members of a parliamentary committee of inquiry into the state of the mass media in France the Giscardian committee members affirmed that since the state was the sole shareholder in the national broadcasting companies and in Sofirad, it was logical that it should be the state, and therefore the government, which should have the role of appointing the management of these companies according to its own criteria.[13] This was an argument which had already been employed by Gaullist Ministers of Information in the past.[14] Documenting the Gaullist colonisation of the state broadcasting services during the first decade and a half of the Fifth Republic, the Giscardian parliamentarians continued:

> Therefore, one has to be very naïve or suffer from a curiously selective amnesia to find in the present situation a worrying innovation. For what reasons should something which was natural twenty five or ten years ago suddenly become scandalous? Other systems of appointment would undoubtedly be possible and perhaps better, in the tradition of the Anglo-saxon democracies. One must, however, understand that they have never been adopted in our country where the weight of tradition is quite different.[15]

Whilst the Giscardian committee members then sought to modify this view somewhat by stating that the authorities appointed the new sets of management 'to apply the new policy of liberalising the media', this seemed only a token acknowledgement of the changes which the 1974 reform had been supposed to introduce.

The 1974 reorganisation of state broadcasting did not, therefore, put an end to the long-established practice of partisan political appointments. On the contrary, these became an integral part of the Giscardian government's means of controlling the political output of radio and television. The frequent criticims voiced by the left-wing opposition and the Gaullists in this domain thus appeared to be fully justified, though it should not be forgotten that the Gaullists had themselves colonised the state broadcasting services during their long period in power.[16]

## Political Coverage

One of Giscard d'Estaing's avowed objectives in breaking up the ORTF was to normalise relations between the government and broadcasting by giving the broadcasters responsibility for programme content. The abolition of the Ministry of Information, the symbol of Gaullist control of the media, was intended to mark the end of government intervention in the news production process.[17] Yet whilst the Gaullist emphasis on direct ministerial control was largely abandoned after 1974, the principles regarding impartiality and balance in news output enshrined in the charters of the programme companies were by no means strictly observed in practice.[18]

Even before the new companies came into operation the government was responsible for establishing the framework within which decisions about news programming would be made, through its control of key appointments and by abusing the procedure whereby ORTF journalists were to be re-employed in the new companies.[19] After the programme companies took over from the ORTF in January 1975, other factors militated against a balanced and impartial political output. For example, within the different news departments the organisation was of a strongly hierarchical nature, with any controversial decisions being made at the top by the Director of News or news editor. The daily meeting within each news department at which the structure and content of the news bulletins was discussed did not reflect a democratic decision-making procedure, since the final decision always lay with the Director of News and his immediate subordinates. For political and/or career reasons, the holders of these key posts were unlikely to want to embarrass the President or his government. Though not all the journalists in the news departments were by any means favourable to Giscard d'Estaing or to the parties of the governing coalition, they had very limited possibilities of making their voice heard. The decision-making structure, the level of unemployment in their profession, the experience of journalists sacked or marginalised on previous occasions, most notably in 1968, and the tradition of political interference in broadcasting, all tended to reduce the likelihood of journalists contesting the decisions of their superiors within the news departments or, *a fortiori*, of opposing them successfully.

Certainly, the excesses of the Gaullist period were now out of fashion. After 1974, cases of overt ministerial censorship became the exception rather than the rule. The Ministry of Culture and Communication, established in 1978, exercised no influence on news programming. Representatives of the Socialist and Communist parties appeared frequently on television and radio. For example, Michel Rocard's standing with the electorate was measurably improved by his television appearances, while Georges Marchais became a television personality in his own right. Moreover, many journalists with Gaullist and Socialist sympathies, though few with Communist leanings, were employed in the state programme companies, some in fairly senior posts.

Other improvements were also made after 1974. A right of reply for the opposition parties was established, albeit within a very limited framework. Party political broadcasts were programmed on the basis of strict equality of time between the *majorité* and the opposition. A daily access programme, *Tribune libre*, was established on FR3, giving some opportunity to minority groups to express their point of view. Furthermore, if one excluded the coverage given the President, there was not a great disparity between the length of time allocated to government ministers and spokesmen of the *majorité* on the one hand, and that accorded representatives of the opposition on the other. In these circumstances it was understandable that many viewers considered that television news programmes after 1974 were more objective than in the years prior to the reform.

However, the political coverage of the state programme companies was neither balanced nor impartial. Nor, given the systemic links which existed between the government and the companies, could it have reasonably been expected to be so. One aspect of this imbalance was the unduly favourable coverage given to President Giscard d'Estaing. The disproportionate amount of time accorded Giscard d'Estaing could not be wholly explained by the importance of his position, nor could the generally obsequious stance adopted by journalists when questioning the President be totally attributable to the supposed reticence of all French politicans on television to indulge in spontaneous dialogue.[20] The uncritical roles performed by such leading television commentators as Patrice Duhamel (TF1), Yves Mourousi (TF1) and Elkabbach (Antenne 2) were particularly evident in televised interviews with the President.

The refusal to deal in any significant detail with controversial topics such as France's commitment to a nuclear-energy policy and the Bokassa diamonds scandal demonstrated the stifling nature of the relationship between the television news departments and the Giscardian regime, as did the tireless reiteration on television news that the quasi-totality of France's economic problems were attributable to the oil crisis. Whether this was true or not, alternative explanations, such as those put forward by the opposition, received short shrift in comparison. Moreover, a defence of Giscardian policies was proposed by several commentators as though this was in the natural order of things.

In contrast with the Gaullist period, controls were largely internalised within the programme companies, with self-censorship making censorship quasi-redundant.[21] The Directors of News and their immediate colleagues replaced the Minister of Information as the key figures in the news production process. A major part of their role was to act as dishonest brokers between the government and the news departments, turning political pressures into professional directives. The consequence of this state of affairs was the partisan political coverage, more qualitative than quantitative, which operated in favour of the President, his supporters and their policies.

This partisan coverage became more noticeable after the 1976 cantonal elections, which were disappointing for the *majorité*, and intensified after Chirac's resignation from the premiership in August of the same year.[22] In the broadcast coverage of the 1977 municipal, 1978 legislative and 1979 European elections Giscardian candidates were favourably treated, particularly in the pre-campaign period.[23] Whilst the result of the 1981 presidential contest showed the all-too-finite limits of broadcasting as an electoral weapon, the coverage of the campaign by the state programme companies offered a useful illustration of the nature of the relationship between the Giscardian regime and broadcasting.

As they have done at every national election since 1965 the broadcasting media constituted a primary source of information for the electorate in the 1981 campaign.[24] During the official campaign period, which began two weeks before the first ballot, an electoral control committee, composed of five top civil servants, supervised the coverage of the different candidates by the state broadcasting services. Strict equality of time allocation was maintained between the different candidates during the official campaign broadcasts, which were shown simultaneously at peak viewing times on both TF1 and Antenne 2. Little can be said about the official campaign broadcasts, except that they represented a limited and very ostentatious attempt at balance in political coverage. Outside of the official campaign broadcasts the committee also intervened to ensure equality of treatment, condemning, for example, the decision by Radio Europe 1 to broadcast an interview with Giscard d'Estaing at the very start of the official campaign period and compelling the state programme companies to balance a statement by General de Boissieu critical of Mitterrand with a counter-statement by Admiral Sanguinetti prior to the second ballot.[25]

Political balance in the official campaign broadcasts did not extend, however, to the coverage of the election in the immediate pre-campaign period. Alleged discrepancies in time allocation and quality of treatment in favour of the 'citizen-candidate' Giscard d'Estaing were condemned by all his rivals. The Gaullist, Socialist and Communist parties regularly published accounts of the amount of time accorded to their candidates in comparison with Giscard d'Estaing, with the latter always the beneficiary. In one television interview the candidate Marie-France Garaud took her interviewers, particularly Patrice Duhamel, to task, stating that:

All the viewers can appreciate the difference between those programmes where one polishes the boots of the citizen candidate – that is of the former President – and those in which one throws the book at M. Debré. Everyone has seen it. Everyone knows it.[26]

Other commentators were also quick to point out the unequal treatment of the different candidates. *Le Monde* and *Le Canard enchaîné* were highly critical, as were the more disinterested correspondents of *The Times* and the *Guardian*.[27] All pointed to the difference in tone and style of questioning between interviews with Giscard d'Estaing on the one hand, and those with his rivals on the other. Like Giscard d'Estaing himself, the interviewers had obvious difficulty in maintaining the abstract distinction between Giscard d'Estaing as President and Giscard d'Estaing as presidential candidate.

The television highlight of the campaign was the face-to-face confrontation between Giscard d'Estaing and Mitterrand before the second ballot which attracted an audience of over 25 million.[28] Whilst the content of the debate was fairly predictable, the controversy surrounding the staging of the televised duel was quite remarkable. Mitterrand and his advisers posed a series of extremely detailed preconditions to the debate's taking place at all. For example, the interviewers were to be chosen among journalists not employed in the state programme companies. There was to be no cutting away from the candidate who was speaking to show the reaction of his opponent. Even the distance between the two candidates was specified by the Mitterrand camp. From the point of view of the professional broadcaster, such conditions naturally made for a very sterile programme. However, Mitterrand obviously considered it necessary to pose such conditions not just because he was generally reckoned to be a poorer television performer than Giscard d'Estaing, but more importantly because he considered he could not trust the state broadcasting companies to maintain equity. For Giscard d'Estaing's presidential rival in 1981, the studios of the state broadcasting services were enemy territory.

With complaints and criticisms from a variety of quarters regarding the broadcast coverage of the campaign, it is not surprising that control of broadcasting was itself a topic in the campaign. This had also been the case in 1969 when Pompidou was forced to reply to the criticisms made by Poher regarding the political partiality of the ORTF. However, while in 1969 there had been a general acceptance of the framework of the state monopoly by the candidates and the main political parties, this was no longer the case in 1981. It was no longer a question of *how* the state monopoly could best guarantee independence and pluralism, but *whether* the state monopoly could perform these tasks. The postwar consensus regarding the organisational principle of the monopoly as the best guardian of a public service broadcasting system had, it seemed, irreparably broken down.

## The State Monopoly

Broadcasting has been a state monopoly in France since the end of the Second World War. During the Fifth Republic the 1964 and 1972 ORTF statutes confirmed the state's broadcasting monopoly which was fiercely defended by the Gaullist party as well as by the Socialist and Communist parties and by the broadcasting trade unions. Attempts to establish a commercial television channel floundered in the face of resolute opposition from the majority of the Gaullist party.

Before 1974, the Giscardians had shown themselves favourable to the abolition of the monopoly, with Giscard d'Estaing's brother, Olivier, introducing a parliamentary amendment to this effect during the debate in 1972 on the new ORTF statute. However, in 1974 Giscard d'Estaing proved himself more Gaullist than his party, refusing to give up the state's overall control of broadcasting. This decision was partly influenced by his lack of a parliamentary majority and his dependence on the Gaullist party to pass his legislation in the Assembly. Moreover, Giscard d'Estaing also wanted to protect the regional press, much of which supported his regime, from the probable losses in advertising revenue which would result if a commercial channel were created.[29]

The 1974 statute, therefore, reaffirmed the state monopoly in programming and transmission. There is still no commercial television channel in France, though brand advertising has been allowed on the state channels since 1968. Local cable television, after an initial experimental period in the early 1970s, also failed to establish itself for both political and economic reasons. With regard to radio, there was no established local radio service by the end of Giscard d'Estaing's presidency. The peripheral radio stations, with their studios in France and their transmitters usually across the French border (though in the case of Radio Monte Carlo also on French territory) infringed the spirit and the letter of the monopoly legislation. However, as the state acting through a holding company, Sofirad, was the most important shareholder in all the peripheral radio stations, with the exception of Radio Télévision Luxembourg, these stations did not provide an independent challenge to the state's control of broadcasting. Thus, the President and his government were responsible for appointments to the important managerial and editorial posts in these stations. For example, at the very beginning of Giscard d'Estaing's presidency the director-general of *Radio Europe 1*, Maurice Siégel, was sacked on the orders of Prime Minister Chirac following a rather irreverent commentary on the premier by one of the station's journalists.[30]

Despite the 1974 statute, however, there were various attempts during Giscard d'Estaing's presidency to break the state's stranglehold over broadcasting, in particular by pirate radio stations broadcasting locally from within French territory. Whilst the pirate radio phenomenon started amongst political fringe groups such as the ecologists, feminists, immigrant workers and regional autonomists, mainstream political organisations also availed themselves of this opportunity to short-circuit the official broadcasting media. Thus, during the latter part of Giscard d'Estaing's presidency the Socialist Party, the Communist Party, the CGT, the CFDT and even the Giscardian party set up pirate radio stations of their own.[31] Pressure groups, such as the Association pour la Libération des Ondes, were formed to lobby for a change in the law.

However, far from giving way to such pressure, the Giscardian government, on the personal instruction of the President, introduced supplementary legislation in 1978 to back up the 1974 statute with tough sanctions for infringement of the state broadcasting monopoly.[32] Giscard d'Estaing's resolute hostility to the pirates was supposedly based on his desire to avoid a replication in France of the 'anarchic situation' in Italy where hundreds of radio stations were competing for listeners in a situation of unrestrained competition. The President was also mindful of the continuing opposition of the regional press to competition from local radio and of the fact that any local radio stations established outside the official state network might be controlled by anti-Giscardian forces. Thus whilst by 1978 the Gaullist, Socialist and Communist parties had substantially modified their previous commitment to the principle of the state monopoly, with the Socialists proposing to allow the establishment of independent local radios of a public service character, Giscard d'Estaing and his government with the reluctant support of many Deputies of the *majorité* shored up the status quo once again.

During 1978-81 the government used the services of the state transmission company to jam the broadcasts of pirate radios and brought several offenders to court, including Mitterrand himself. At the same time the government established on an experimental basis three local radio stations under the control of the state radio company, Radio France. Thus, whilst seeking to repress the pirate stations, the government also attempted in a very limited fashion to accommodate the demand for local broadcasting within the existing legislative framework. Essentially, however, there was little difference in practice between Giscard d'Estaing and his Gaullist predecessors on the question of defending the state broadcasting monopoly during the period 1958-81.

## Broadcasting: a Case Study of *Giscardisme*

This chapter has so far concentrated on the relationship between government and broadcasting during Giscard d'Estaing's presidency. However, broadcasting may also be used as a case study to exemplify certain general features of the Giscardian regime.

First, the evidence of this chapter tends to support the view that under Giscard d'Estaing the regime of the Fifth Republic became even more presidential in character than under his two Gaullist predecessors.[33] While the Prime Minister, the Minister of the Interior and the Minister of Culture and Communication all played some role after 1974 in supervising the formulation and implementation of particular decisions regarding the running of the broadcasting companies, the source of major policy initiatives was the Elysée. The 1974 reform was drawn up by a leading member of the President's staff, Cannac, under Giscard d'Estaing's overall supervision. Appointments to key managerial and editorial posts within the state companies and peripheral radio stations reflected the views of Giscard d'Estaing, as did the government's continuing support for the principle of the state monopoly. Thus, during the Fifth Republic responsibility for broadcasting moved from the Ministry of Information (1958-69) to the office of the Prime Minister (1969-72) and then to the Elysée.

Just as the President had no rivals within the political executive, so there was a lack of checks and balances to his power elsewhere in the system. The civil service as a corporate entity had virtually nothing to do with the running of the broadcasting companies. Parliament had neither the authority, the time, nor the information to challenge the dominance of the executive in this field. The Haut Conseil de l'Andiovisuel was a toothless body, which in any case was not directly involved in the management of the broadcasting companies.

Within the companies themselves all the possible countervailing forces were subject to a variety of constraints. For example, the broadcasting unions, already divided along functional and political lines, were further weakened by the break-up of the ORTF and then by specific measures designed to reduce their capacity for effective corporate action, including legal limits on their right to strike. The journalists had little power or incentive to challenge their superiors within the news departments. They in turn were either political appointees or at least unwilling for career reasons to act as a buffer between the journalists and the authorities. The boards of governors exercised very little power in the day-to-day management of the companies and were in any event dominated by persons appointed directly or indirectly by the state. Finally, the broadcasting management were tied to the government through their method of appointment. Moreover, unlike the director-general of the ORTF, none of the heads of the broadcasting companies set up in 1974 was in charge of the whole state broadcasting network. Thus, even in the unlikely event of a difference of opinion between the President and one of the company heads, the whole system was not affected.

Secondly, this chapter has illustrated Giscard d'Estaing's policy of demolishing 'the Gaullist state' by replacing Gaullist appointees in key areas with his own supporters.[34] The break-up of the ORTF was itself primarily a political act best understood within this context. During his presidency Giscard d'Estaing's antipathy towards the Gaullists became especially overt after 1976. Increasingly broadcasting was colonised by supporters of the President and his regime, including former members of the Elysée staff, while political coverage was intended to enhance the reputation of the President and the Giscardian fraction of the increasingly shaky governing coalition at the expense of the Gaullists and the Socialist–Communist opposition.

Yet whilst wishing to minimise the role of the Gaullist party on the Right of French politics, Giscard d'Estaing was obliged to depend on its support in Parliament where he lacked a Giscardian majority. Between 1974 and early 1976 Giscard d'Estaing was able to use Chirac to secure this support, on the reorganisation of broadcasting for example, with the notable exception of the abortion reform which was passed with Socialist and Communist support in the face of widespread Gaullist opposition. After the spring of 1976, however, Gaullist support was harder to obtain. Thus, Giscard d'Estaing's proposed capital-gains tax reform in that year was savaged in the National Assembly. Giscard d'Estaing's antagonism towards the Gaullists, which had helped bring about de Gaulle's downfall in the 1969 referendum, was repaid in kind during the 1981 presidential elections when Chirac gave only muted support to Giscard d'Estaing before the second ballot, an act which helped secure the latter's defeat.

Thirdly, the 1974 reform of broadcasting highlighted the centralist nature of the Giscardian regime. Though thought to be in favour of a devolution of power to the regions at the time of his election in 1974, Giscard d'Estaing later declared his opposition to such a policy. In the field of broadcasting the President's centralist stance was perfectly evident. Regional radio and television consisted mainly of news bulletins and a few locally produced entertainment programmes and documentaries, which taken together supplied a supplementary service for national radio and television rather than substantial competition.[35] The regional broadcasting committees, whose creation was provided for in the 1974 statute, were in fact never set up for fear that they might become dominated by opposition politicians. Cable television and independent local radio were either not encouraged or positively outlawed. At the same time the Giscardian government pushed ahead with plans to introduce direct broadcasting by satellite in the mid-1980s. The advantage of satellite broadcasting was that, as with the state broadcasting companies, it could be easily controlled from the centre. Once again, possible checks and balances in the broadcasting system were eschewed.

Finally, the relations between government and broadcasting during Giscard d'Estaing's presidency demonstrated the limits in practice of the President's much-vaunted claims in favour of an advanced, liberal society. The measures taken against ORTF journalists at the end of 1974, the non-renewal of Jullian's contract at the end of 1977, the government's repressive policy against the pirate radios, its support of stricter anti-strike proposals within the broadcasting companies in 1979 and the distortions in political output, all contrasted sharply with promises made at the time of Giscard d'Estaing's election. The liberal rhetoric of the Giscardian *septennat* could not disguise a relationship between government and broadcasting which was different in form but similar in substance to that of the de Gaulle and Pompidou presidencies. Thus, in broadcasting as in other policy areas, particularly in the field of civil liberties, the reformist commitment of the 1974 campaign had by 1981 manifestly failed to live up to expectations.[36]

## The Mitterrand Presidency

Whatever the causes of Giscard d'Estaing's electoral defeat, the victory of Mitterrand promised to open up a new era in French politics. Mitterrand's election platform emphasised the desirability of change in the social, political and economic life of the nation. Moreover, as the gradualist 'change without risk' of Giscard d'Estaing's 1974 campaign had proved politically bankrupt, Mitterrand espoused a radical policy of change, including, for example, a more interventionist role for the state in economic policy-making.

In the field of broadcasting, too, change was the order of the day. Just as it had done at the start of Giscard d'Estaing's presidency in 1974, so in

1981 the problem of the government's relationship with the state broadcasting media posed itself at the very beginning of Mitterrand's term of office. Two matters in particular had to be dealt with almost immediately: first, the fate of the Giscardian appointees holding important posts in the broadcasting companies; and secondly, the necessity of legislation to govern the operations of the pirate radio stations which had sprung up in the latter half of Giscard d'Estaing's term of office. A third question, the wholesale reorganisation of French broadcasting, was to be the object of new legislation in the first parliamentary session of 1982.

## Appointments

The election in 1981 of a Socialist President immediately called into question the position of those Giscardian appointees in key posts in the broadcasting media. Understandably the new administration regarded these appointees as 'yesterday's men', an integral part of the Giscardian regime which had been rejected by the electorate. In the case of the heads of the state broadcasting companies, however, the Socialist government faced the problem that under the provisions of the 1974 statute, that is, the existing legislation, the former had been quite legally reappointed for another three-year term of office at the end of 1980. A new broadcasting statute introduced quickly at the start of Mitterrand's presidency, as Giscard d'Estaing had done in 1974, would have resolved this problem. However, the Socialist reform proposals in this field were not yet finalised and a variety of interested parties, including the broadcasting unions, insisted on their right to make their own contribution to the debate. Moreover, since they had severely criticised Giscard d'Estaing for steamrollering his own broadcasting Bill through Parliament in 1974 without adequate consultation of those affected, the Socialists were reluctant to lay themselves open to similar protests. In any case, other legislative proposals concerning the de-centralisation of power to the regions and *départements* and the early nationalisation measures took precedence over a structural reorganisation of broadcasting. Thus, the new Socialist administration had somehow to rid broadcasting of the old Giscardian guard without at the same time being seen to indulge too overtly in a political witch-hunt.[37]

The Socialist response to this problem was to apply pressure on certain directors of news and company heads to resign 'voluntarily' either directly through ministerial meetings with those concerned or indirectly by urging the broadcasting staff, particularly the journalists, to force the issue within the companies. The new minister in charge of the media, Georges Fillioud, himself a former broadcasting journalist, was especially vitriolic in his condemnation of those pro-Giscardian elements who still retained their posts after the change of presidency. Yet while the means employed by the new government left many broadcasting staff with an uncomfortable frisson of *déjà vu*, they did succeed gradually in attaining their goal of easing out the Giscardian appointees from their positions of responsibility. As a result, by autumn 1981 the heads of six of the seven state broadcasting companies had been removed, only one Director of News in the four programme companies still held his post and widespread changes had also taken place among the management of the peripheral radio stations.[38] In addition, certain well-known broadcasting journalists excluded from the state networks as a result of Gaullist and Giscardian purges in the past now returned to fill important positions.[39] On the other hand, the Communist Party still maintained with some justification that journalists with Communist sympathies were under-represented in the news teams, particularly at editorial level.[40]

Not all the new appointees could be regarded as having pro-Socialist views, and indeed some possessed an impressive record of professional competence and political independence. None the less, the manner in which the change-over at the top of the broadcasting companies was handled by the government raised doubts about the extent to which a commitment in principle to public service norms regarding impartiality and independence could be reconciled with the well-established practice of partisan political appointments. The Socialists might argue that they were merely clearing out the Giscardian residue prior to making a fresh start. However, the allocation of top posts in French broadcasting has traditionally formed part of a *de facto* spoils system on American lines, a political fact of life which is apparently accepted by a majority of the French electorate as 'normal'.[41] The structural reorganisation of broadcasting may make such partisan politicisation more difficult in the future. Certainly, any attempt by the Socialists to colonise broadcasting in the manner of their Gaullist and Giscardian predecessors will be firmly resisted by the broadcasting journalists among others. None the less, the temptation will still be present and fears that the Socialists will be unable to resist this temptation are scarcely allayed by statements such as that made by President Mitterrand in the autumn of 1981:

> We do not want a purge, but nonetheless a certain number of command controls have to be held by men and women whose views correspond with those of the majority of the country. We must ensure that the policies desired by that majority, which we are putting into practice, are really implemented.[42]

Applied to the field of broadcasting, Mitterrand's statement has a hauntingly Gaullist ring about it.

### Radios libres

The second immediate problem facing the new Socialist government concerned the situation of the previously outlawed pirate radio stations.

Naturally those involved in running pirate stations and the different pressure groups in which they were organised reacted favourably to Mitterrand's presidential election success, hoping that as a former strong critic of Giscard d'Estaing's control of broadcasting Mitterrand would introduce more liberal legislation than his predecessor in this area by relaxing the state's broadcasting monopoly. New pirate stations began broadcasting in the summer of 1981, whilst others which had closed down their transmitters in the face of Giscardian repression started up again in this period of post-election euphoria. The organisers of some stations, due to appear in court on charges of infringing the state monopoly, were amnestied as part of the presidential amnesty for minor offences.

However, the legislation governing this area of broadcasting remained the 1974 statute, strengthened by the supplementary 1978 law in support of the state monopoly. Prior to the introduction of new legislation which would make the judicial position accord with the new political situation, the Socialist government was determined that political and commercial groups should not take advantage of the period of flux to establish their own stations and thus present the government with a *fait accompli* when new legislation was eventually introduced. Thus, ironically for a time the Socialists continued the practice of the previous Giscardian government of jamming the broadcasts of certain pirate stations. When this proved unpopular, a voluntary code was drawn up between the minister and relevant pressure-groups to try to prevent the situation from getting out of hand. However, it was clear that new legislation would be required to restore order to the airwaves.

After consultations with the pirate radio pressure-groups the government introduced a Bill in Parliament in September 1981.[43] This Bill allowed certain exceptions (*dérogations*) to the state monopoly in the field of radio transmission. Private local radio stations would be allowed to broadcast up to a maximum distance of 30 kilometres. Transmission licences would be granted by the Prime Minister or a minister appointed by him for this purpose on the basis of advice given by a committee chaired by a *conseiller d'Etat* and whose members would include representatives of the relevant pressure-groups. A specified person or group of persons would be permitted to run only one private station so as to prevent chains of local stations being established. Municipal radio stations were not to be allowed, a move designed to frustrate not only the Gaullist-Giscardian opposition, but also the Communist Party who had previously campaigned in favour of such an option. Finally, and most controversially, commercial advertising was forbidden as a source of revenue for the local private stations.

The decision not to allow advertising, while it pleased the regional press lobby, sparked off most protest. The Gaullist-Giscardian opposition, many of whom had supported the state's monopoly over broadcasting while in power, now suddenly discovered good reasons why the Socialist proposals were too timid. The government itself was split on this particular question, with the minister in charge of the media contradicting himself on a number of occasions as the government dithered. The Socialist Party in Parliament was also divided, with supporters of Michel Rocard seemingly more in favour of allowing advertising. Finally, the pressure-groups themselves could not agree. Thus, while the Association pour la Libération des Ondes opposed the ban on advertising, the less representative Fédération Nationale des Radios Libres supported the no advertising policy of the Socialists.

The decision not to allow advertising on the local private stations disappointed many of those involved in the running of the former pirate stations, who argued that deprived of this source of revenue they would be unable to compete with the national and peripheral radio stations. The Socialists replied that to allow advertising would be to open up this sector of communication to well-organised commercial interests ideologically opposed to the new regime who would kill off the lesser competition. Both views have some validity, though it is not clear why limited advertising could not have been permitted. It certainly seemed ironic that in the very week that Mitterrand should benefit from his own amnesty, with charges against him over the Radio Riposte affair being finally dropped, the Socialists should introduce legislation which many pirate stations regarded as inimical to their well-being.[44]

The Socialist government has thus made a small, hesitant step in dismantling the state's broadcasting monopoly. Private local radio stations will now be legalised. At the same time Radio France is pushing ahead with its own plans to establish more local radio stations under its own control on the lines of the experimental stations set up towards the end of Giscard d'Estaing's presidency. Thus, France is gradually acquiring on a largely piecemeal and ill-planned basis a system of local radio run partly by private (but not commercial) interests and partly by a state broadcasting company.[45]

## The Socialist Broadcasting Reform

While in the short term the new Socialist administration concentrated on *ad hoc* responses to the specific problems of replacing the Giscardian appointees in top broadcasting posts and introducing legislation to regulate the situation of the private local radio stations, a full-scale structural reorganisation of broadcasting still formed an integral part of its plans. To this end an advisory committee was set up by the government in July 1981 composed of persons with undoubted professional competence in the cultural and broadcasting fields, many though not all of whom had political sympathies for the Socialist regime.[46] Chaired by Pierre Moinot, a top civil servant and former governor of the ORTF, the committee produced its report in October.[47]

Following general principles laid down by the government, the report stressed the need to make the state broadcasting services politically independent. A wide-ranging structural reform of broadcasting was essential if this end were to be achieved. The report proposed, therefore, the creation of an executive body provisionally entitled the High Authority (La Haute Autorité) which would act as a buffer between the government on the one hand, and the broadcasting companies on the other. This High Authority would have nine members: three appointed by the President of the Republic; three drawn from top judicial bodies such as the Cour de Cassation and the Conseil d'Etat; and three persons co-opted from a list of names put forward by the National Council for Broadcasting (see below). The chairman would be elected by the members of the High Authority, who would enjoy a guaranteed six-year non-renewable term of office. The High Authority would be given power to allocate frequencies (for example, to local private radio stations), to appoint one-third of the members of the boards of governors in the national broadcasting companies and to allocate licence and advertising revenue among the different companies. It would also ensure that the provisions of the broadcasting charter were observed by the companies.

The report also proposed the creation of a National Council for Broadcasting (Conseil National de l'Audiovisuel), which would take over from the Haut Conseil de l'Audiovisuel the role of the think-tank in broadcasting matters. This consultative assembly, whose function in the formulation of broadcasting policy might be compared to that of the Economic and Social Council in economic policy-making, was to consist of sixty members: twelve representing the political parties; twelve representing the economic forces of the nation (trade unionists and management representatives); twelve representing professional groups; twelve representing the creative arts; and twelve representing the public. Consulted on a variety of broadcasting issues by the High Authority, the National Council for Broadcasting would also have the task of drawing up the broadcasting charter which would lay down the norms governing the activities of the broadcasting companies. Three representatives from the Council would appoint one-third of the members of the boards of governors of the national broadcasting companies.

The organisation of the broadcasting companies themselves would also be reformed. A national television company grouping together the present TF1, Antenne 2 and SFP, would be established. Competition between the two national television channels would be abolished in favour of complementary programme scheduling. As in the case of the other national companies, the board of governors of this new television company would consist of nine members: three chosen by the High Authority; three by the National Council for Broadcasting; and three representatives of the company staff. The chairman of the company would be elected by the board from among its members. The Moinot Report also provided for the establishment of a national radio company (the equivalent of Radio France but without any responsibility for local radio), an archive conservation institute (a slimmed-down INA) and a transmission company (similar to TDF).

In line with the de-centralist commitment of the new Socialist government the second major aim of the Moinot Report was the geographical de-centralisation of responsibility for broadcasting to the regions and localities. Regional communication councils would be established to fulfil a function similar to that served by the National Council for Broadcasting at the national level. In each region a radio company would supervise the establishment of public-service local radio stations. Thus, the perennial conflict between Radio France and FR3 as to who should manage local radio would be resolved. Private local radio stations would also be allowed to broadcast provided that they respected certain public service norms. Moreover, these private stations would be allowed to use advertising as a source of revenue, though within strictly defined limits! Lastly, regional television was to be encouraged, managed by nine regional television companies using the present television facilities of FR3.

Generally accepted by the Socialist government as the basis of the new broadcasting statute, the implementation of the Moinot Report will entail a complete reorganisation of French broadcasting. The 1982 reform will not just involve papering over the cracks in the system established in 1974, for example, through the establishment of a central federating body, the High Authority. Nor will it merely entail a return to the status quo ante 1974, the unitary structure of the ORTF. Rather it will be an attempt to learn from the defects of both the Gaullist and Giscardian experiences and prepare French broadcasting for the technological innovations of the 1980s, such as direct satellite transmissions. If successful, the 1982 statute will achieve two objectives which the 1974 reform failed to attain: an improvement in programme quality and the removal of broadcasting as an issue of political controversy.

## Conclusion

While it is on the basis of the 1982 reorganisation that the Socialist pledge to reform broadcasting will be judged, in the interim some improvements have already been made. For example, television programmes on the nuclear-power issue were shown at the time of the debate in Parliament. The film *Le Chagrin et la Pitié*, a realistic account of attitudes to the Nazi occupation in one French town (Clermont-Ferrand), has finally been shown on television, more than ten years after being screened in the cinema. Other early signs, however, including most notably the fierce attack on 'the lack of objectivity' of television news made by Claude Estier,

Socialist Deputy and close political ally of President Mitterrand, are not so encouraging.[48]

It is too early to say whether the previously stifling relationship between the government and the broadcasting media in France can be significantly altered. Structural reorganisation can certainly play a part in helping to cut the links which historically have always tied the broadcasting media to the government. Even here, however, it is by no means clear that the High Authority, the body at the top of the pyramidal structure proposed by the Moinot Report, will be able to fulfil its allotted role as a buffer between the government and the broadcasting companies. Largely this will depend on the strength of will and political resilience of those chosen to serve on this body. If the chairman of the High Authority were sympathetic to the Socialist administration or politically pliable, the High Authority might well lose its claim to independence and become a political tool of the government within the broadcasting system. Alternatively, the High Authority may find itself bypassed as governmental pressure is exerted directly on the radio and television companies.

Accompanying the structural reorganisation of broadcasting, therefore, must be a change of attitudes. The acceptance of governmental interference in broadcasting is at present a recognised part of French political culture at both the mass and elite levels. Somehow the Socialist government has to change this belief. Commitment to public service goals of independence and impartiality are all very well during periods of opposition and in the post-election honeymoon period. The depth of this commitment will be put to the test, however, when as a result programmes critical of government policy are accepted as a normal part of French life. When there is a clash between the government's professed support for the public service norms and its natural desire for favourable publicity, then and only then will the Socialist broadcasting reform be meaningfully tested. The Giscardian reform noticeably failed this test in the period after 1976. Moreover, as in many other aspects of contemporary French politics, it may well be the attitudes and behaviour of the President which will prove crucial in this respect.

At this stage of the new presidency judgement must necessarily be tentative. One does not have to be particularly cynical, however, to foresee circumstances in which the Socialist government will seek to use the broadcasting media, as their predecessors have done, in a partisan fashion to defend controversial policies. As in the performance of the French economy, the consequences of the policy of radical change in the field of broadcasting are as yet mainly verbal.

## Notes: Chapter 7

1   V. Giscard d'Estaing, *Démocratie française* (Paris: Fayard, 1976).

2   *Journal Officiel, Documents Assemblée Nationale*, 'Rapport fait au nom de la commission de contrôle de la gestion financière de l'Office de radiodiffusion et télévision française, rapporteur – Roger Chinaud, annexe au procès-verbal de la séance du 20 juin 1974', No. 1072, 1973 –4.

3   *Journal Officiel, Lois et décrets*, Law no. 74-696 of 7 August 1974.

4   On the system of financing the Giscardian broadcasting companies, see R. Kuhn, 'Government and broadcasting in France: the resumption of normal service?', *West European Politics*, no. 2, 1980, pp. 207-10.

5   *Le Monde*, 18 January 1975.

6   Giscard d'Estaing, op. cit., p. 99.

7   M. Jullian, *Délit de vagabondage* (Paris: Grasset, 1978), pp. 28-35.

8   ibid., pp. 129-34.

9   C. Durieux, *La télécratie* (Paris: Tema, 1976), pp. 82-5; and J. Diwo, *Si vous avez manqué le début* (Paris: Albin Michel, 1976), pp. 264-5.

10  Antenne 2, Minutes of the *comité d'entreprise*, 3 March 1977.

11  See F. Mitterrand, *Ici et maintenant* (Paris: Fayard, 1980), pp. 99-113.

12  *Le Monde*, 16 June 1978.

13  *Journal Officiel, Documents Assemblée Nationale*, 'Rapport fait au nom de la commission d'enquête sur les conditions de l'information publique, présenté par Claude Martin, dépôt publié au *Journal Officiel* du 18 septembre 1979', No. 1289, 1979, p. 28.

14  *Journal Officiel, Débats Assemblée Nationale*, 16 June 1972, p. 2521.

15  *Journal Officiel, Documents Assemblée Nationale*, 'Rapport fait au nom de la commission d'enquête sur les conditions de l'information publique, présenté par Claude Martin, dépôt publié au *Journal Officiel* du 18 septembre 1979', No. 1289, 1979, p. 29.

16  Mitterrand, op. cit., pp. 99-113.

17  A. Peyrefitte, *Le Mal français* (Paris: Plon, 1976), pp. 69-78.

18  *Journal Officiel, Lois et décrets*, 'Arrêtés du 25 avril 1975 fixant les cahiers des charges des sociétés nationales de télévision et de radiodiffusion.'

19  Kuhn, op. cit., pp. 214-15.

20  A. Duhamel, *La République giscardienne* (Paris: Grasset, 1980), p. 100; see pp. 81-104, for Duhamel's rather optimistic view of broadcasting during Giscard's presidency.

21  R. Cayrol, 'Radio télévision et pouvoir politique', paper presented to Conference on the French Mass Media, Association Française de Science Politique, Paris 1978.

22  F. Giroud, *La Comédie du pouvoir* (Paris: Fayard, 1977), pp. 162-76.

23  On the broadcast coverage of the 1978 legislative elections for example, see S. Bauman and A. Ecouves, *L'Information manipulée* (Paris: Editions de la Revue politique et parlementaire, 1981), esp. pp. 171-84; and R. Cayrol, 'The mass media and the electoral campaign', in H. R. Penniman (ed.), *The French National Assembly Elections of 1978* (Washington, DC: American Enterprise Institute, 1980), pp. 144-70.

24  J. G. Blumler, R. Cayrol and G. Thoveron, *La Télévision fait-elle l'élection?* (Paris: Presses de la Fondation Nationale des Sciences Politiques, 1978).

25  *Le Monde*, 14 April and 10-11 May 1981.

26  *Le Monde*, 10 April 1981; and *Le Canard enchaîné*, 15 April 1981.

27  *Le Monde*, 8 May 1981; *Le Canard enchaîné*, 22 April 1981; *The Times*, 15 April and 20 May 1981; and *Guardian*, 18 March 1981.

28  *Le Monde*, 2, 3-4, 5 and 6 May 1981.

29  *Télé-7-jours*, no. 821, 7 February 1976.

30  *L'Express*, no. 1217, 4 November 1974; and *Le Nouvel Observateur*, no. 521, 4 November 1974.

31  F. Cazenave, *Les radios libres* (Paris: PUF, 1980).

32  *Journal Officiel, Lois et décrets*, Law no. 78-787, 28 July 1978.

33  V. Wright, *The Government and Politics of France* (London: Hutchinson, 1978).

34  See article by Y. Agnès, 'L'Etat-Giscard', *Le Monde*, 2–3 March 1980.

35  D. Descollines, 'Propos sur la télévision régionale', *Projet* no. 112, February 1977.

36  J. Frears, *France in the Giscard Presidency* (London: Allen & Unwin, 1981), esp. pp. 175–97.

37  The Socialists were initially very conscious of the need to avoid undesirable publicity which might surround a political witch-hunt; see, for example, the interview with Lionel Jospin in *L'Express*, no. 1558, 22 May 1981.

38  The following list gives an indication of the extent of the change-over in top broadcasting and related posts:

> Jean-Louis Guillaud, head of TF1, replaced by Jacques Boutet, July 1981;
> Maurice Ulrich, head of Antenne 2, replaced by Pierre Desgraupes, July 1981;
> Claude Contamine, head of FR3, replaced by Guy Thomas, June 1981;
> Jacqueline Baudrier, head of Radio France, replaced by Michèle Cotta, July 1981;
> Antoine de Clermont-Tonnerre, head of the SFP, replaced by Bertrand Labrusse, June 1981;
> Gabriel de Broglie, head of INA, replaced by Joël Le Tac, August 1981;
> Jean-Pierre Elkabbach, Director of News Antenne 2, replaced by Henri de Virieu, July–August 1981;
> André Sabas, Director of News FR3, replaced by Maurice Séveno, August–October 1981;
> Roland Faure, Director of News Radio France, replaced by Jérôme Bellay, June 1981. Of the Directors of News in the state programme companies, only Jean-Marie Cavada, TF1, still retained his post by the autumn of 1981.
> Xavier Gouyou-Beauchamps, head of Sofirad, replaced by Michel Caste, June 1981;
> Yves Cannac, head of Havas, replaced by Pierre Nicolay, June 1981;
> Michel Bassi, head of Radio Monte Carlo, replaced by Jean-Claude Héberlé, July 1981;
> Etienne Mougeotte, Director of News Radio Europe 1, replaced by Philippe Gildas, August 1981.

> Changes in personnel were also to be found in other top posts, such as Channel Director and News Editor in the different companies.

39  They included Maurice Séveno, sacked after the 1968 strike at the ORTF, appointed Director of News at FR3 in October 1981; Edouard Guibert, former secretary-general of the Syndicat National des Journalistes, who had resigned in 1974 in an act of sympathy with journalists sacked at the time of the break-up of ORTF, appointed special adviser to the head of FR3 in charge of relations with the journalists, September 1981; and Christian Guy, purged from the news team on Elkabbach's arrival at Antenne 2 in the spring of 1977, who returned to the news team in June 1981.

40  Some Communist journalists were given posts, however. These included Roland Passevant and François Salvaing at TF1, Michel Cardoze at Radio France and Marcel Trillat at Antenne 2.

41  According to an Ifres opinion poll, 53 per cent of the population judged the changes in broadcasting management to be 'normal', *Le Monde*, 11 August 1981.

42  *Le Monde*, 29 September 1981.

43  For the provisions of the Bill, see *Le Monde*, 11 September 1981.

44  The main provisions of the Bill emerged intact from parliamentary discussion. At the time of writing of this chapter (November 1981) the Gaullist-Giscardian opposition has asked the Constitutional Council to rule on the constitutionality of the legislation.

45  See *Le Point*, no. 471, 28 September 1981; *Le Nouvel Observateur*, no. 881, 26 September 1981; and *L'Express*, no. 1578, 9 October 1981.

46  For the composition of the Moinot committee, see *Le Monde*, 8 July 1981.

47  A summary of the main recommendations of the Moinot Committee was published in *Le Monde*, 16 October 1981.

48  On the controversy sparked off by Estier, see *Le Nouvel Observateur*, no. 886, 31 October 1981.

# 8

# Central Control and Local Resistance

*YVES MÉNY*

Elected President of the Republic despite his party's weakness and lack of grass-roots support, Giscard d'Estaing sought from the beginning of his seven-year term to consolidate his personal success at national and local level. But in view of the political structure, solid on both the Left (Socialist and Communist parties) and the Right (the Gaullists), the new President's room for manoeuvre was rather limited. The construction of a Centre party implied the development of local foundations by rallying round the presidential movement the unorganised or dispersed elite of the traditional 'marais'. For whilst the centrists had practically disappeared as an important political formation nationally, their influence at local level remained strong, especially among the thousands of 'apolitical' mayors or town councillors. These local representatives could constitute not only a valuable support for the strengthening of the presidential party, but also a counterweight to the opposition parties or to the Gaullists, thanks to their means of putting pressure on and intervening with the administrative and legislative machinery of the state: their role in electing Senators, and the tradition of *cumul des mandats* (that is, the possibility of simultaneously occupying several seats, both local and national) made them the essential elements of national political life.[1]

The question of de-centralisation and regionalisation was therefore not only a technical problem or even a political choice as to the best way to organise the state, but also one of the instruments through which Giscard d'Estaing hoped to achieve his major aim: to constitute a powerful Centre party and reduce the Communist and Gaullist parties to the smallest possible dimensions.

Like de Gaulle, Giscard d'Estaing had to seek to conquer the periphery, but the means could not be the same, if only in view of the results of the conflict there had been between the first President of the Fifth Republic and the local representatives throughout his eleven years in power.

As regards de-centralisation, the de Gaulle period (1958–69) can be typified schematically by three features:

(1) A permanent endeavour to reform the system locally. From December 1958 to April 1969 attempts were multiplied in all possible forms: laws, decrees, orders under special powers, circulars, financial incentives, and political and administrative pressure, experiments and, finally, referendums constituted a continuous and unprecedented effort to change the structure, the financing and the elites of the local system. This included the creation of the districts (1958), the urban communities (1966) and the new towns (1968–70); the reorganisation of the Paris region (1964); and the attempts at regional reform. These innovations constantly pursued two goals, the modernisation of the local structures and the endeavour through various means (creation of new assemblies or committees, reform of the electoral law in towns of over 30,000 inhabitants in 1965) to eliminate the local bastions of opposition to Gaullism. The high stakes at play explain why the decentralisation issue was the object of passionate debate throughout the period.[2]

(2) The fact of failure was no less striking than the continuity of the effort. In 1969 there remained 37,000 municipalities out of the 38,000 that were to have been reduced to a 'more reasonable' figure; the reform of local finance, the principles of which had been set out in 1958, was still not achieved;[3] local elites had maintained their positions, and the referendum on regional reform and the Senate of 1969 had brought this ill-starred series of attempts to a final end.[4]

(3) The resistance of local elites to the penetration of Gaullism into the municipalities and *départements* was likewise an essential factor of the wider political game: the opposition parties, excluded from power and severely shaken by the setting up of the Fifth Republic, consolidated their local bastions, whilst the traditionally 'apolitical' representatives of the Right and Centre refused pure and simple allegiance to Gaullism. Whilst generally faithful to de Gaulle on questions of national importance (Algeria, the Constitution, and so on), moderate local representatives were at the very least hesitant with regard to the local level reforms aimed at by the Debré and Pompidou governments. Being in agreement on the main points the great mass of mayors, like the population as a whole, were disinclined to show themselves anti-Gaullist (except in 1969) by refusing the central government's proposals. For the local authority reforms were never presented as 'a vital obligation' (by contrast with the national plan) or as an essential element of government policy. Moreover, where authoritarian measures were provided for, they were practically never applied (for instance, the government had recourse only once to constraint in order to oblige municipalities to co-operate in a district), or else were applied with much circumspection (as with the four urban communities created in 1966 at Lille, Lyons, Bordeaux and Strasbourg).

The combined shock of the 1968 May events and the 1969 referendum induced Georges Pompidou to implement a policy of prudence and of winning back the *notables*. In doing so he was obeying both his personal convictions and the political needs of the moment. His mistrust of the region and his profound connivance with the local political ambience impelled him towards the reconciliation he had always hoped for with the political groups of the Centre. As Prime Minister in 1962–8 he had constantly sought to ensure support from the Independent Republicans, despite the tensions between their leader, Valéry Giscard d'Estaing, and General de Gaulle from 1967 onwards. He had also since 1962 tried to associate the centrists of the MRP in government. De Gaulle's biting irony about Europe did not allow the experiment to last for more than a month. Finally, in 1969 as candidate for the presidency, Georges Pompidou ensured himself of support from one centrist group (led by Jacques Duhamel), and after the 1973 legislative elections, he broadened his political base still further by incorporating some of the remainder of the Christian Democratic family, which had remained in opposition under the wing of Jean Lecanuet. The centrists, and the moderates in general, controlled a very large number of local or departmental seats, especially in traditionally Catholic regions such as Alsace or the west where the Gaullist successes in national elections had also been most marked. Pompidou's strategy at the Centre therefore implied a policy of appeasement of rank-and-file elected representatives, traditionally influential and powerful thanks to the *cumul des mandats* and to their privileges as electors of Senators.

Pompidou's policy was therefore a compromise between the Gaullist heritage (the region, the imperative of reform) and his own ideas (hostility to any upsetting of the local system). The 1971 law aiming at reducing and restructuring municipalities was a model of prudence, and the 1972 law creating the regions was a step back by comparison not only with the regionalist demands, but also with the referendum law of 1969 (limited powers and budget, no direct election of regional Assembly members).

When Valéry Giscard d'Estaing was elected President in 1974, he 'inherited' two reforms, one of which had not been exploited to its full potential (the number of communes was reduced by only about 1,000, from 37,000 to 36,000) and the other had barely entered into application. The options were therefore wide open, especially since the newly elected President's doctrine had until then been remarkably unclear.[5] His declarations in favour of local de-centralisation never went beyond the level of the fine words that all political parties ritually proclaim, and his regional options, whilst obscure, gave hope to all those who were looking for a more powerful regional level. Had not Giscard d'Estaing, in his ambiguous formula, 'refused his yes' to the 1969 referendum, on the pretext that the proposed regional reform was insufficiently bold? The vague nature of the formula in 1969 was already a significant pointer to

Giscard d'Estaing's wish to attract one side without disappointing the other: fashionable regionalist stances, but support for the local representatives and for the Senate, threatened by the reform, without any clear declaration of opposition to General de Gaulle's project. The 'refusal of the yes' in no way meant support for the 'no'. This all-things-to-all-men attitude is revealing for his later strategy in his seven-year mandate: how to please the centrist local representatives without altering the controls (especially financial) by central government over the municipalities and *départements*? The Giscardian reforms sought by other ways and other methods what the Gaullist had aimed at in vain for fifteen years: to control the periphery in order to give the presidential party a more solid local foundation and render it better able to dispose of the political resources needed to exercise power.

On the other hand, the new instruments used reflected the decline in planning which until the early 1970s had been the framework for local and regional policy, and they served as a formal cover for a policy of patronage and influence such as had been familiar in the Radical Third Republic.[6] Instead of a plan whose various sectoral and regional components were organised as a function of objectives laid down by the political power in association with the 'social partners', there appeared 'priority action programmes' along with specific regional plans drawn up as a function of the economic demands or political problems of the moment. Very often these plans had no other merit than that of organising, in a document that was little more than political marketing, the separate measures decided on by the various ministries (see Chapter 6 by Jack Hayward). The contractual policy, founded on the 'co-operation that must become the rule in relations between the state and the regions',[7] is another example of the use of flexible and apparently rational techniques in the service of a partisan policy.

## The Giscardian Strategy: the Line of Least Resistance

It is undeniable that the paternity of Giscard d'Estaing's local policy is to be sought, if anywhere, more in Pompidou's practice than in that of General de Gaulle. Both of them expressed distrust of ambitious, comprehensive reforms, a refusal of any over-hasty change and the need for a reconciliation with the *notables*. But this political line was still more needed by Giscard d'Estaing, who, once elected, still had to build the majority party that de Gaulle and Pompidou had benefited from.

This strategy could not be achieved except through reconciliation with the *notables*. Only they could, by their local roots, counterbalance the Gaullist party organisation. Finally, the new President could hope to make, towards those Radicals or Socialists frightened by the prospects of the 1972 left-wing Common Programme, an 'opening to the Left'. But in this case, too, the possibilities of an opening were much greater in the direction of the traditional 'red *notables*' than in that of the new elites of the Socialist Party.

Starting from the objective of winning back the local representatives for central government the problem was no longer which reform was most desirable, most rational, or most liberal, but to define the most effective method of blandishment. The first stage in this strategy was the break with the past, however recent, wherever it injured the feelings of the mayors or the local councillors. Giscard d'Estaing, although a member of government throughout the Fifth Republic, and responsible as Minister of Finance for the reform of local taxation, refused to identify himself with the previous policies. He went so far as to declare:

The Fifth Republic has given France stable, effective and democratic political institutions which will, of course, be respected and protected. But the renewal introduced has effected only the national institutions. Our local institutions, in the *départements* and municipalities, are still governed essentially by century-old laws.

This ignoring of fifteen years of reforms under de Gaulle and Pompidou was again apparent in the rejection of the report that President Pompidou had commissioned from a group of experts chaired by Alain Peyrefitte. Presented to President Pompidou on the eve of his death the report was to remain a mere study document. It is significant that none of it was made public until the time when another commission was set up, the Commission on the Development of Local Responsibilities, created on 26 November 1976 and chaired by Olivier Guichard, a loyal Gaullist, who was, however, more attracted by the centrist line of Pompidou and Giscard d'Estaing than by Chirac's rightist attitudes. Both documents were published in 1976, but only the Guichard Report was – briefly – treated as an official working document.

The desire to attract the local representatives was already clear in the composition of the Guichard Commission. For the first time, almost all the members (eight out of ten) were local representatives, and only one came from the body of prefects. Even though several of these representatives had themselves been high officials and exercised national responsibilities, the innovation was remarkable, given the strength of the custom of recourse to the top civil service in preparing reforms. Pierre Sadran and Jean Dumas, for instance, have shown that out of the 102 members making up the four working groups behind the principal proposals on de-centralisation, no fewer than eighty-four were top civil servants.[8] Despite this notable change in attitude by central government (for the first time two opposition members were also appointed), the report received a very lukewarm reception from most local representatives. The Guichard Commission proposed rather radical, rigorous solutions, not very different in substance from the innumerable projects which since 1958 had caused local representatives to mobilise against central government: new distribution of powers, financial reform and especially the constitution of a two-tier local administration, municipalities and communities of municipalities, an idea that had always been rejected by local representatives. This gap between the hopes placed in the commission and the results obtained was not, however, as surprising as might seem at first sight. The commission's composition shows that after the resignation of the two opposition members, there remained only the (four) members close to Gaullism and followers of Giscard d'Estaing, or representatives who had had important responsibilities in the *départements* or as mayors. The great chorus of elected representatives of the small municipalities, profoundly hostile to territorial reorganisation, had not been heard, and could not accept proposals that threatened, even partially, their existence.

This abortive attempt at attracting the municipal councillors was combined with a policy of appeasement towards the assemblies of the *département*, the general councils. For them, the principal item at stake was the competition that the region might constitute to the traditional administrative level. After having attempted to empty the regional economic development commissions (CODERs) set up in 1964 of their substance, brought about the failure of the 1969 referendum and controlled from within the regional bodies created in 1972, the general councillors feared that the regionalism taken on by Giscard d'Estaing might constitute a new threat. Yet appeasement came and quickly dampened the enthusiasm of the President's regionalist supporters. As early as November 1975, Giscard d'Estaing was saying that 'France is not rich enough to be the only country in the world with four tiers of administration. It is too divided to want to introduce new political games where reflection and consultation already prevail'.[9] But gliding over the ambiguity, he asked himself: 'Should we choose the regional level or the *département* level for the administration? It is clear that we cannot have both.' But at the same time he implicitly underlined his preferences by describing the *départements* as 'the pre-eminent centre for harmonious administration of the country, and they must be affirmed and used as such'. Later he reiterated his opposition to any regional authority (speech at Thann, 14 May 1979), stating during the 1981 presidential election campaign that if the choice had to be made between *département* and region, it would be by popular referendum. The cumbersomeness of such a procedure boded ill for the future of the regions, and appeared as nothing more than procrastination to avoid making the choice. This latest episode of the electoral campaign was, however, more significant than it seemed as to Giscard d'Estaing's refusal to make specific commitments, the ambiguity of his policies and his attempts to satisfy some without annoying the others. Thus, in February 1981 many decrees were published regulating the powers of the regional bodies, particularly in the economic sphere. The measures were an attempt before the presidential elections to appease the demands of the more dynamic regions without upsetting the supporters of the *départements*. However, these 'clever' tactics misfired: while they did sometimes succeed in deceiving, they ended up by accumulating discontent, without arousing warm support. The 'reasonable' regionalists (the word favoured by the ex-President), who were meant to have been satisfied by changes in line with principles they had often urged, saw these as only sham reforms. The first decision by the new Socialist Prime Minister, Mauroy, on 27 May 1981, was to announce the abrogation of decrees he had pressed for, the final text of which he judged to be inadequate and centralist.

All in all, despite the pledges given to the local representatives, the initiatives of Giscardian governments met with a merely lukewarm reception: on the one hand the moderate representatives felt their real demands had not been met (in particular, on local finance), and on the other the local elections of 1976 (general councils) and 1977 (municipal elections) exacerbated the tensions between central government and the Left opposition that had remained solidly anchored in the town halls and *départements* throughout the Fifth Republic. The voting reform in towns with more than 30,000 inhabitants in 1965, and the progressive bi-polarisation of French political life, merely heightened the tensions. Specifically, the local elections constituted a privileged field for testing and reinforcing the application of new left-wing alliances, finally breaking the previous agreements between Socialists or Radicals and those centrists who nationally belonged to the right-wing governing coalition. The success of the Left alliance in particular in the towns (two-thirds of the towns with more than 30,000 inhabitants were won by the Left) helped to strengthen the 'nationalisation' of local political life and make it still more urgent to win back the local representatives.

Such a strategy implied paying attention primarily to the mayors of the small and medium-sized municipalities, where the vast majority of local representatives are to be found, at the expense of big city mayors, who were for the most part politically too opposed to the government for there to be a hope of winning them over. After the 1977 municipal elections, Giscard d'Estaing launched a reform which, on the eve of the presidential elections, was still awaiting a final vote in Parliament. A general mobilisation was launched: consultation of the mayors of the 36,394 municipalities: the appointment of a junior minister in the Ministry of the Interior with the task of mobilising the local representatives and sorting and analysing the 16,229 replies received by the government. The summary produced by the Aubert working group did not teach anything that was not already known. From the demands of the mayors' associations and the reactions of the elected representatives to the government reforms and the numerous reports and counter-proposals drawn up over some twenty-five years, the diagnosis of 'the local sickness' was perfectly well known. It was the remedies over which the parties, the representatives and the administration were divided.

The reform, prepared with great care (one of the President's advisers, Richard, was in 1978 appointed head of the Directorate-General for Local Authorities), in large part took up the mayors' demands and totally neglected the structural reforms, such as mergers of municipalities, which had always mobilised the representatives against central government.

Three major texts were proposed by the government, two of which were adopted. In January 1979 various government subsidies to local authorities were brought together under a single heading, the 'overall operative appropriation'. Thanks to their continuous pressure (and to initial erroneous estimates made by the Ministry of Finance), these payments, to be used at will, constituted a very important resource for the local authorities. Apart from the fact that the appropriation grows more rapidly than government resources, it represents more than 34 per cent of municipal and *département* resources or the equivalent of the proceeds of local taxes. Furthermore, in January 1980 local taxes were adjusted and the principle of progression introduced. VAT payable by local authorities on their investment expenditure was thereafter reimbursed by the government, and systems of loans were facilitated, especially for municipalities with fewer than 10,000 inhabitants. The local representatives clearly knew how to take advantage of a President looking for a broader political base.

The third plank of the reform did not reach a final vote. Only the Senate discussed it, adopting a draft that was transformed and sometimes mutilated by numerous amendments. Shuttling between the two assemblies would have required a lot more time, as well as compromise, but it is unlikely now that the planned reform will ever see the light of day. The government, by dissociating the three drafts under pressure from local represenatives and from parliamentarians, had already lost some of its trump-cards: the financial texts that in the representatives' eyes were the main point had already been adopted. There then remained three major sectors to reform: the status of local representatives, the distribution of power between government, the *départements* and the municipalities, and new forms of citizen participation and information. Despite the interest of these drafts, one must perforce conclude that they left the most important problems untouched: for instance, the *cumul des mandats*, which everyone condemned without being willing or able to eliminate it, or active participation by associations and the population (for instance, by way of referendum), which the local representatives rejected despite favourable declarations of principle.

Without being secondary, the proposed reforms all too often concerned only the most irritating *forms* of relationships between government and local authorities. Under the twin pressure of the top civil service, which was ill-disposed to give up its prerogatives, and the *notables*, who despite their protestations had very little wish to take the responsibility for unpopular measures, the Giscardian reforms aimed more at tampering with rather than at a substantial change in the centralised structures of the state. The Socialist Party has other projects which will condemn the Giscardian reforms to remain dead-letters.

President Giscard d'Estaing also hoped that apart from the content of the reforms, the procedures implemented might set up a new type of relationship between government and local authorities. Not only did the project to develop local responsibilities give rise to consultation on a gigantic scale, albeit often of a window-dressing nature, but numerous presidential initiatives were aimed at improving the atmosphere: the negotiation of the 'Great South-western plan' with representatives of that region, the open-hand policy towards Radical or Socialist mayors (Giscard d'Estaing's two trips to Lille and his interviews with the Socialist mayor, Mauroy, were widely commented symbolic gestures) and finally the contractual policy. Here too, however, the Giscardian initiatives were frequently looked at suspiciously by opposition representatives, who saw in them merely political cajolery or deceptive illusions. Though Giscard d'Estaing had stressed 'the usefulness of co-operation to mobilise energies and choose actions that are well adapted to local possibilities' (5 December 1979), many of his hearers had the feeling that the co-operation related more to details than to the main point, especially when interests to which the government gave priority were at stake (the Fontevrault and Larzac military camps or nuclear-power stations, for example).

Finally, this policy of consultation, which Giscard d'Estaing wanted to extend to other social categories or groups, engendered its own contradictions. For instance, in seeking to develop his influence with the Ecologists and the associations, the ex-President brought upon himself the almost unanimous opposition of the local representatives, who were reluctant as to the associations and most frequently hostile to the idea of local referendums. By interfering with habit and touching on old taboos without bringing about major reform, Giscard d'Estaing aroused the mistrust of his natural allies without reducing his adversaries' hostility.

### The Paradoxes of Giscardian Politics: Structural Uniformity and Differences of Treatment

One of the myths best rooted in French political culture is that de-centralisation worthy of the name can exist only strictly within the framework of direct universal suffrage. The existence in other democratic countries of non-elected executives (burgomasters in the Netherlands or city managers in the USA, for example) is, in every sense of the word, foreign to the French. The uniformity of statute linked to this political creed and strengthened by tradition constitutes another requirement of local and national elites: after the laws of 1871 and 1884, all towns and *départements*, with the notable exception of Paris which central government regarded as dangerous, had an identical charter. In 1946 the 'departmentalisation' of the oldest French colonies (such as the French West Indies) was unanimously regarded as a great 'Republican' conquest.

Uniformising anything that has not yet been almost automatically confers a 'Republican' image on the person responsible, whereas the differentiation attempts of de Gaulle were always presented and felt as marks of authoritarianism. After his election in 1974, the new President sought to reinforce the 'liberal' image he had tried to give himself during the election campaign. Thus, for the first time since the Paris Commune, the capital city was given essentially the same charter as the other local authorities, and was in 1977 empowered to elect a mayor – though, in the event, at the expense of the President's party. Likewise, the Paris region (the Ile-de-France) was given in 1976 a similar charter to that for the other French regions. The same applied to Corsica, which was given the status of a region, although it constituted only a single *département*. This 'anomaly' was righted not by granting the special status that the island's cultural and other peculiarities deserved, but by the creation of a second *département*. The island, with only 250,000 inhabitants, now has two general councils, one regional council and two prefects. Finally, departmentalisation was continued in the West Indies and Réunion, not stopping short at the most damaging consequences for their social and economic equilibrium.

This structural uniformity, erected into a dogma by almost all the parties, can only inadequately cover an irreducible diversity. The status of Paris and the Ile-de-France, for example, was 'normalised' only at the expense of numerous derogations, such as the grouping of *département* and municipality functions given to the Paris council. From this point of view, Giscard d'Estaing's policy contradicted the philosophy it was claiming to be applying, namely, the need for 'diversity', the affirmation that French society was not 'dedicated to levelling out and uniformity'.[10]

This policy of diversity was instead applied intensively in the *procedures* used by the government *vis-à-vis* its local partners. For about a decade, especially during Giscard d'Estaing's seven years, the methods of assigning government financial aid were multiplied, over and above the appropriations calculated on objective criteria. Though most of the methods used by the Giscard d'Estaing presidency had been initiated in the Pompidou period, the fact remains that the use made of them and the framework they were applied in constituted a perversion of the initial intentions. Moreover, as Hayward shows in Chapter 6, the planning system was seriously cast in doubt at the beginning of the 1970s, whilst new town-planning policy instruments were worked out and experimented with. These new planning tools had recourse to the 'contractual' method, and were used, initially without success, with urban communities ('plan contracts'), and then with medium-sized towns'. What might have been an innovatory tool of de-centralised planning became in a short time, with the decline of the plan, the vehicle of a policy which smacked of propaganda and masked a barely disguised form of patronage. Instead and in place of regional planning, for instance, specific programmes were superposed, being claimed as making a special effort for each region, although when added together, the effect was to generalise their application to the whole country. Thus, special development programmes were adopted for the Massif Central (October 1975), the other mountain areas and Corsica (1975 and 1978), the border areas (1976), the west and the coastal hinterlands (1975), the Great South-west (1979), and the Ile-de-France and Nord-Pas-de-Calais (1980). Just in case some areas might have been left out, there was a further special industrial adjustment fund set up in 1978 (Lorraine, Nord, the Loire country and Provence) and an inter-ministerial development and rural planning fund that covered thirty-three *départements* (1979). Apart from the 'showbusiness-politics' aspect that these plans, announced in a great blaze of publicity by the government, too often had, it is undeniable that they no longer had much in common with the original plans implemented at the end of the 1960s. All-round coherence was discarded in favour of one-off operations over which the central machinery kept a controlling hand.

At the local level this 'blow-by-blow' policy was complemented by the way the contractual techniques were more or less used as patronage. The principle was fairly simple: it consisted most often in laying down as riders to general rules based on objective criteria (for instance, the overall operative appropriation) provisions for flexibility at the discretion of central government. The fundamental mechanism was always the same: hard law, soft practice. The originality of the system lay in the procedures used and the latitude it left the government in its choice of partner. The contract technique experimented with by Chaban-Delmas in 1970–2 became increasingly widespread: apart from contracts from medium-sized towns and the countryside (70 and 240 contracts respectively were signed during 1974–80), contracts were set up for suburbs, for rural planning, for land or for loans, for cultural charters, and so on. Some contracts existed only in very limited numbers (for instance, those with Lille and Marseilles in favour of immigrants) or even had to be, by definition, unique (the contract with Strasbourg to meet its 'obligations as the capital of Europe'). This procedure presented numerous advantages for the central government.

In the first place, it was free to choose its partners more or less as it wished, because of the woolliness of the criteria adopted. For instance, medium-sized towns were defined in such a way that the government had almost total, not to say arbitrary, discretion. The multiplication of narrow and therefore discriminatory policies strengthened this trend, whilst avoiding, because of the formal nature of the procedures, the reproach of patronage. Moreover, despite appearances that seemed to strengthen 'partnership' between the government and the local authorities and attenuate the hierarchical nature of traditional relations, the local representatives were constrained to become beggars whose requests were more or less well received by the government and its departments.

In the second place, this technique allowed the reintroduction into the centre–periphery relationship of both prefects and the external field services that the local representatives occupying a national seat had sometimes short-circuited thanks to their direct access to the ministries. The requests were submitted by the prefects, made out by the field services and passed on to the central departments, where the decision on how to follow up was taken. Control by the prefects over the municipalities was a tradition that no regime or government had until then been able to give up, but Giscardian practice strengthened it still more, despite the declarations of good intent on local autonomy. The prefects were 'Giscardianised' or shifted from post to post, giving some of them greater autonomy *vis-à-vis* the local elites, at the expense however of making them dependent on their administration for want of adequate knowledge of local people and local problems. In seven years, only nine *départements* (out of ninety-six) had not more than two prefects, and the others had at least three (and in the two Corsican *départements*, five and six). Another illustration of the increasing politicisation of planning policy was given by the reattachment of the DATAR (the major body with the task of industrial decentralisation) to the Ministry of the Interior in 1974–6, the period when Giscard d'Estaing's closest adviser, Poniatowski, held the post. Nor did the latter hesitate to ask prefects to indicate the political 'colour' of municipalities in applications for contracts. As the very official Guichard Commission prudently and decorously stressed, 'the contractual policy all in all gives good political results. The temptation to use the contractual procedure to give government action better impact is a very real one'.

The balance-sheet of Giscardian policies amounts ultimately to very little. Valéry Giscard d'Estaing did not succeed in mobilising local elites in his favour, nor, for lack of time, did he complete the municipal reform placed before Parliament, but adopted only by the Second Chamber, the Senate. He was the latest victim of the Gaullist reforms, but with his fall he also brought down General de Gaulle's heirs, who had sought by every political and institutional means to polarise French political life by organising it into two opposing blocks, at the expense of the Centre. He was likewise a victim of the sociological change that reached its apex in the 1970s: rapid urbanisation, industrialisation and particularly growth of the tertiary sector at the expense of traditional sectors like agriculture. Finally, he was the victim of his own errors of analysis and strategy. Giscard and his advisers minimised too much the successive losses undergone in the 1976 (cantonal elections) and the 1977 (municipal elections), that benefited the Left and especially the Socialist Party. These victories not only consolidated the local base of the Socialist Party, created at the 1971 Epinay Congress (growth of militancy, network of influence, patronage and sources of party finance), but strengthened its power to extend towards the Centre in a system still characterised by the cumulation of local and national elected office.

Giscard d'Estaing's strategy perhaps gave him the support of thousands of local representatives of the small- and medium-sized municipalities, but was incapable of assuring him support from the towns where the major part of the population is now concentrated. The alliance between the bourgeoisie and the local *notables* was a success at the right time, during the Third Republic. Other days, other ways.

## The Victory of the Left: New Prospects for De-centralisation?

After François Mitterrand's victory, which was confirmed and amplified by the general elections in June, one of the first issues to be opened up by the new government was that of de-centralisation, presented by Prime Minister Pierre Mauroy as the 'grande affaire du septennat'. The speed – some might say the haste – with which the new Minister of the Interior and of De-centralisation, Gaston Defferre, brought his Bills before Parliament aroused considerable astonishment, not to say criticism: were there not, stressed the opposition, some top civil servants and part of the press, more pressing problems?

To this criticism Gaston Defferre replied with the need for speed, so as to take advantage of the so-called 'period of grace' following the presidential election and avoid the inevitable obstructionism of the upper civil service. As Ezra Suleiman stresses,

> while every (political) group may have reasons for preferring a particular form of decentralisation or deconcentration, there seems to be little doubt that there is an intimate link between the structure of administrative institutions (particularly the *grands corps*) and the centralisation of power. The ability of the various corps to preserve their power and to offer such wide liberties to their members reposes on the concentration of power. The corps, therefore, constitute one of the most powerful forces in the society opposing a genuine decentralisation of the state apparatus.[11]

Nevertheless, apart from the usual desire to catch the opponents unawares, the reform bears witness to the belief of the new government in structural reform as an instrument of social change. De-centralisation and nationalisation are considered as essential parts of the policy of economic, political and administrative change that the Socialist government is seeking to pursue.

From this point of view, the new rulers have not adopted an attitude or a strategy that is any different from that of the Michel Debré government in 1958. The major structural reforms were adopted during the first six months after his taking office, and since he lacked a coherent, disciplined majority like that elected in 1981, Debré acted using the full powers allowed by the Constitution for a six-month period. The experience of the initial phase of the Fifth Republic was to provide some guidance for those who twenty years later ventured along the same path: in many sectors, particularly in respect of de-centralisation, the structural reforms had remained a dead-letter. It took fifteen years to make a start on implementing the local taxation ordinances, and twenty years to bring the number of municipalities down from 38,000 to 36,000!

One is therefore entitled to wonder whether the Defferre reform will go any further than the symbols that it abolishes and those it sets up, and if so, what will be the consequences of the new provisions for centre–periphery relations. The Bill on 'the rights and liberties of municipalities, *départements* and regions' introduces several changes which at least appear to constitute serious breaks with the past government: control over the acts of local authorities is abolished, with *a posteriori* checks through the courts replacing the *a priori* administrative and political censorship; the prefects cease to be the executives of the *département* and the region, becoming mere 'commissioners of the Republic', responsible for the co-ordination of the state's field services; and local authorities can now take measures to ensure 'the protection of the economic and social interests of the regional population'.

These three major changes seem to be radical, and the opposition has not failed to bring out the usual scarecrows from the Jacobin cupboard: 'threats to the unity of the Republic', say some; 'waste, disorder and muddle', cry others. In truth, the reform deserves 'neither that honour, nor this indignity', if looked at from a realistic viewpoint.

On the suppression of the preliminary supervision: the Defferre law completes a development that began in 1959, and continued during the 1970s, that is, it consigns to oblivion an archaic supervisory system that had become pointless. It is, for instance, hardly any use to check administrative or financial measures for their legality when it is very well known that in most municipalities they have been prepared by the government's own field services. The crucial question in recent years has not been supervision by the prefectures, but that of the Ministry of Public Works or the Treasury. On the other hand, while checks through the courts theoretically ensure more guarantees, it is not certain that they will differ substantially from the previous administrative control: both the administrative tribunals and the future regional courts of auditors will be, by virtue of their composition, steeped in the values and traditions of the administration. Finally, the personal responsibility of elected representatives, which is the logical accompaniment to the elimination of the supervision, ought according to the Bill to be accentuated. In fact, the French Deputies have already limited their personal financial responsibilities to the amount of the annual allowance they receive, and it is a matter of public notoriety that the French system shrinks from applying individual responsibility. For instance, the Court of Budgetary and Financial Control, already competent for judging civil servants, will now be so for locally elected representatives. It is interesting to note that during 1968–81 only twenty-eight civil servants had been sentenced, the majority to very light penalties. Should one therefore conclude that the administration had functioned perfectly?

The transformation of the prefects into commissioners of the Republic has certainly constituted the most spectacular aspect of the reform. One cannot wipe out with impunity two centuries of such solid and continuous tradition! However, the 'revolutionary' nature of the change is moderated by several considerations. In the first place, Socialists and Communists had already provided in the 1946 Constitution for the elimination of the prefect as executive of the *département*. Yet that reform was never put into practice. To be sure, the present governing coalition, in contrast with previous governments of the Fifth Republic, has time on its side. However, one may wonder whether such a change will not be vulnerable in the event of a political or social crisis. On the other hand, many presidents of departmental councils will be tempted, as in the past, to leave things to the prefect, who from behind the scenes will retain the central role he has exercised hitherto.

However, this assumption is likely not to be the case in the most urbanised and industrialised regions or *départements*, where leaders of national stature will take full advantage of the new rules of the game. One possible consequence might be the development of patronage relations and the strengthening of the parties at local level. This 'Italianisation' of French political life would, however, meet with resistance from the state administration. This is very powerful at local level. Only a few big cities, *départements* and regions have sufficiently well-staffed services to counterbalance the state administration. Elsewhere the latter will retain its primacy, except that the triangular relations between prefect, departmental ministries and elected representatives will probably give way to a bi-polar confrontation: between representatives of the ministries and the prefect on the one hand, and the administration and the elected representatives on the other.

The third major aspect of the innovation is the authorisation given to regions, *départements* and municipalities to take measures in the economic sphere. The reform in actual fact ratifies practices that the previous government had sought to prevent but had not been able completely to forbid: both Pierre Mauroy at Lille and Gaston Defferre at Marseilles, to cite only two examples, had thought up and created numerous instruments and procedures aimed at circumventing the prohibition, so as to come to the aid of firms in difficulties. Now the same policy can be extended and applied without encountering a veto from central government.

With these largely symbolic provisions adopted, the list of potential reforms remains a long one: neither the powers nor the resources of the three tiers of regional, departmental and local government have been redefined. And these are two areas where the Fifth Republic has continually met with setbacks. But while the present government in principle has better cards to play than the Giscardian coalition had, it is nevertheless the case that the potential conflicts are many: between supporters of the *département* and those of the region (knowing that one of these two tiers will have to be made privileged), between those who favour autonomy of revenue and those who would prefer to have autonomy in expenditure, between planners and de-centralisers, between rural representatives and those from the towns. Not only do these cleavages sometimes separate the governing coalition and the opposition, but they also divide parties into several internal tendencies.

The first reforms adopted reveal, despite appearances, some options that are already clear. First, the *départements* have been favoured at the expense of the region, the reform of which, while adopted in principle, will not be applied until later. Secondly, big cities with well-staffed, competent services have been favoured, since only they will be able to benefit from the increased autonomy. For the others, the proclamation of 'liberties' will remain a pious wish, and they will be forced willy-nilly to go back to using the state field services. Thirdly, local *notables* have been favoured against the prefects. It is significant that the declared intention to reduce the plurality of offices held has been put in very circumspect terms, and that preparation of the reform has been entrusted to a Member of Parliament who holds several national and local offices!

Whilst we do not wish to indulge in polemics, it is probable that the Mauroy government reveals in this area more continuity than change. If this is the case, it would once again prove true that local changes are slower and more out of phase than those at the centre.

## Notes: Chapter 8

1  P. Birnbaum, 'Office holders in the local politics of the French Fifth Republic', in J. Lagroye and V. Wright (eds), *Local Government in Britain and France* (London: Allen & Unwin, 1979), pp. 114–26.
2  Y. Mény, *Centralisation et décentralisation dans le débat politique français* (Paris: Librairie Générale de Droit et de Jurisprudence, 1974).
3  Y. Mény, 'Financial transfers and local government in France: national policy despite 36,000 communes', in D. E. Ashford (ed.), *Financing Urban Government in the Welfare State* (London: Croom Helm, 1980), pp. 142–57.
4  V. Wright, 'Regionalisation under the French Fifth Republic: the triumph of the functional approach', in J. Sharpe (ed.), *Decentralist Trends in Western Democracies* (London: Sage, 1980), pp. 194–234.

5  See the special issue of *Pouvoirs* devoted to 'Giscardisme' (no. 9, 1979).
6  See Chapter 6 in this volume.
7  V. Giscard d'Estaing, *Le Monde*, 6 December 1979.
8  J. Dumas and P. Sadran, 'Le processus de réforme des collectivités locales en France', Congress at Metz, October 1980, mimeo.
9  V. Giscard d'Estaing, speech at Dijon, 26 November 1975.
10  V. Giscard d'Estaing, *Démocratie française* (Paris: Fayard, 1976), p. 53.
11  Ezra N. Suleiman, 'Administrative reform and the problem of decentralisation in the Fifth Republic', in William G. Andrews and Stanley Hoffman (eds), *The Impact of the Fifth Republic on France* (Albany, NY: State University of New York Press, 1981), pp. 74–5.

# 9

# Europeanisation and the Pursuit of National Interests

*R. FORMESYN*

## Giscard d'Estaing, Convinced but Cautious European, 1974-8

When Valéry Giscard d'Estaing announced in the *mairie* of Chamalières his candidacy for the French presidency on 4 April 1974, there was very little electoral gain to be made from projecting himself as a fervent European. Indeed, Europe was seen by many as heading for a very uncertain future, perhaps in danger of collapse. As recently as January, President Pompidou had preferred to see the franc driven out of the 'snake' - after having spent 1 billion dollars in support of the exchange rate - rather than accept a generous German offer to assist the franc during its difficulties. In February, as the oil crisis worsened, disunity within the EEC had increased, as several members hurriedly signed bilateral contracts with individual Gulf countries, leaving the Netherlands, which had been singled out by an Arab embargo, to fend for itself. Michel Jobert, who had just signed an important deal with Saudi-Arabia, expressed great apprehension about the desirability of a communal European approach: any such move could be seen by the Arab countries as a new concerted attempt, similar in character to the recent Nixon–Kissinger initiatives, to unite Western consumer countries against 'unjustifiable' Arab pressure. France did not want to be associated with any such possible impression; indeed, Jobert was not at all sure that his EEC partners would be prepared to show the same appreciation of Arab grievances about American policies in the Middle East that France herself had shown over the last years. Thirdly, since the beginning of 1974 Europe had been paralysed by a spate of political changes in the major member-states: Edward Heath had been defeated in Britain, the death of President Pompidou had suspended all initiative in the field of French foreign policy and in the Federal Republic, Chancellor Brandt had been succeeded by Schmidt. To complete this unpromising scene there were noises about the new Wilson government demanding renegotiation of the conditions of UK entry into the EEC; there were even noises of possible withdrawal, although they were later played down. As a result, Giscard d'Estaing made little reference to European policies or plans in his presidential campaign. He simply assured the French that he would follow in the footsteps of his predecessor who wanted to 'create Europe' by 1980. As he had to win the Gaullist vote at the second ballot, the one-time enthusiastic supporter of Europe, and Deputy who had voted in 1957 in the National Assembly for the ratification of the Treaty of Rome, cautiously refrained from making statements about Europe which could be interpreted as deviations from Gaullist orthodoxy.

There was hardly any hint of innovation in foreign policy when Jacques Chirac presented the new government to the National Assembly: the three objectives were to maintain national independence, to continue existing defence policies and to 'achieve Europe' by 1980. There was, however, an unmistakable indication that Giscard d'Estaing intended to be in charge of foreign policy: the new Foreign Affairs Minister was Sauvagnargues, a career diplomat, used to the role of implementing faithfully instructions given from above, now the President. As to European policy, the first Giscardian views emerged only at the June Franco-German summit: both leaders agreed that they wanted to 'stop the process of weakening which is taking place in the Community'; that there was no chance of economic recovery 'through protectionist measures'; but that recovery could be guaranteed only through 'common measures with regard to monetary, economic and international problems'. President Giscard d'Estaing clearly did not conceive of any possibility of achieving durable French prosperity without careful co-ordination of economic policies within a European dimension. European inter-dependence was for Giscard d'Estaing a reality which had to be recognised. This was the new dimension for the neat planning mind of the President. As to the new style of French European policy, Giscard d'Estaing let it be known at the Elysée reception for the diplomatic corps (20 June) that co-operation, flexibility and liberal attitudes would prevail. The previous conflictual Jobert approach would disappear; it had isolated France and created an atmosphere which was not conducive to the successful launching of French initiatives.

A major opportunity for Giscard d'Estaing to prepare initiatives in Europe occurred on 1 July 1974 when the half-yearly presidency of the EEC Council of Ministers, which is taken in rotation by the Nine, fell to the French. Giscard d'Estaing wished to mark the occasion by inviting all EEC heads of government to dinner at the Elysée Palace towards the end of the year, the declared aim being to discuss freely together in a relaxed atmosphere. At this time there were indeed many very serious problems in Europe: the Fourcade proposals for monetary union were unceremoniously rejected by the German H. Apel as ignoring the need for economic discipline by all partners involved. A few days later the Agricultural Ministers of France and Germany had taken diametrically opposed positions: the French insisting on an increase in the CAP financial arrangements – the overall French priority being to fight unemployment, the Germans resisting the increase, as they saw the fight against inflation to be their top priority. Nevertheless, in Giscard d'Estaing's view these difficulties together with many others could be solved only within a 'European construction' and therefore had not to be allowed to jeopardise the overall, long-term progress towards that ultimate objective. At his press conference of 24 October 1974 Giscard d'Estaing repeated his earlier invitation to the EEC leaders and announced, clearly as a major gesture of good-will, that in matters which were not of major national interest he would no longer insist on a rigid observance of unanimity voting in the Council of Ministers in Brussels, thereby demonstrating that France now accepted 'in certain circumstances a transfer of sovereignty, beginning with small issues'. These words were indeed important, as they reversed at least in tone and attitude, although not much in substance (as the minor issues had to be identified by unanimity voting), the intransigent stand taken by General de Gaulle in 1965 against article 148 of the Treaty of Rome, which requires majority voting in the Council. Giscard d'Estaing, once he had decided on a long-term European strategy, remained undeterred by a set of practical setbacks in Europe: soon after the French government found itself again in opposition to its EEC partners, who wanted the Community to attend and speak with one voice at the US-convened International Energy Agency; the French refused to join as they feared indeed that the collective EEC position will not accurately reflect their own with regard to the Arabs in a matter of such crucial importance to France. At the same time they also saw their plan for an EEC-Arab dialogue postponed *sine die*.

When the nine heads of government met in Paris in December 1974, Giscard d'Estaing showed himself capable of considerable flexibility with regard to UK demands for a correcting mechanism affecting its EEC budget contribution and equally with regard to the setting up of the European Regional Fund – a proposal for which he felt little enthusiasm; and in spite of Gaullist opposition, he agreed to direct elections to the European Assembly in 1978. But Giscard d'Estaing's courteous diplomacy was not unrewarded: at the meeting he secured a major strategic success as he obtained general support for his proposal to set up a new European institution, the European Council: heads of state or government shall meet 'at least three times per year' and 'whenever necessary'. The European summit meetings, first called by Pompidou, would now be institution-alised: 'Le Sommet européen est mort, vive le Conseil Européen!' That which de Gaulle, under the Fouchet plan, never got through, as it was seen as part of a plan to replace the EEC institutions by inter-governmental agencies, was now accepted. It was the creation of a veritable para-Community institution. Giscard d'Estaing's personal style and reasonable flexibility were no doubt largely responsible for this success, although not unaided by the presence of two new partners in the EEC, the UK and

Denmark, both averse to the federal tendencies built into the treaty institutions. M. Poniatowski may have spoken for the President when he declared that the 'European Council may progressively become a kind of European cabinet, taking major decisions, developing plans for the future on a continental scale'. Giscard d'Estaing, indeed, seemed to be working towards a kind of Europe which he approved of – as it was going to be Europe which he would increasingly need.

A further significant declaration of Giscardian foreign policy was made at a press luncheon on 21 May 1975, when the European dimension was extended to encompass a global dimension: successful government requires 'problems to be tackled on a worldwide scale ... From the moment that one part of the world wants to deal with them, another part of the world will not be able to ignore them; indeed this must be the dominating idea of our policy'. No doubt the successive oil crises had prompted the neat Giscardian mind to take into account a wider dimension for French advance planning. Subsequent statements would now increasingly demonstrate Giscard d'Estaing's keen interest in influencing global policies more effectively and no doubt he wanted to occupy the 'driver's seat' in Europe. Europe was seen as an instrument for maximising French policy influence in the world; Europe was no longer just a target, but a stepping-stone towards the further target of global influence. Both Chirac in the Senate and Sauvagnargues in the National Assembly sought, in the summer of 1975, approval for a number of delicate EEC measures basing their arguments on the importance of strengthening Europe as an instrument for French influence in world affairs.

As the dollar and oil crises deepened and the weakness of American leadership in the West became more apparent, there was an acute awareness amongst other European leaders of the need to have an impact on world events. Even Chancellor Schmidt had now come round to Giscard d'Estaing's thesis of the need for a European role in the world. Equally the Brussels Commission was now taking this view and developing Giscardian arguments: in its submission to the Tindemans Report it stressed the inadequacy of the individual states to respond adequately to the global dimension of the problems they faced. It suggested that, in order to make the member-states more effective, all 'competences which can no longer ... be effectively exercised by the individual states should be transferred to the Community'. A similar awareness appears in the declaration of the December 1975 European Council which now accepted the Giscardian theory that the fight against the recession required 'a concerted action of a structural monetary kind also involving the United States and Japan'.

The growing consensus in Europe on the need for a global economic and political strategy encouraged the French President to press ahead with renewed fervour with his plan for a North–South conference, which would be much wider in scope than the Nixon–Kissinger-created International Energy Agency. Giscard d'Estaing sought a more even-handed tripartite participation involving not only the oil-producers (seven of whom wished to be considered at the same time as developing countries) and the industrialised countries, but also the poorer developing countries. This demonstration by Giscard d'Estaing of a more sophisticated understanding of the 'South' not only led to the conference effectively taking place in December with the result that four commissions were set up to study common problems, but Giscard d'Estaing achieved a growing French influence in the world, placing him in a favourable position to pursue forcefully a Euro-Arab dialogue. This would, of course, mean in practical terms, the creation of an independent European voice in the world, separate from American views and policies.

The 1976 Tindemans Report met with polite silence from the French President. Strengthening of the Brussels Commission and complete abolition of the unanimity vote in the Council were not amongst his favourite objectives. What he, in fact, preferred is to be found in the communiqué of the February Franco-German summit: a strengthening of the European Council and the setting up of a European *directoire* very much along the lines of a similar proposal by General de Gaulle in 1958, but improved by a system of rotation. The proposal was, however, unacceptable to the European Council in April, a meeting characterised by a depressed atmosphere: the Tindemans Report was buried, monetary union was collapsing, and the UK and Denmark were unwilling to commit themselves to direct elections in 1978. At the closing press conference Giscard d'Estaing was the only member to believe that 'progress has been made'. Was this perhaps an indication of how much Giscard d'Estaing's European policy was basically long-term: planning and patiently setting up useful structures for the future in chess-game fashion.

It can be argued that one of the major reasons for the break-up between Jacques Chirac and Giscard d'Estaing in the summer of 1976 was economic policy within France and Europe: the former aiming primarily at full employment, the latter increasingly approving of the German approach of first dealing with inflation as the cause of all evils. The new Prime Minister Raymond Barre, greeted by the President as 'France's best economist', was much more in tune with Giscard d'Estaing's analysis of the situation: France's competitiveness had to be restored in the foreign markets if durable employment was to be achieved. The change in leadership in France was welcomed in the European capitals, since it meant not only the disappearance of a man with views which were often felt to be too Gaullist, but particularly because the Federal Republic and the Benelux countries felt that now a real measure of economic policy co-ordination could be organised. The later reshuffle in the second Barre government, after the Left's victory in the 1977 local elections, had very little to do with responding to the electorate's verdict on economic policies; on the contrary, it aimed at a deliberate further strengthening of the Giscardian economic team within the government. Although throughout 1977 there were no spectacular events on the European level, there was none the less quiet and solid progress towards streamlining economic strategy in Europe, as the French and German leaders particularly showed a growing conviction that in dealing with unemployment, inflation, balance of payment problems and exchange rates there was a close interlocking between the national situation and the European situation; this should now be 'managed'. This view was also increasingly appreciated by French public opinion (*Aurore Publimetrie*, 10 December 1977) which saw the need for linked policies at the European level as one of the main reasons justifying further steps towards unification in Europe, such as going ahead with direct elections to the European Assembly.

## Giscard d'Estaing, Liberated European, 1978–81

The March 1978 victory of the Giscard-Gaullist coalition, when the Giscardian UDF considerably increased its strength (139 seats as against 119 previously) in relation to the Gaullist RPR (150 seats reduced from 183), appeared dramatically to liberate Giscard d'Estaing from Gaullist constraints. With the European Commission's ex-Vice President Barre reappointed as the Prime Minister of a confident team, the opportunities to launch initiatives in Europe were there to be grasped: first of all, a number of issues such as Greek, Spanish and Portuguese entry into Europe were simply waiting for decisive action; and secondly, new problems were throwing up a range of tasks which would give scope for new initiatives, for example, in the sphere of monetary stabilisation.

### One Money for Europe?

There is no doubt that the President saw France as irrevocably enmeshed in the European economic framework: as there is political and economic interdependence, there must also exist opportunities for tackling recession and unemployment more effectively within this wider context. However, easy solutions for reflation were out. Full employment could be more permanently ensured only if France, in the words of Giscard d'Estaing, 'makes a considerable effort in competitiveness. If not – perhaps she does not fully realise this – she will be condemned to a decline in living standards and in resources, as history has shown for many countries'. As an immediate step, the Barre government decided to liberalise price controls in order to increase business profitability. If there was going to be a reflation, the aim was to make it an investment-led one enabling French industry to establish itself on a sound financial basis and, in the words of M. Monory, the Finance Minister, 'able to compete with the best in Europe'. The traditional devices of protectionism and devaluation had to be abandoned as they did not cure the fundamental weakness of the national economy. Giscard d'Estaing did not waste time: he invited Chancellor Schmidt to Rambouillet on 2 April 1978 and sketched out a major initiative in Europe: with great effort, an area of European monetary stability had to be created. At the Copenhagen summit the proposal took the form of the creation of a European unit of account, the proposer being Schmidt, 'speaking very much with the authority of a recent convert to closer monetary union'. Giscard d'Estaing, with the prestige of the only head of state who had always been enthusiastic about progress towards monetary union, stressed the need for interventions within the 'Boa-snake' to be made in EEC currencies instead of dollars as was the case, as well as the 'importance of co-ordinating national economic policies in parallel with tightening currency links'; he also pointed out that it was politically important that all member-countries should participate in the system and that there was therefore a need for some concession – at least in the beginning – as to the exact margins of flexibility for weaker currencies. After the July Bremen European Council which agreed on a scheme which would be backed by pooled reserves, Giscard d'Estaing was keen to stress the political significance as he saw it: 'closer European co-operation is the key to a greater independent European decision-making capacity.' The Gaullist philosophy aiming to free Europe from all hegemonies, with France occupying a leading position in Europe, was never far from Giscard d'Estaing's mind; his views, however, were more pragmatic, his approach more gradualistic and his action better timed. Paradoxically, however, much of the Giscardian progress in Europe was the result of constant 'Franco-German duetting' which was seen with increasing annoyance by the other Community partners as hegemony politics within Europe, highly 'unEuropean' in spirit, smacking of the old prewar diplomatic wheelings and dealings in search of power and influence. The German Chancellor was aware of the dangers of this intense bilateral diplomacy and firmly put the brakes on from mid-1978: in statements after such meetings he now carefully referred to 'further consultations' with other partners. At the Brussels European Council in December 1978 the European Monetary System was finally approved. However, at the last moment Italy and Ireland were unable to obtain acceptable conditions for joining and so stayed out. Incomprehensibly it was Giscard d'Estaing who had refused further concessions. Was the much-heralded European dimension now abandoned? Had not the initiative now turned into a European disaster? Certainly, for the French President it was not only the 'most important step in the organisation of Europe since the creation of the EEC', but also an important move towards increasing European independence in the world. It was thought that Giscard d'Estaing had perhaps decided that enough concessions had already been made: indeed, just before the summit, Giscard d'Estaing had had a rough time at home. The National Assembly had thrown out his EEC VAT Bill and the Gaullist RPR mercilessly pursued him personally for allowing France to participate in what they saw as the dangerous game of direct elections to a supra-national European Assembly. Above all, Giscard d'Estaing had been angered by the European Assembly's decision to make a huge increase in the Regional Aid Fund, well beyond what were the authorised limits, and so taking out of his hands the very means he may have wished to bargain with in order to obtain the Italian and Irish agreement to join the EMS. Given his known aversion for the kind of economic soft options represented by simple 'transfers of resources' either regional or across countries, given the need to demonstrate for those critics at home that he was no easy push-over for an aggressive European Assembly, the President, as 'a Republican monarch', was in need of bolstering-up political support within France. He had therefore to be seen to take a firm stand for France in the European arena. However, by 15 December concessions had been made and both Italy and Ireland had joined a fully fledged European system. It can be argued that very similar domestic political reasons forced Giscard d'Estaing almost immediately to take a hard stand on the early phasing out of the agricultural Monetary Compensatory Amounts (intended to compensate producers for exchange-rate fluctuations between the Nine), thereby delaying the putting into operation of the EMS until 13 March 1979. Similarly, his rather grand invitation – at short notice – to the three Western supremos to join him in January in the Guadeloupe for an agenda-less summit can safely be seen as a further means for Giscard d'Estaing to improve in France his image as a world leader and host in true Gaullist style.

The EMS functioned, and it was coping reasonably well with the continued instability in the financial world market. The French attributed the success to three major factors: the strong-willed perseverance of their Prime Minister and government in pursuing orthodox economic policies; the German resolve to support the system rather than allow the mark to become an international reserve currency; and finally, the willingness of member-countries to take appropriate steps when their currency moved out of line. However, in March 1981 when the question of introducing 'Stage Two EMS' arose, Giscard d'Estaing and Chancellor Schmidt agreed to delay. Giscard d'Estaing particularly did not want the political issue of national sovereignty, implied in the second stage of EMS, to complicate further his electoral campaign.

## One Assembly for Europe?

The Gaullists had, in essence, continued to take the General's attitude of disdain for 'régimes d'Assemblée' and certainly for such compounded absurdities as a supra-national Europe controlled by a strong supra-national Assembly. The attitude of Giscard d'Estaing in 1978 was subtle. First, there was clear support for the early implementation of the European Council's decisions in 1974 and 1976 to organise direct elections; this support had to be seen by the other EEC members as a clear token of Giscard d'Estaing's commitment to European progress. Secondly, there was a clear awareness of the fact that as the powers of the Assembly were defined by the treaty, these elections merely changed the mode of designation of the new members of the Assembly, in line with the requirement of article 138. This point was sharply emphasised on three occasions: to H. Schmidt, to W. Brandt and to the Luxembourg Premier G. Thorn. It was also during the run up to these direct elections that the French President pronounced the two most extensive expositions of his view on 'European construction'. The first was delivered at a press conference on 21 November 1978 and constituted the President's European constitutional doctrine. In essence, he declared that he

> looks forward to an organisation of Europe which is confederal . . . in which no one can impose his will on anyone . . . which does not entail the possibility of . . . being compelled to follow a line with which one does not agree; if at present Europe would be of a federal type, it would be subject to American influence . . . We must see Europe as it is . . . a continent on which has been accumulated the longest history, the greatest variety of national temperaments and of tradition. It is, therefore, natural that the structure of Europe reflects this situation and that it has a confederal aspect. My position [on the powers of the Assembly] has not changed since I voted in favour of the Treaty of Rome as a very young member of Parliament. I have maintained exactly the same course, which is the application of the Treaty of Rome *dans son interprétation en direction d'une confédération*. The powers . . . can only be changed by a modification of the Treaty . . . I remind you that the article relating to the revision of the Treaty of Rome submits the consideration of such revision to the unanimous agreement of the Council of Ministers . . . It is sufficient that one country . . . does not agree for the Treaty to be applied as it stands.

Would the President recommend a right choice for the European election? 'No.' Would the President at any future date agree to extended powers?

> I think that as long as a confederal Europe is not fully organised and until it has demonstrated its capacity to survive, I am not in favour of an extension of the powers . . . Modification of the Treaty of Rome requires . . . the unanimous support of the European states . . . if there were to be, however, an important modification it is probable that it would pose institutional problems and that it would require a modification of the French Constitution. At that point we would have to apply the procedure for the modification of our Constitution . . . But if the reform of the Constitution would entail a transfer of powers for example to a European institution, I think that in that case it is an essential point

in our national life that the procedure of revision to be used is the vote of the two Assemblies and a referendum.

Very similar views were restated in Hoerdt in Alsace on 15 May 1979, just before the European elections, perhaps with greater reference to some Gaullist objections: 'The principle of the election is unassailable.' It is not only enshrined in article 138 of the treaty, but it is inconceivable that old democracies should wish 'to take away from their citizens the right to designate themselves their representation'. As to the kind of Europe: 'I have never changed my position: the application of the Treaty of Rome, not more, not less *dans la perspective d'une organisation confédérale.*' When the European elections came (10 June 1979), the voters tilted further the balance of support in the country towards the Giscardian UDF, which gained twenty-seven seats against fifteen for the Gaullists; whatever had been said before by Barre about the elections not having any internal French significance, the results did not fail to boost government morale and standing. On 18 July Mme Veil was elected president of the European Assembly on a liberal ticket: one of the ablest and the most popular Giscardian ministers and Giscard d'Estaing's personal choice as leader of the UDF list she enjoyed an outstanding position of delicate power in the European Assembly. Giscard d'Estaing's prestige as a European had never been higher.

## Greece, Spain and Portugal for Europe?

After a number of earlier vacillations, the new 1978 Barre government did not hesitate long before choosing a deliberate policy of support for the second enlargement. When in May 1978 the commission published its report assessing the life of a twelve-member Community and laid stress on the need for the negotiation with the three countries to be conducted separately, it ran into rough waters in the Council: many ministers would not have been unhappy to refer the whole study back to the commission for further work. But the new French government took a vigorously positive attitude and supported quite enthusiastically the commission's proposal for a scheme involving rapid progress. It was understood in Brussels that the Giscard d'Estaing presidency had now come to the clear conclusion that without support for the Greek entry, there was no possibility of a successful French Mediterranean policy; and once Greece was admitted, it would have been politically absurd to resist Spanish and Portuguese entry – although there were real economic problems. This stand was now to be given ample publicity by Giscard d'Estaing in a state visit to King Juan Carlos' Spain (28 June 1978) and soon after to Portugal. The press of both countries, while appreciating Giscard d'Estaing's role as cheer-leader for the second enlargement, made clear its impression that underneath the statements of 'the need to strengthen the southern flank of the

Community', there was the unspoken ambition of the French to play a leading role in this bloc.

As to the institutional problems to be settled before the creation of the twelve-member Community, Giscard d'Estaing called urgently for a committee of three wise men, with solid experience in the EEC administration, to prepare a thorough report. However, when they (R. Marjolin, E. Dell and B. Biesheuvel) produced their views in early 1979, Giscard d'Estaing had lost interest. The demand for thorough reports – typical of the Giscard d'Estaing administration within France – seems also here, as in the case of the Tindemans Report earlier, to have been the usual well-known device of the President: namely, to elicit potentially interesting proposals from a committee, with the intention of promoting them with the added authority of the committee, if they fitted in well with French policies, but allowing them to slip into oblivion most courteously, if they did not suit government policy. As to the question of enlargement, near the end of 1978 there were overriding political and long-term considerations in favour; even the expected economic problems of the southern French wine-growers and fruit-farmers appeared no longer to be an obstacle. As during the EMS negotiations, there was a point when Giscard d'Estaing firmly considered the political stakes first and the economic stakes second. Politics overshadow economics: a true Gaullist attitude indeed. Later rumours that Giscard d'Estaing wanted to delay the new entries were firmly dismissed at the Elysée press conference of 26 June 1980.

## One Foreign Policy for Europe?

The fourth major area of Giscardian initiative was the promotion of closer co-operation in foreign affairs between the EEC members. This was to be achieved not only through making good use of the mechanisms set up in the early 1970s by the Davignon Reports as regular meetings of the foreign affairs ministers and setting up of a European political committee, but particularly since 1974 by bringing the major issues of foreign policy to the forefront of the discussions at the European Councils. The definition of a common European position on a number of international issues was increasingly becoming the key topic at the European Council's meetings. The objective was to give Europe its independent and legitimate role in the world; Giscard d'Estaing stressed that this had not to be seen as a new attempt 'to exercise world power in an imperialistic form ... It is a new form of presence in the world that Europe envisages', that is, a moving away from the 'two hegemonies' situation. Whereas in 1974 the Nine had hoped that the then rapidly emerging Giscard d'Estaing-US détente and new cordiality might have led to the gradual reintegration of France within the Atlantic sphere, by 1978 quite the opposite was taking place, as Giscard d'Estaing, very much helped by a deteriorating world situation, increasingly asserted the need for Europe to decide its own policy independently from the USA, and furthermore was able to bring the other Europeans, including the West Germans and the British, to abandon what André Fontaine called their political *suivisme*, that is, automatically following American policy lines. There was during Giscard d'Estaing's presidency European differences of policy with the USA over:

(1)  the attitude to adopt towards the oil-producers: Europe insisted on a more understanding approach towards the oil-producers, particularly those which were themselves developing countries, and the need for a North–South dialogue and for worldwide co-operation;

(2)  the ways of combatting world inflation: the need for reducing European and American dependence on oil;

(3)  the responsibility and role of the dollar in achieving greater international monetary stability;

(4)  détente with the Soviet Union: the disapproval of what was seen as the noble but naïve pursuance by President Carter of human rights in Russia, and which was seen there as an external campaign to undermine the Soviet state. Détente had to be brought about by subtler means and 'human rights' would gradually follow. Since the Afghan invasion, however, the practice of détente has become less appropriate, and alone among the Europeans Giscard d'Estaing began arguing for substitution of détente by a policy of restraint towards the USSR;

(5)  the solution of the Middle East problems: far more understanding for Arab and Palestinian grievances was essential to any settlement. Hence, deep scepticism towards the Camp David proposals and European political overtures towards the Egyptians (Sadat in Luxembourg), the Saudi-Arabians and indirectly the PLO.

The long-term French campaign for closer European 'concertation' of foreign policy was rapidly gaining ground. Strong, though much less anti-American, support seemed to be coming from the British Foreign Office. The swift and stern European Council's warning to the Russians about Poland seemed indeed to augur more decisive action. The further question of the ultimate need for a European defence was sharply brought to the forefront of the discussions at the Franco-German summit in July 1980 and received considerable encouragement from the German Chancellor.

It was clear that all European political co-operation bore a strictly intergovernmental character. Both Giscard d'Estaing and the British wished to maintain the co-operation within this limit, whereas the Germans, the Italians and the Benelux countries supported moves towards a European Union and a Community foreign policy.

## Political Implications

### Political Background of France and the EEC

As a country with an almost unbroken tradition of foreign-policy ambitions, France has constantly been in search of the means of strengthening and extending her foreign-policy capacity. This ambition was extraordinarily explicit in de Gaulle's policies and has been strongly present ever since. The Gaullist Republic has even claimed that the previous Fourth Republic lacked a foreign policy, apart from that towards Germany. Paradoxically, however, the most outstanding creation in postwar Europe, the European Economic Community, was the work of Fourth Republic politicians. And on close examination one detects the reason why Gaullist politicians came to this negative verdict: the Fourth Republic was one of the very rare periods in modern French history in which narrow nationalistic policies were not crudely pursued. The glory of nationalism was much tainted by the cruel experiences of the Second World War; in the Europe of 1945 there was a widely held feeling that the anarchy of the nation state was a situation which could not continue. It was in this particular climate that the creation of the European Community was conceived, planned, ratified and set up. It is, in fact, the only period in recent French history during which such an un-nationalistic, Community-spirited, European-interest-minded organisation could probably have been set up and contributed to by France. Admittedly, the EEC treaty does not exhibit the evident supra-national features of the earlier European coal and steel community treaty, when six European governments accepted voluntary limitations on their national sovereignty 'in respect of a vital part of their economic life with the avowedly political aim of surmounting their centuries-old conflicts and going forward together towards a united federal Europe' (R. Morgan). Nevertheless, the treaty of 1958 represented a move towards European supra-nationalism in a gradual and more subtle way. Its institutions are not overtly supra-national, but the working party of experienced politicians including Mollet, Spaak and Monnet at Val Duchesne created, adroitly, some internal mechanisms within the institutions which would act as 'motors' towards supra-nationalism:

(a) the commission's members shall be completely independent in the performance of their duties and no government shall seek to instruct them (article 157). It shall act by a majority vote (article 163). Where, in pursuance of the treaty, the Council acts on a proposal from the commission, unanimity shall be required for an act constituting an amendment to that proposal (thereby tilting the balance towards the European Commission) (article 149);

(b) the Council of Ministers shall act by a majority of its members or by a weighted majority where required (article 148); this being a key mechanism towards supra-nationalism;

(c)   the European Assembly can dismiss the commission by a motion of censure (article 144). It also now has the final say on the Community budget (article 203);

(d)   the European Court of Justice has the monopoly of interpretation of Community Law and therefore claims in this matter precedence of Community jurisdiction over national jurisdiction.

The European Community thus started its life as something more than a traditional inter-governmental organisation. It is not overtly federal, but has the built-in internal mechanisms which will make it federal.

The intellectual climate which allowed this treaty to be drawn up and signed did not prevail in the Fifth Republic. An almost opposite climate was created by General de Gaulle, and it soon pervaded French politics. Many European politicians feared that de Gaulle in 1958 would refuse to accept the Treaty of Rome as it stood. But, however much de Gaulle disliked the treaty, he avoided a head-on collision with the other Five and accepted to work within its framework. The General's co-operation, however, lacked the previous spirit of openness and pursuance of wider European interest; his co-operation was completely utilitarian and narrowly nationalistic: the only progress he wanted was the setting up of the Common Agricultural Policy, which was pursued unashamedly with the French interest in mind. Some Europeans felt that European co-operation was turned into European exploitation. And fundamentally the Treaty of Rome did not fit in with French politics any longer: it 'did not correspond any more to France's need.'[1] The Fouchet Plan was the first attempt to set up an alternative organisation (allowing the EEC to fall into disuse): it provided for the setting up of a Council of Heads of Government, a European Assembly with sole supervisory role and a European Political Commission. The plan was rejected by the other Five as a poorly disguised attempt to replace the Treaty of Rome with a new, purely inter-governmental organisation. But, for France, the de Gaulle-Fouchet Plan had become the official plan for Europe: not only did Pompidou work towards its implementation by introducing 'summitry' in Europe, but it was in substance the blueprint for Giscard d'Estaing's policy. France needed Europe. But the reasons for European construction before 1958 were very different from the later reasons. The first were basically European: France wanted to integrate within a European Community; the old emphasis on the nation state was not only obsolete, but dangerous; and one has to remember in this respect the special significance of the term 'Community' in the postwar intellectual climate, as designating 'togetherness of feelings and interests, and abolition of barriers'. The post-1958 reasons were nearly the opposite: Europe was perceived as an instrument for furthering narrow national economic interest and the extension of national foreign policy influence. The emphasis on integration disappeared. President Giscard d'Estaing continued to see the reasons for what he called 'organising Europe' very much along the same Gaullist–Pompidou lines: in his Hoerdt speech he gave strong reasons for organising Europe, none for 'integrating'. Indeed, the term 'integration' was absent from Giscard d'Estaing's vocabulary. European interests as the wider and greater interests of the peoples of Europe increasingly disappeared from the argument. They were replaced by the interests of France. The European dimension was more central to Giscard d'Estaing's economic and foreign policies than to any of the other EEC members, but for reasons which were Gaullist rather than close to those of the founding fathers. So, what kind of Europe did Giscard d'Estaing want?

## EUROPE OF THE TREATY OF ROME?

What credence can be given to Giscard d'Estaing's claims that the Europe he wanted to see was the Europe of the Treaty of Rome? A careful analysis of what the President 'said' and 'did' reveals statements and actions that were *incompatible* with the Treaty of Rome:

(1)  Giscard d'Estaing, following the stand of General de Gaulle taken in 1966, refused to implement article 148 requiring majority voting in the Council, thereby resisting any transfer of national sovereignty and blocking the main mechanism of evolution towards a more federal Europe. His 1974 gesture to allow majority voting on minor issues was purely cosmetic, since unanimity voting was still required for deciding which issues were to be designated as minor.

(2)  France ignored the Euratom Treaty provisions relating to nuclear supply policies and wanted its supra-national character changed.

(3)  The French, supported at home by the Constitutional Council's ruling of 30 December 1976, frequently ignored the rulings of the European Court in Luxembourg. The French refused to call on the Court over what they angrily called the 'illegal' supplementary Euro-budget for 1980.

(4)  The President was ambiguous; the two policies that he pursued – the Europe of the treaty, nothing more, nothing less, and on the other hand, *dans la perspective d'une organisation confédérale* or *en direction d'une confédération* – were conflicting. General de Gaulle straight-forwardly stated the incompatibility between the terms of the Treaty of Rome and the confederal Europe he wanted, and therefore proceeded to submit the Fouchet Plan. Giscard d'Estaing tried to gloss over this.

(5)  In addition, as French domestic attitudes are more naturally disposed to accept the need for change or revision, at intervals, of constitutional documents, so there is in the European sphere evidence of the same phenomenon: revisionism. On all accounts the demand for

revisionism in the EEC was, until the British joined, an exclusively French phenomenon.

Other initiatives of Giscard d'Estaing *reduced*, if not *replaced*, the role of established treaty institutions. The European institution which was most vigorously promoted by Giscard d'Estaing was not a treaty institution but a new, superimposed or 'para-Community' institution: the European Council. It now takes all major initiatives and decisions. In important matters, such as the setting up of the EMS, the Council of Ministers was reduced to the status of a badly informed and unconsulted onlooker. The Commission, although represented in the Council through its President, was increasingly reduced to the status of a technical secretariat, working out complicated solutions for the European Council. The once-famous decision-making process through the Commission–Council of Ministers dialogue, established by the treaty and designed to foster progress towards federal integration, was bypassed in important matters. This Giscardian assault on the treaty was not frontal, it was more subtle; the new process was not in flagrant breach of the treaty, but outside the treaty, and in practice replaced the treaty institutions. The de Gaulle–Fouchet Plan of the 1960s, much combated then by the federal-minded Five, had under the gentle hand of Giscard d'Estaing almost surreptitiously come into being. The strong Giscard d'Estaing support for the Davignon procedures which provided for inter-governmental co-operation in the field of foreign affairs represented another instance of the development of European agencies which were outside the orbit of the treaty institutions. The French insisted on maintaining a sharp dividing-line between Davignon business and strict EEC business so as to avoid all stain of supra-nationalism on the 'concertation' of the European foreign policies.

A number of Giscard d'Estaing initiatives were *not in the spirit* of the treaty. His regular assertions of the importance of the Franco-German special relationship as a keystone of the European constitution was a constant reminder to the other members of their inferiority. Similarly, the constant Franco-German 'duetting' as a consultative process excluding all the others, and this on a regular basis, was felt to create a small secretive 'Community within the Community' and smacked of Franco-German hegemony in Europe. Neither was Giscard d'Estaing's very personal diplomacy towards the new applicant countries much appreciated amongst either the old or the new members. It was felt that he used Europe to boost his own country's status. Thirdly, the emphasis of Giscard d'Estaing and Jean François-Poncet on the need for a stronger southern bloc within the EEC was distinctly perceived as unnecessary political manoeuvring. No other Community country speaks such language of rivalry. Finally, there were the attempts by Giscard d'Estaing to use the Community for new purposes, close to French preoccupations, such as anti-Americanism, but alien to the other members' or the treaty aims in general. Similarly, there was the constant French attempt to interpret the European Council's decisions in a way unsupported by a general Community consensus, for example, as steps towards complete European independence.

## A CONFEDERAL OR A FEDERAL EUROPE?

In his press conference of 21 November 1978 Giscard d'Estaing quoted three reasons for wanting a confederal structure: first, a federal Europe would probably be subject to American influence; secondly, no country in Europe would accept decisions imposed upon it by a federal authority; and thirdly, Europe could not imitate the United States federation as its history was much longer, its national temperaments more varied and its cultural traditions very firmly embedded in the different countries. In his first TV broadcast, 'One hour with the President of the Republic', on 18 April 1979, Giscard d'Estaing developed a *fourth* reason: the confederal European Council was in his view 'the most effective and important way to achieve European progress'. At Hoerdt on 15 May 1979 Giscard d'Estaing added a *fifth* reason: confederal Europe was the kind of Europe that found most support in France, 'Never has there been greater consensus'. Finally, after his visit to Portugal, he formulated a *sixth* reason: the Community of the Twelve needed structures which were less cohesive than those imposed by the existing treaty rules. There was no doubt that the second and the fifth reasons were most readily understood in France. But what kind of assessment can be made of the Giscardian rationales? There are, indeed, strong arguments in favour of a confederal structure in Europe, and it would be wrong to proceed to federalism just because it is written into the treaty, irrespective of whether or not there is overwhelming popular support. However, federalism has long been popular in postwar Western Europe, and still is amongst the original Five. France, indeed, constitutes a problem; but it ought to be pointed out that its rigid anti-supranationalism is very much 'manufactured by politicians' and the result of Gaullist pedagogy after 1958. The problem is, therefore, self-inflicted and there is much scope for the *de*-indoctrination of the present French popular attitudes.

But cannot it be argued that present confederal procedures allow for dynamic and decisive political action at top level: is not the European Council a much stronger executive than the Commission? Are not the modern Western democracies moving towards stronger governmental powers and decreased parliamentary powers? And is therefore the pursuance of a stronger European Assembly, more parliamentary control over the Commission in Brussels, not an outmoded strategy? Certainly, a strategy for 'immobilism' in the French eyes. Professor Duverger[2] has suggested that if one was further to apply political textbook theories of the 1930s to Europe, prescribing a strong parliamentary federal regime, this European 'federal government would be as unstable and weak as that of the

Italian Republic of today, of the Third and Fourth Republics, of the Weimar Republic and of all the regimes in which there is no coherent and disciplined majority'. M. Duverger then presented President Giscard d'Estaing as a second-generation European who is aware of the new needs of modern government:

His faith in the Community is certainly not less than that of Monnet. But it has taken into account the evolution of the circumstances and of the mentalities over the thirty years which followed the ECSC initiative. The President certainly hopes for a supranational Europe in the end. But with the same realism as Pope Jean-Paul II hopes for the advent of the Kingdom of God on earth. The declaration about a confederal Europe must be seen in the context of the initiative taken in 1974. In a proposal to the Heads of Government of the Community to meet from then onward three times a year and whenever necessary together with the Commission's President, M. Giscard d'Estaing has persuaded them to set up a new Community institution not foreseen in the texts, the 'European Council'. This has progressively become the true executive of the Community.

Duverger thus supports a confederal type of Europe on the ground that it allows for a stronger and more effective executive in the form of the European Council than the cumbersome executive which the EEC institutions provide.

But did Giscard d'Estaing really want a more powerful European executive? Did he not rather want more power *over* the European executive? The latter seems to be the case. It seems more plausible to read the whole French government attitude more as a gradual move to bring political initiative in Europe back to the individual member-governments, dismantling subtly and from within what he saw not only as the politically cumbersome, but also the potentially more independent Commission-Council dialogue mechanism, further taken out of his hands by the interference of the European Assembly. His motive for pursuing confederalism was to make sure that at no time in the future would France be obliged to bow to a European supra-national authority. The French government under Giscard d'Estaing was extremely active and adroit in the European arena and it constantly exploited the European dimension to achieve the success of its policies. However, the government was always unwilling to see an organic, political Europe coming into existence of which France would be a part. It was only prepared to play the European dimension for the pursuit of national economic interest and the extension of its foreign policy influence in the world. Giscard d'Estaing's approach was more courteous, less inflexible but no less determined in its objective than de Gaulle's or Pompidou's. It is difficult to agree with Duverger's analysis that President Giscard d'Estaing was creating the European Council as a preliminary step to the emergence later of a powerful European President, elected directly by European suffrage: a kind of temporary European 'praesidium'. It is difficult to see how the extremely inter-governmental, strictly confederal practice represented by the European Council, and the strict insistence on continued unanimity voting in the Council of Ministers, could in any way be construed as a move towards a supra-national presidential system in which the President would have strong federal powers similar to those of the American Presidents until the Nixon era. There was very little, if any, evidence of such aims in the Giscardian strategy. It seems more realistic to take Giscard d'Estaing's action very much at face-value: courteous but strong insistence on national sovereignty and as close a European co-operation as was compatible with French national interest. But nothing beyond this. Not supra-nationalism, but close inter-governmentalism was the limit. All available evidence suggested that the French government saw confederalism as the best structure for Europe and one which responded to France's main require-ments: influence in the world and unfettered national independence.

## Mitterrand, Socialist and Committed European

### 'L'espace social européen'

When Raymond Aron, in a reference to the electoral in-fighting within the Right, claimed that 'The former right-wing coalition was not defeated. It committed suicide', he perhaps had overlooked the critical importance of the issue of unemployment in the presidential contest. Not only did unemployment affect nearly 2 million voters, but it was forcefully taken up by the opposition as a battering-ram against Giscard d'Estaing's record. Soon after his victory at the subsequent legislative elections, Mitterrand called for the creation of 210,000 new jobs. As a convinced European, with a minister in his government for European Affairs, André Chandernagor, the new President has no doubt that this initiative required a European framework and called for an EEC-wide reflation: a concerted effort by the countries of Europe to create a 'European social area'. The long-standing constructive attitude of Mitterrand towards Europe replaces the rather critical attitude he had shown during the presidential campaign: forgotten now the accusations against Giscard d'Estaing not having served French national interests in Europe, having been 'insufficiently vigilant' in resisting the British demand for budgetary rectification and in protecting the livelihood of French farmers and fishermen. Now the emphasis is again on Europe not simply as a useful, but an essential, framework for Mitterrand's social plans to succeed. At his first European Council meeting on 30 June 1981 in Luxembourg Mitterrand stole the show: somewhat to the surprise of his partners he brought social and economic affairs to the forefront of the discussion, stressing the impossibility of tackling the 'scourge of unemployment' in isolation. He invited the heads of government in Europe to consider five possible lines of pragmatic action within the EEC:

(1) to make greater use of Euro-loans for approved new industries;
(2) to give a greater chance of success to certain key industries (for example, computers and energy) by encouraging development on a European scale;
(3) to take into account, in any economic strategy, the overriding need to achieve social objectives, so as to create a 'peaceful European social area';
(4) to study in-depth means of reducing the working week;
(5) to encourage Europe to see its development in relation to the poorer countries of the world and to be aware of the need for a North–South dialogue and co-operation.

These new French topics for reflection were received sympathetically by the small EEC countries and Italy but with polite scepticism by Chancellor Schmidt and Mrs Thatcher. However, everybody was pleased about Mitterrand's clear declaration of commitment to Europe and his frank enthusiasm for new goals; many were equally pleased when he let it be known through his Foreign Minister Claude Cheysson that, while France recognised the need for close relations with West Germany, there would no longer be a 'Paris–Bonn axis', that is, not the same exclusive relationship that was pursued by Giscard d'Estaing towards an increasingly reluctant Chancellor Schmidt.

Later in July at the Franco-German summit in Bonn Mitterrand and Delors, his Economics Minister, announced a major French initiative would set out concrete proposals for an EEC-wide plan for reflation and agro-budgetary reform. However, by October the French attitude towards reform of CAP and the Euro-budget, while not totally changed, had considerably hardened. Perhaps Mitterrand was taking up a bargaining position: French concessions in the above areas would have to be offset by British and German willingness to support reflation in Europe. The more detailed plan for reflation within a 'European social area' (called by Rocard 'Europe's new deal') now comprises: an evolution of the EMS beyond the existing scope; greater use of the EEC's social fund to create jobs; increased borrowing for the Community for approved investment projects; more consultation between unions and employers' organisations; and enhanced co-operation over energy, research and development. These are all plans involving long-term measures, and little or no action can be expected to be forthcoming immediately. But Mitterrand now repeatedly asserts that he will be in power for seven years, with a majority in the legislature for five years: no European leader has such power.

Among the more immediate steps the French government took for improving the employment situation were: an approach to the German Chancellor asking for immediate support for the French franc, support which was forthcoming; a proposal to disconnect European interest rates from USA rates by creating a European two-tier system, a proposal which was not well received by the German Federal Bank as it would entail the imposition of control of capital movement; and a request that French deficit spending be tolerated for up to two years in order to achieve growth. On 4 October 1981 realignment within the EMS equivalent to a 3 per cent devaluation of the French franc and a 5.5 per cent revaluation of the deutschmark was seen by many as a 'German sacrifice'. This realignment had become necessary not only to stop the drain on reserves (£3·5 billion since the elections), but to 'activate exports' (J. Delors). The move was accompanied by measures for price control and an invitation to the unions to discuss wage restraint. The June 1982 devaluation of the French franc was preceded by tough negotiations in Brussels, with the Germans insisting on the French taking measures to curb inflation.

These French proposals and early measures obviously foreshadow a very clear move away from the previous Giscard d'Estaing–Barre policies: it seems paradoxical that those also were intended and introduced primarily as part of a campaign to combat unemployment. Whereas Giscard d'Estaing–Barre seemed to have concentrated on strategies for a long-term cure of the illness, the response of Mitterrand–Mauroy seems more emotional and designed to create immediate relief – in the view of the sceptics, however, a very ephemeral relief and possibly leading to greater unemployment in the end. It was, in any case, very clear that in 1981-2 (in spite of the austerity measures of June 1982) France was moving away from the German economic and financial strategy. The French returned to Keynes, whilst the Germans remain unmoved in their scepticism. This divergence of policy poses the question of whether instead of inviting greater European co-operation, the new French policies will lead to a near break-up of specific European achievements such as the EMS, which postulates for its proper functioning and development a solid convergence of national and European economic and financial policies.

The growing divergence in Europe was revealed again, later in October 1981, by the different reactions of the EEC countries to the Commission's document on 'Economic policy guidelines': the body of the plan, which was drawn up before Mitterrand's election, was criticised by the French for some of its monetarist assumptions, whereas the Germans found the foreword, drawn up by the Frenchman, Ortoli, after the elections, somehow too Keynesian. The question therefore must arise: is there now a real danger that the EEC could be immobilised, even move apart under the pressure of the opposing demands of its principal partners? Or will Mitterrand be able to bring his European partners round to see things his way? Both are possibilities, but at present the first one looks more probable than the second.

## INSTITUTIONAL CHANGES?

In view of the lack of consensus on the fundamental approach to the present problems in Europe, it seems reasonable to expect that neither Schmidt nor Mitterrand nor Mrs Thatcher will have any inclination to move beyond the present confederal arrangements – allowing for flexible inter-governmental co-operation in Europe – and the present practice of unanimity voting in the Brussels Council of Ministers. It seems, indeed, hardly conceivable that Mitterrand would wish to reverse the present French opposition to majority voting in the Council, thereby accepting a decision-making process which could clearly place him in a minority position and require him to abandon, or at least obstruct, his policies for a demand-led reflation, his demand to maintain basic aspects of the agricultural policy (such as Community preference), his nationalisation plans and a number of other Socialist policies. At present Europe seems set to retain the institutional status quo of the celebrated 1966 Luxembourg compromise: co-operation indeed, but only with the rule of unanimity and, as Pompidou later suggested, '*à la carte*', thus co-operation set clearly within the limits of a confederal nature. Article 148 of the Treaty of Rome seems condemned to remain dormant for quite a while.

It is, however, fair to observe that there are at least some encouraging, if very general, indications from the French side for some integrative progress in Europe. On 26 October 1981 Chandernagor, the Minister for European Affairs, announced before the Council of Europe's Assembly that the new French government would now fully accept the European Convention on Human Rights, thus allowing French citizens to take on their own government in the European Court in Strasbourg. This acceptance means a small and belated, but nevertheless real, extension of European supra-national jurisdiction in France, inconceivable under the Gaullists or Giscard d'Estaing. There is a second sign: the new French proposal for giving the European Commission the right to take part in the Community's foreign policy consultations: this represents a real change of heart by the French and has been widely credited to the present Foreign Affairs Minister, Cheysson, who was until June 1981 a member of the Commission in Brussels. It means an improvement in the status of the Commission and an extension of its area of influence which until now has been exclusively confined to the economic arena, as there was no provision in the Treaty of Rome for harmonising foreign policy. This participation had always been opposed by French Presidents as they particularly insisted on national and sovereign rights in foreign policy matters. This move is even more significant as it gives the Commission access to an active and expanding sector of European co-operation for which there is all-round strong support, including the British and the Germans: 'political co-operation' in pursuance of a common European foreign policy. The EEC members' support for the Saudi-Arabian plan for Middle East peace (which will put pressure on the American administration, at least not to reject it easily) and the plan for a European peace-keeping force in the Sinai demonstrate Europe's intention to pursue its own active and independent foreign policy. It is encouraging to note that at present there is no evidence that President Mitterrand is wanting to use the European platform as a means for the extension of French foreign policy influence.

## CONFEDERALISM ADEQUATE?

Amongst the present French Socialist leaders there might not be the strong ideological objection to progress beyond confederation that used to exist with de Gaulle, Pompidou and Giscard d'Estaing; however, there is little to encourage them in that direction. There is far too little sympathy for Mitterrand's plans for reflation, which would lead him to seek successful implementation of his plans through powerful support from strengthened EEC institutions. If the majority of the ministers in the Council were to be in sympathy with Mitterrand's Socialist strategies, this would constitute a perfectly good reason for moving towards majority voting a Brussels. At present, however, there is no such support; it is hard for Mitterrand to see any specific important function or task, pursued by himself, which could be realised more effectively by a federal Europe. On the contrary, with the present membership, it would not doubt be obstructed. For the same reason, there is little chance of the Genscher–Colombo initiative for a 'European Act', aiming at federal progress, receiving French support. At present, any steps towards supra-nationalism and majority voting in Europe must appear to Mitterrand as a move which would make his immediate and declared priority tasks more difficult.

Functionalist theories may still be proved valid in the end: only in given circumstances, in which the case for close integration becomes apparent to all, is it likely that popular support will be generated of a sufficient strength to transfer old loyalties, in certain specific areas, from the nation state to a new, more effective, functional centre of loyalty, a European centre.[3] The economic, political and defence necessities generated by world circumstances may indeed bring Europe, including France, closer together by functional means rather than by academic argument. This way of European progress by pressure of circumstances in certain sectors is not new. Was not Monnet after all a functionalist?

## Notes: Chapter 9

1 C. de Gaulle, *Mémoires d'Espoir. I, Le Renouveau* (Paris: Plon, 1973), p. 231.
2 M. Duverger, 'La lumière et les taupes', *Le Monde*, 18 November 1978; 'Le Présidium de la Communauté', *Le Monde*, 7 December 1978; 'Confédérale et Supranationale', *Le*

*Monde*, 26 December 1978; 'L'Europe à deux vitesses', *Le Monde*, 13–14 May 1979; 'Les Européistes contre l'Europe', *Le Monde*, 20 June 1979; and 'La diplomatie de Janus', *Le Monde*, 1–2 June 1980.
3  P. Taylor, 'Functionalism: the theory of David Mitrany', in P. Taylor and A. J. R. Groom (eds), *International Organisation* (London, Frances Pinter, 1978), pp. 236–51, and chs 9 and 10.

## Chapter 9: Bibliography

Cousté, P.-B., and Visine, F. (1974), *Pompidou et l'Europe* (Paris: Librairies techniques).

Couve de Murville, M. (1969), *La Politique européenne de la France* (Paris: Secretariat du gouvernement).

Couve de Murville, M. (1980), 'Réflection sur la nature de la crise internationale', *Politique etrangère*, no. 3, pp. 599–608.

Debbasch, C. (1974), *La France de Pompidou* (Paris: PUF).

Delamare, C. (1979), 'Quelle amitié franco-allemande?', *Revue politique et parlementaire*, May–June, pp. 33–41.

François-Poncet, J. (1980), 'Diplomatie française: quel cadre conceptuel?', *Politique internationale*, no. 6, p. 9.

de Gaulle, C. (1970), *Mémoires d'Espoir* (Paris: Plon), pp. 207–339.

Giscard d'Estaing, V. (1976–81), *Discours et déclarations du président de la république française* (Paris: La Documentation française).

Giscard d'Estaing, V. (1976), *Démocratie française* (Paris: Fayard).

Grosser, A. (1976), *Les Politiques Européennes dans la crise* (Paris: Presses de la Fondation Nationale des Sciences Politiques).

Grosser, A. (1980), *The Western Alliance* (London: Papermac).

Haas, E. B. (1968), *The Uniting of Europe*, 2nd rev. edn (London: Stanford University Press).

Haurieder, W. F., and Auton, G. P. (1980), *The Foreign Policies of West Germany, France and Britain* (Englewood Cliffs, NJ: Prentice-Hall).

Hodges, M. (ed.) (1972), *European Integration* (London: Penguin Education).

Hoffmann, S. (1981), 'L'Europe et les Etats-Unis entre la discorde et l'harmonie', *Politique etrangère*, no. 3, pp. 553–67.

Jouve, E. (1967), *Le Général de Gaulle et la construction de l'Europe* (Paris: Librairie générale de droit et de jurisprudence).

Kolodziej, E. A. (1974), *French International Policy under de Gaulle and Pompidou: The Politics of Grandeur* (Ithaca, NY: Cornell University Press).

Masclet, J.-C. (1978), *L'Union Politique de l'Europe* (Paris: PUF).

Massip, R. (1963), *de Gaulle et l'Europe* (Paris: Flammarion).

Merlé, M. (1978), 'Les élections législatives de mars 1978 et la politique extérieure de la France', *Etudes internationales*, December, pp. 467–505.

Monnet, J. (1976) *Mémoires* (Paris: Fayard).

de Montbrial, T. (1981), 'Réflexions sur l'Europe politique', *Politique etrangère*, no. 3, pp. 23–4.

Morgan, A. (1976), *From Summit to Council: Evolution in the EEC* (London: Chatham House/PEP).

Morgan, R. (1972), *West European Politics since 1945: The Shaping of the European Community* (London: Batsford).

Morse, E. L. (1973), *Foreign Policy and Interdependence in Gaullist France* (Princeton, NJ: Princeton University Press).

Noel, E. (1979), *Les rouages de l'Europe* (Paris: Natan).

Poniatowski, M. (1979), *L'avenir n'est écrit nulle part* (Paris: Albin Michel).

Pryce, R. (1981), *The Politics of the European Community* (London: Butterworth).

Reuter, P. (1978), *Les Organisations européennes* (Paris: PUF).

Rideau, J. (1975), *La France et les communautés européennes* (Paris: Librairie générale de droit et de jurisprudence).

Schutze, W. (1979), 'L'Europe des Neufs: état présent et perspectives de la construction européenne', *Politique etrangère*, no. 2, pp. 273-91.

Simonian, H. (1981), 'France, Germany and Europe', *Journal of Common Market Studies*, no. 3, pp. 203-19.

Taylor, P., and Groom, A. J. R. (1978), *International Organisation: A Conceptual Approach* (London: Frances Pinter).

Vaughan, R. (1979), *Twentieth Century Europe* (London: Croom Helm).

Wallace, W. (1980), 'Independence and economic interest: the ambiguities of French foreign policy', in P. G. Cerny and M. A. Schain (eds), *French Politics and Public Policy* (London: Frances Pinter), pp. 267-90.

Wright, V. (1981), 'The change in France', *Government and Opposition*, Autumn, pp. 414-31.

Zorgbibe, C. (1978), *La Construction politique de l'Europe* (Paris: PUF).

# Index

## DATE DUE

| 4 Apr 84 | | | |
|----------|--|--|--|
| | | | |
| | | | |
| | | | |
| | | | |
| | | | |
| | | | |
| | | | |
| | | | |
| | | | |
| | | | |
| | | | |
| | | | |
| | | | |
| | | | |
| | | | |
| | | | |
| | | | |
| GAYLORD | | | PRINTED IN U.S.A. |